A COMPLETE GUIDE

HAWAII'S BIG ISLAND

Call Lava tours
2/9/11

Salt spray cools a roadside picnic spot in the Puna district of the Big Island.

A COMPLETE GUIDE

1ST EDITION

HAWAII'S BIG ISLAND

Elizabeth Blish Hughes

The Countryman Press
Woodstock, Vermont

In memory of my mother, Ann MacLean Hughes

ISBN 978-1-58157-091-5

Cover photo © Douglas Peebles
Interior photos by the author unless otherwise specified
Book design by Bodenweber Design
Page composition by PerfecType, Nashville, TN
Maps by Mapping Specialists Ltd., Madison, WI © The Countryman Press

Published by The Countryman Press, P.O. Box 748, Woodstock, Vermont 05091

Distributed by W. W. Norton & Company, Inc., 500 Fifth Avenue, New York, NY 10110

Manufactured in the United States of America

10 9 8 7 6 5 4 3 2 1

GREAT DESTINATIONS TRAVEL GUIDEBOOK SERIES

Recommended by *National Geographic Traveler* and *Travel + Leisure* magazines

[A] CRISP AND CRITICAL APPROACH, FOR TRAVELERS WHO WANT TO LIVE LIKE LOCALS.
—*USA Today*

Great Destinations™ guidebooks are known for their comprehensive, critical coverage of regions of extraordinary cultural interest and natural beauty. The authors in this series are professional travel writers who have lived for many years in the regions they describe. Each title in this series is continuously updated with each printing to ensure accurate and timely information. All the books contain more than one hundred photographs and maps.

Current titles available:

THE ADIRONDACK BOOK

ATLANTA

AUSTIN, SAN ANTONIO
& THE TEXAS HILL COUNTRY

THE BERKSHIRE BOOK

BERMUDA

BIG SUR, MONTEREY BAY &
GOLD COAST WINE COUNTRY

CAPE CANAVERAL, COCOA BEACH
& FLORIDA'S SPACE COAST

THE CHARLESTON, SAVANNAH
& COASTAL ISLANDS BOOK

THE CHESAPEAKE BAY BOOK

THE COAST OF MAINE BOOK

COLORADO'S CLASSIC MOUNTAIN TOWNS

COSTA RICA: GREAT DESTINATIONS
CENTRAL AMERICA

THE FINGER LAKES BOOK

THE FOUR CORNERS REGION

GALVESTON, SOUTH PADRE ISLAND
& THE TEXAS GULF COAST

THE HAMPTONS BOOK

HAWAII'S BIG ISLAND

HONOLULU & OAHU:
GREAT DESTINATIONS HAWAII

THE JERSEY SHORE: ATLANTIC CITY TO CAPE MAY

KAUAI: GREAT DESTINATIONS HAWAII

LAKE TAHOE & RENO

LOS CABOS & BAJA CALIFORNIA SUR:
GREAT DESTINATIONS MEXICO

MAUI: GREAT DESTINATIONS HAWAII

MICHIGAN'S UPPER PENINSULA

MONTREAL & QUEBEC CITY:
GREAT DESTINATIONS CANADA

THE NANTUCKET BOOK

THE NAPA & SONOMA BOOK

NORTH CAROLINA'S OUTER BANKS
& THE CRYSTAL COAST

PALM BEACH, FORT LAUDERDALE, MIAMI
& THE FLORIDA KEYS

PALM SPRINGS & DESERT RESORTS

PHOENIX, SCOTTSDALE, SEDONA
& CENTRAL ARIZONA

PLAYA DEL CARMEN, TULUM & THE RIVIERA MAYA:
GREAT DESTINATIONS MEXICO

SALT LAKE CITY, PARK CITY, PROVO
& UTAH'S HIGH COUNTRY RESORTS

SAN DIEGO & TIJUANA

SAN JUAN, VIEQUES & CULEBRA:
GREAT DESTINATIONS PUERTO RICO

SAN MIGUEL DE ALLENDE & GUANAJUATO:
GREAT DESTINATIONS MEXICO

THE SANTA FE & TAOS BOOK

THE SARASOTA, SANIBEL ISLAND & NAPLES BOOK

THE SEATTLE & VANCOUVER BOOK

THE SHENANDOAH VALLEY BOOK

TOURING EAST COAST WINE COUNTRY

WASHINGTON, D.C., AND NORTHERN VIRGINIA

YELLOWSTONE & GRAND TETON NATIONAL PARKS
AND JACKSON HOLE

YOSEMITE & THE SOUTHERN SIERRA NEVADA

If you are traveling to, moving to, residing in, or just interested in any (or all!) of these enchanting regions, a Great Destinations guidebook is a superior companion. Honest and painstakingly critical, full of information only a local can provide, Great Destinations guidebooks give you all the practical knowledge you need to enjoy the best of each region. Why not own them all?

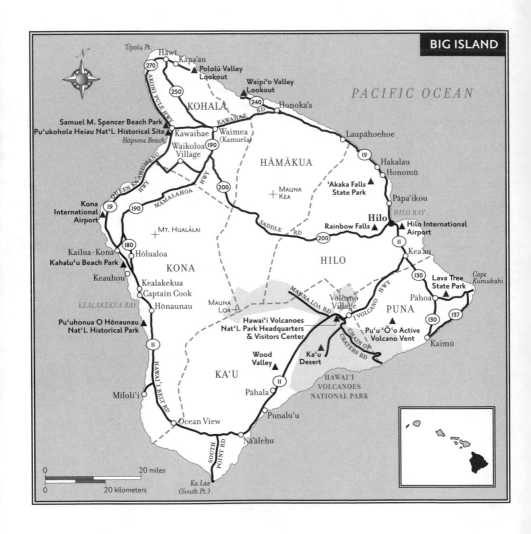

BIG ISLAND

PACIFIC OCEAN

Ūpolu Pt.
Hāwī
Kapa'au
270
▲ Pololū Valley Lookout
250
Waipi'o Valley Lookout ▲
240
KOHALA
RD
Honoka'a
KAWAIHAE
Samuel M. Spencer Beach Park ▲
Pu'ukoholā Heiau Nat'l. Historical Site ▲
Kawaihae
Waimea (Kamuela)
Laupāhoehoe
19
Hāpuna Beach
Waikoloa Village
190
HĀMĀKUA
Hakalau
Honomū
HWY
200
'Akaka Falls State Park
+ MAUNA KEA
Pāpa'ikou
HILO BAY
Kona International Airport
19
190
MAMALAHOA
SADDLE RD
200
Rainbow Falls
Hilo
Hilo International Airport
+ MT. HUALĀLAI
180
Hōlualoa
Kailua-Kona
KONA
HILO
Kea'au
11
Kahalu'u Beach Park ▲
Keauhou
Kealakekua
Captain Cook
Hōnaunau
130
Lava Tree State Park
Cape Kumukahi
KEALAKEKUA BAY
MAUNA LOA RD
MAUNA LOA +
Volcano Village
Pāhoa
137
Pu'uhonua O Hōnaunau Nat'l. Historical Park ▲
Hawai'i Volcanoes Nat'l. Park Headquarters & Visitors Center
VOLCANO HWY
PUNA
130
Kaimū
11
Pu'u 'Ō'o Active Volcano Vent ▲
CHAIN OF CRATERS RD
Wood Valley ▲
KA'U
Ka'u Desert ▲
HAWAI'I VOLCANOES NATIONAL PARK
Miloli'i
Pāhala
11
HAWAI'I BELT RD
Punalu'u
Ocean View
SOUTH POINT RD
Na'ālehu
Ka Lae (South Pt.)

0   20 miles
0   20 kilometers

Contents

Acknowledgments 9

Introduction 10

The Way This Book Works 13

1
History
From Island Formation to the Present
21

2
Transportation
Getting Here, Getting Around
37

3
Lodging
Not Just for Sleeping
51

4
Culture
What to See, What to Do
95

5
Sacred Sites, Ancient Ruins, and Natural Wonders
Places of Revelation
129

6
Restaurants and Food Purveyors
Breakin' da Mouth
155

7
RECREATION
Fun in the Sun
197

8
SHOPPING
Island Style
226

9
BEST BETS
If Time Is Short
243

10
INFORMATION
Practical Matters
255

GENERAL INDEX   270
LODGING BY PRICE   283
DINING BY PRICE   285
DINING BY CUISINE   287

MAPS:
    BIG ISLAND   6
    HILO   15
    HAWAI'I VOLCANOES NATIONAL PARK   16
    KAILUA-KONA   17
    PUNA DISTRICT   18
    LAVA HAZARD ZONE   19

Acknowledgments

Many thanks to friends who have traveled with me to the Big Island or who have shared their appreciation of the place: Gail Bensinger; Lynn Myers Berger; Bob Gallo and Joe Giordano; Charlie Harmon; James R. Hughes; Althea and Eleanor James; Denise Alexandre LeComte; Elizabeth McDonald; Jim, Lucia, Natalie, and Thomas Sayre; Emilia Simonelli; and Chris Osburn. Thanks also to Barbara Berkeley, Ron Burt, Laura Cerv, Ben Collins, Jen Fogarty, Anastasia Hendrix, Alan and Alison MacLean, Anne O'Moore and Christine Petrozzo. Special mention must be made of Althea James, who provided needed administrative assistance at just the right moment.

Phil Donian, an independent Mac consultant, and the Stonestone Apple Store's Genius Bar in San Francisco deserve kudos for tech support that included help with Hawaiian-language issues and data retrieval from a crashed hard drive.

Thanks to Kim Grant, Kermit Hummel, Susan Barnett, Jennifer Thompson, and Doug Yeager at The Countryman Press.

While writing, I consumed the following varieties of Big Island coffee: Aikane Plantation, Kaʻu-grown medium-dark roast; Greenwell Farm Kona grown dark roast and Full City roast; Hilo Coffee Mill, dark roast Puna Estate; and Ono Kono medium-dark roast Hāmākua District. They are all worth seeking out.

I am grateful to have had the opportunity to experience the Big Island many times with my late mother, who made the trip from Connecticut to Hilo for the Merrie Monarch Festival until her early 90s. Like her, I find the Big Island to be a source of strength and healing, and its people to be filled with a spirit I have come to cherish as aloha.

Introduction

For many people, Hawai'i is the most foreign part of the United States.

Its location alone guarantees it a level of exoticism—a chain of islands surrounded by the Pacific Ocean about 2,300 miles from San Francisco.

The island of Hawai'i is the state's largest. That is why it is often referred to as the Big Island. Here the rolling hills of up-country ranchland evoke the West's Big Sky country, until you realize ancient now-dormant volcanoes shaped the land. Not far away, new eruptions add to the island's landmass. Much of the terrain looks like little on the North American continent. Narrow valleys knife deep into the islands, their steep, almost perpendicular walls covered with a lush tangle of jungle greenery. There are white-sand beaches and ones of green and black, too. The mountains are some of the world's highest, and the waters offshore some of the deepest.

There's some of the best hula in the world, and a mad, fierce cowboy culture centered in a town known by two names: Waimea and Kamuela. Waimea at one time referred to both a small, up-country community and an *ahupua'a,* a traditional Hawaiian method of land division. It is also the name of communities on neighboring islands. The postal service, built on efficiency, not the poetry of ancient naming conventions, wanted to eliminate confusion. For the Big Island's Waimea, Kamuela it would be. The name chosen is the Hawaiian variant of Samuel, the scion of a prominent local family, the Parkers.

It is an island marked by its physical contradictions.

Then there are the people, a glorious rainbow of ethnicities, races, and cultures. People speak English, Japanese, Cantonese, Mandarin, Vietnamese, Thai, Cambodian, Spanish, and a local lingo, pidgin, that blends English with Hawaiian while grabbing words from other immigrant groups as they were needed. So while a first-time visitor may hear English spoken with a musical lilt, understanding what is being said may take some adapting.

This, however, is part of what makes the Big Island both delightful and challenging to visit. Some preparation will tilt the scale toward more of the former and less of the latter.

As you explore, travel with better maps than those provided by vehicle rental companies. Street signs are plentiful in built-up areas but quickly become sparse. On main highways, track your progress with mile markers. If you ask for directions, expect instructions that include the terms *mauka,* toward the mountains, and *makai,* toward the ocean. For the first-time visitor, this can be a brain-changing exercise, like being asked to go through the day flip-flopping the concept of left and right. If you're unsure of where you're being told to go—"you know, turn where the laundry used to be"—ask again, or ask another person who doesn't assume you know the island like a local.

Always call in advance to make sure an attraction, restaurant, or business is open. While hours may be advertised, expect variations based on the season, family demands, and the flow of business. It is also smart to ask for an up-to-date physical address because smaller enterprises may move while retaining their phone number and mailing address.

Make travel plans well in advance to avoid disappointment. Hawai'i truly is an international destination, so what a resident of the United States may consider an off-season isn't for visitors from another hemisphere. The sooner you can solidify your travel plans, the more choices you will have.

At many attractions or events, you will encounter a two-tiered pricing system, one for visitors and one for *kama'aina,* or state residents. Let it slide. Unless you live in a high-cost-of-living state like California or New York, prices for food, gasoline, housing, and other basics can be a shocking introduction to the "paradise tax." While there are signs of great wealth clustered in many locations that draw visitors, you don't have to look hard to see signs that there are vast disparities in the incomes of local residents. So consider that extra dollar or two you pay to rent snorkel gear an investment in good karma and remember what goes around comes around.

Tourism is one of the main economic drivers on the Big Island, and service is usually pleasant, efficient, and skilled. If something goes wrong, however, anger and loud remarks will serve little purpose. You'll just look like an ill-behaved outsider, and that will decrease your chances of getting what you want. A quiet word in private with a supervisor, manager, or concierge will be more effective, as the local practices often hew to a more Asian model.

Accept that island time is a different. Take a deep breath upon arrival and slow down, because everything around you will be moving at a pace that may test the patience of a Type A. Be patient and flexible. You're on vacation, and what's 15 minutes here or there when even the shopping center has a sunset view?

Do not underestimate the intensity of the sun or the variability of the climate. Wear sunblock all day, stay hydrated, and carry layers of clothing with you. Within an hour's drive you may experience a 30-degree variation in temperature and just as dramatic changes in the weather. Hilo is one of the wettest places on the planet; Kohala, on the other side of the island, is one of the driest.

Be smart and stay safe around the ocean. Do not turn your back on the water. Obey posted warning signs. If in doubt, stay out even if other people are swimming, surfing, or tide-pooling.

If there are Civil Defense warnings about volcanic eruptions or tsunami, follow instructions. These are very much a part of life on the Big Island. Evacuation route signs are posted and maps of safety zones are available wherever you are staying.

The payoff for this preparation will be a vacation filled with experiences of a lifetime. The Big Island's unparalleled variety of climate, topography, and recreational options make it a perfect vacation spot.

The contradictions and contrasts only heighten the sensation of the place. You may experience rain forests and snow in one day. High-level scientific research is undertaken yards from ancient sacred places where believers still make offerings. Tomorrow's eco-technologies exist in tandem with traditional ways in fields such as aquaculture. Shake a tree for an out-of-this-world fresh papaya for breakfast, then have dinner at a world-class restaurant. Stay in a tree house or stay in a resort with so many stars it's a constellation representing outrageous luxury. Choose endurance training or lazy time on the beach.

Be prepared for these extremes and let them jolt you alive. Be open to the Big Island and its seductive powers; let it lead you deeper into its complicated persona. You may find that this island, often described as the least stereotypically Hawaiian of the state's islands, is indeed *your* Hawai'i, one so captivating a single vacation leaves you wanting more. No matter how many times you return, the Big Island will offer you something new.

—Elizabeth Blish Hughes

The Way This Book Works

This book is divided into 10 chapters, each with its own introduction. If you are particularly interested in one chapter, head right there and you can start reading without the feeling of starting in the middle. You can read from start to finish as you plan your trip months in advance or flip through it on the plane as a way to organize the final details of your visit. You can also carry it with you as you explore the Big Island. There are maps and telephone numbers to assist you in planning a day's activities or figuring out where to find lunch as you wander on back roads. Cell phone coverage on the Big Island gets better by the month, so you really can use this guide on the road. If you can't complete a call from your mobile, wait and try again a few miles down the road.

To find a place to sleep or eat, try looking first at the lodging or dining indexes at the end of the book. These are organized by area and price. Then turn to the pages cited and read the specific entries for the places that appeal to you.

Entries within most of the chapters are arranged by location, as if you were circumnavigating the island district: Kohala Coast, Kona Coast, South Kona, South Point, Hawai'i Volcanoes National Park, Puna; Greater Hilo, Hāmākua Coast, North Kohala, and Waimea.

Some entries, most notably those in chapter 3, Lodging, and chapter 6, Restaurants, include information in blocks at the head of each entry for easy reference. There is an accessibility note in these blocks. It specifies "Full," "Partial," or "None." Full access means just that, while partial access means efforts have been made to provide accommodation, but there may be problems for some travelers. When in doubt, call ahead. All detail in the information blocks, as well as all the phone numbers, addresses, and Web locators in others parts of the book, was checked as close to publication as possible. However, these and other details change more frequently than one would expect, so call and check.

The inevitability of change is why there's a price range or a base price rather than

Price Codes

	Lodging	Dining
Inexpensive	Up to $100	Up to $25
Moderate	$100–225	$25–40
Expensive	$225–350	$40–85
Very Expensive	Over $350	Over $85

Credit cards are abbreviated as follows:
AE: American Express
CB: Carte Blanche
D: Discover Card
DC: Diners Club
MC: MasterCard
V: Visa

specific prices. Lodging price codes are based on a per-room rate, double occupancy. Check online or call ahead for specific rates and reservations. Calling can result in a better rate than is available online. When you are planning your vacation, do check the most current schedule of holidays, festivals, and conventions at the Big Island Visitors Bureau's Web site, www.bigisland.org. Room rates can double, if there's even space available, when a big event is going on.

Restaurant prices indicate the cost of an individual meal including appetizer, entrée, dessert, tax, and tip. The cost of alcoholic beverages, with or without those tiny paper tropical umbrellas, is not included.

Hawai'i has one area code, 808. You do not need to dial it for interisland calls, but they are charged at long-distance rates. For directory assistance, call 411 for numbers on the Big Island and 1-555-1212 for numbers on other islands.

The best source for up-to-the-minute year-round tourist information is the Big Island Visitors Bureau, www.bigisland.org. The organization has offices in East Hawai'i at 250 Keawe St., Hilo. They are open 8—4:30 weekdays, 808-961-5797. In West Hawai'i they are at the Waikoloa Kings' Shops, # B-15, 69-250 Waikoloa Beach Dr., Waikoloa, HI 96738, 808-886-1655. There is a trip planner on the Web site, and you can sign up for an e-mail newsletter for updates. If you want to book tickets for Hawaiian-music performances, go to www.mele.com, which maintains a comprehensive schedule of concerts on all the islands and on the mainland.

Once you're on the island, check the calendar listings of the *Hawaii Tribune-Herald* for Hilo-side listings, and *West Hawaii Today* for Kona-side information. They're both widely available and the best way to make sure you don't miss hula or music performances, a craft fair, or a fund-raiser with true, local-style food.

For up-to-date advisories on closures at Hawai'i Volcanoes National Park, call 808-974-4221 or go to www.nps.gov/havo/closed_areas.htm.

For best results while planning your trip, do your research while listening to one of the many Internet music feeds, such as www.kaparadio.com, www.alohajoe.com, or www.hawaiianrainbow.com. It's a good way to figure out which music you like, so you can buy some CDs or downloads to have for your flights and in the car. Radio reception on the Big Island can be spotty. With those CDs or downloads playing, planning your trip and the flight to Hawai'i will become part of your vacation.

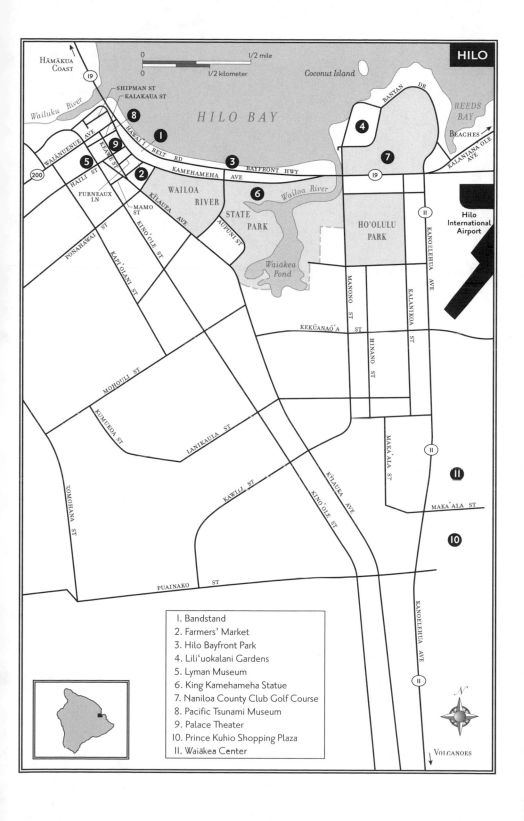

HILO

HĀMĀKUA COAST

Wailuku River

HILO BAY

Coconut Island

REEDS BAY

BEACHES

BANYAN DR

SHIPMAN ST
KALAKAUA ST

HAWAIʻI BELT RD

WAIĀNUENUE AVE

KEAWE ST

BAYFRONT HWY

KAMEHAMEHA AVE

KALANIANAʻOLE AVE

HAILI ST

FURNEAUX LN

MAMO ST

KĪLAUEA AVE

KINOʻOLE ST

AUPUNI ST

WAILOA RIVER

Wailoa River

STATE PARK

Waiākea Pond

HOʻOLULU PARK

Hilo International Airport

PONAHAWAI ST

KAPIʻOLANI ST

MANONO ST

HINANO ST

KALANIKOA ST

KANOELEHUA AVE

KEKŪANAOʻA

MOHOULI ST

KUMUKOA ST

LANIKAULA ST

MAKAʻALA ST

ʻOMOHANA ST

KAWILI ST

KINOʻOLE ST

KĪLAUEA AVE

MAKAʻALA ST

PUAINAKO ST

KANOELEHUA AVE

N

VOLCANOES

1. Bandstand
2. Farmers' Market
3. Hilo Bayfront Park
4. Liliʻuokalani Gardens
5. Lyman Museum
6. King Kamehameha Statue
7. Naniloa County Club Golf Course
8. Pacific Tsunami Museum
9. Palace Theater
10. Prince Kuhio Shopping Plaza
11. Waiākea Center

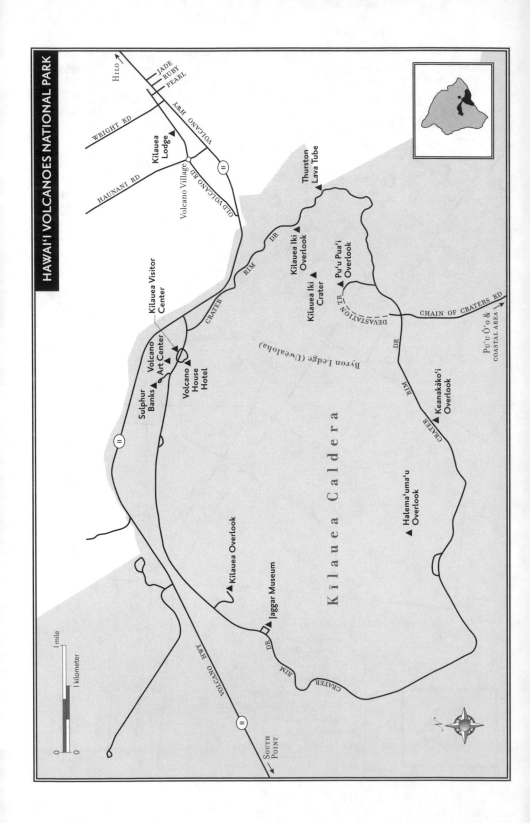

HAWAI'I VOLCANOES NATIONAL PARK

HILO

JADE
RUBY
PEARL

WRIGHT RD

Kilauea
Lodge

HAUNANI RD

Volcano Village

VOLCANO HWY

OLD VOLCANO RD

Thurston
Lava Tube

Kilauea Iki
Overlook

Pu'u Pua'i
Overlook

Kilauea Iki
Crater

DR

RIM

CRATER

Kilauea Visitor
Center

Volcano
Art Center

Sulphur
Banks

Volcano
House Hotel

DEVASTATION TR

CHAIN OF CRATERS RD

PU'U O'o &
COASTAL AREA

Byron Ledge (Uwealoha)

DR

RIM

CRATER

Keanakāko'i
Overlook

Kilauea Caldera

Halema'uma'u
Overlook

Kilauea Overlook

Jaggar Museum

VOLCANO HWY

DR

RIM

CRATER

SOUTH
POINT

1 mile

1 kilometer

0

0

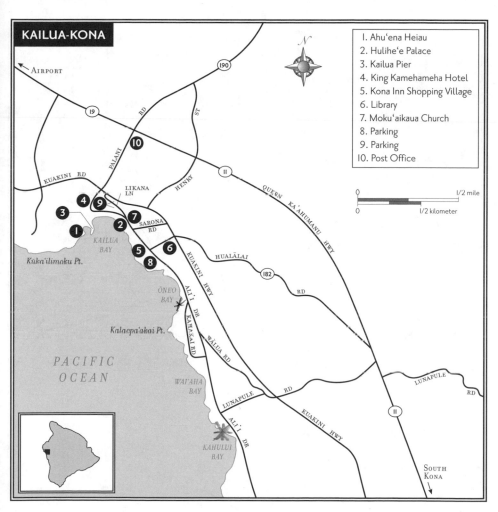

KAILUA-KONA

1. Ahu'ena Heiau
2. Hulihe'e Palace
3. Kailua Pier
4. King Kamehameha Hotel
5. Kona Inn Shopping Village
6. Library
7. Moku'aikaua Church
8. Parking
9. Parking
10. Post Office

* where we stay 2/2011

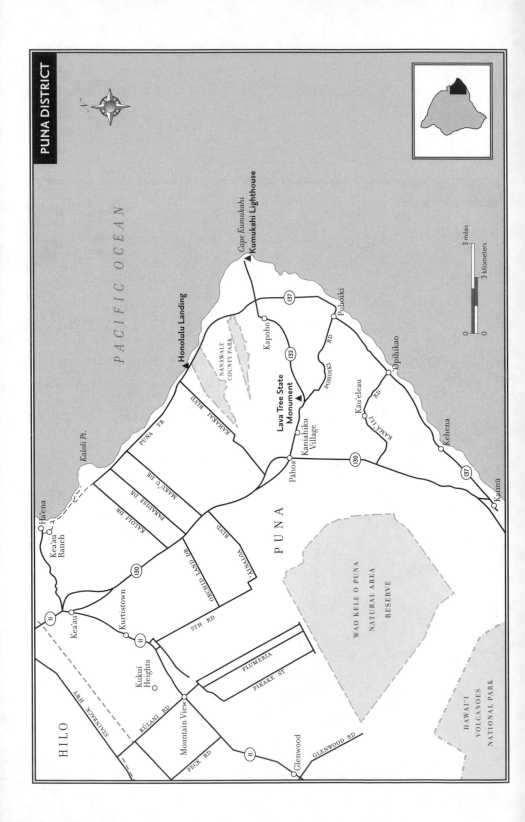

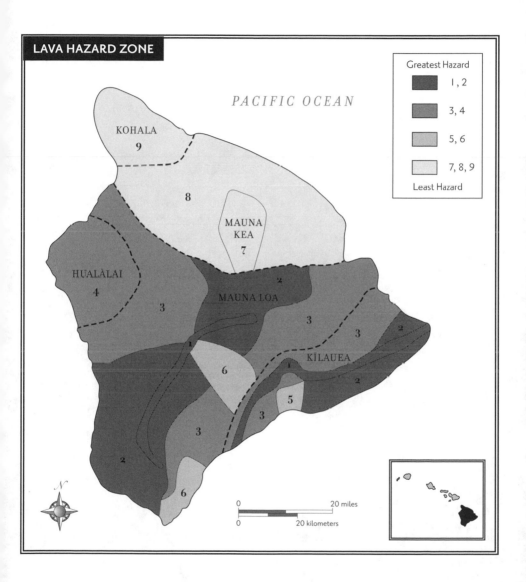

The first Polynesians are believed to have arrived in the South Point.

HISTORY

From Island Formation to the Present

Scientists and the Kumulipo (the chanted record of the creation of Hawai'i; see The Creation Chart sidebar in chapter 5) differ on the age of Hawai'i. Science tells us it is the youngest of the Hawaiian islands, just over 1 million years old. The oral history of the island, transmitted from generation to generation by chanters, says the Big Island, as it is known, is the first "island child" of Wākea, the sky father, and Pāpā, the earth mother.

That discrepancy encapsulates the conflict in tracing the island's history. Science offers an almost endless recitation of facts and figures offering proof positive that this is a unique landmass and environment. Yet for a visitor, it is virtually impossible to ignore the counterweight offered by the legends that pervade every inch of the island, and indeed the state of Hawai'i, often explaining the emotional impact of an area that science can merely quantify or explicate.

The raw, extreme beauty and rich bounty of the island of Hawai'i have been attracting visitors for centuries. Each time it has been discovered, the word brought home has been "we've discovered paradise," triggering in many the need to see this place for themselves. Upon arrival, many have stayed, changing the life they found with their presence, leaving their own mark on the place, and then finding themselves facing newcomers. They've kept coming by sailing canoes, tall ships, clippers, steamers, airplanes, and jets. The land, with its varied climates and omnipresent power, has changed each group, upending their beliefs and customs, from ancient Polynesian mariners, European explorers and traders, American whalers and missionaries, and laborers imported from Asia to a globally representative selection of adventurers, dreamers, artists, spiritual seekers, and ordinary folks drawn to an isolated place with abundant water, a temperate climate, seas rich in fish, and bountiful land.

Despite this, and even though the Big Island has the most repeat visitors of any Hawaiian island, the island of Hawai'i is not for everyone, defying as it does the stereotype of a tropical island. It is a place of extremes. Of the world's 23 climate zones, the Big Island has 21, and you can drive through them all in one hard day behind the wheel. The ideal of Hawai'i, a place of winsome hula dancers and handsome surfers, is a created place of radio programs, travel advertising, television, and movies. The real Big Island, with its black-sand beaches and white snowfields, its astronomers and cowboys, its Alpine meadows and seething lava, is a more complex place.

NATURAL HISTORY

Eight islands and numerous atolls with a total landmass of 6,423 square miles make up the state of Hawai'i. All told, the islands form the most extensive archipelago on Earth. The islands are the visible peaks of the Hawaiian Emperor seamount chain, formed as the Pacific plate moved slowly over a hot spot in the Earth's mantle. Because the Pacific plate speeds northwest at about 32 miles every million years, the islands in the northwestern part of the state are the oldest.

The southernmost and easternmost island in the Hawaiian Islands, Hawai'i is not only the youngest, about 800,000 years old, but also the largest, about the size of Connecticut. The island, with a landmass of over 4,000 square miles, continues to grow, thanks to Kīlauea's eruptions pouring lava into the ocean since 1983. The island was created by Kīlauea and Mauna Loa (the largest shield volcano on the planet), which are still erupting, and Mauna Kea, Hualālai, and Kohala, which are considered dormant.

Lō'ihi is a new volcano about 20 miles offshore and 3,000 feet below sea level. Fired by the same hot spot that gave birth to the other volcanoes, it should be visible above the Pacific in another 60,000 years. Reserve your oceanfront-view lot now.

The island of Hawai'i isn't called the Big Island for nothing. The Big Island accounts for more than 60 percent of the state's total landmass. You can put two of every other island on the Big Island with hundreds of acres to spare. It has 266 miles of coast. It is 80 miles from east to west, and Cape Kumukahi is the easternmost point in the state. It stretches about 95 miles north to south, with Ka Lae (South Point) the southernmost point in the United States, which is believed to be where Polynesians first arrived.

Of all the Hawaiian Islands, the Big Island is closest to Polynesia, about 2,500 miles to the south. On a map of the Pacific Ocean, Hawai'i is the tip of part of a vast watery triangle

Trees and scrub bow before winds in the South Point area.

anchored below the equator by New Zealand to the southwest and Easter Island to the southeast. Inside are Samoa, Fiji, and the Marquesas. Above the equator, there's Christmas Island, as well as atolls such as Palmyra and Johnston.

Geography has played a large part in creating the natural world of Hawai'i and the Big Island that we experience today. It is the most isolated island group in the world. The nearest continent, North America, is more than 2,500 miles away. This isolation meant few animals and plants migrated here because it was so difficult to survive the ocean or air passage.

Some seeds and plants floated here. Others stuck to birds. Others blew in on the jet stream. The same serendipitous forces brought in animals. However, on average, only one invertebrate successfully survived in Hawai'i every 70,000 years, a plant once in every 100,000 years, and a bird once in every million years. Once on land, their evolution sped up, due to the absence of predators and the mild climate.

Given those odds, it isn't surprising that about 90 percent of the plants now found on the Hawaiian Islands arrived after the Europeans.

Some have adapted too well. Indigenous plants and animals have one of the world's highest rates of extinction, and almost half the U.S. birds classified as endangered live in Hawai'i. Of Hawai'i's more than 90 native bird species, 28 percent are extinct and another one-third are listed on the federal threatened and endangered species lists, according to figures released in 2000 by the U.S. Fish and Wildlife Service. The Hakalau Forest Wildlife Refuge was the first national wildlife refuge established in the United States for forest birds. There's even an effort to raise some of the endangered species in captivity. Family groups of the smallest of the endangered Hawai'i creepers, 'akepa, raised under a San Diego Zoo conservation program, were released in protected areas off the Big Island's Saddle Rd. in the fall of 2007. Invasive species have run through the Big Island's ecosystem, causing havoc. For example, a recent arrival, the miconia tree, native to South and Central America, was introduced to Tahiti in the 1930s and to Hawai'i in the 1960s. The trees grow quickly and close together. Their shade crowds out other forest plants, and their shallow root systems can cause landslides and erosion. Efforts are being made to eradicate it from the Big Island and from the rest of Hawai'i. The coqui frog, native to the Caribbean, arrived on the Big Island from Puerto Rico sometime around 1988. There were 200 at first, and the population has grown exponentially. Aside from being a noisy nuisance, their appetite puts Hawai'i's unique insects and spiders at risk. They also compete with endemic birds and other native fauna that rely on insects for food. They're adaptable, found in different ecological zones and elevations throughout the island, from sea level to 4,000 feet elevation.

SOCIAL HISTORY

The First Voyagers

The first Polynesians probably arrived in Hawai'i by chance. Fishermen or warriors blown from familiar waters returned home to Bora Bora, Moorea, and Tahiti to describe a huge, lush land with incredible *mana* or power, plenty of water, and seas rich in food. Or so ancient navigational chants suggest. Passed from father to son, the chants laid out routes to Hawai'i, passages navigated using the sun by day; the stars by night; and subtle signposts such as seabirds, the direction of swells, currents, and cloud formations.

A model of an ancient Hawaiian shelter at Pu'uhonua O Hōnaunau.

The first planned migrations to Hawai'i are estimated to have started between A.D. 300 and 500 from the Marquesas, 11 islands in eastern Polynesia. Chants suggest that the Mo'okini *heiau* on the Big Island was built around A.D. 480. The inhabitants were cannibals, tattooed in blue designs and patterns from head to toe. They built double-hulled canoes, catamarans as long as 80 feet, with a cabinlike hut in the center for shelter. Each could carry an extended family unit of 30 or so members. For starting anew in Hawai'i, they brought the roots of *kalo* (taro) and *uala* (sweet potato); *pua'a* (pigs), *'ilio* (dogs), *moa* (chickens), *niu* (coconut), *mai'a* (banana), *ko* (sugarcane), and other plants they could eat or use for medicine.

Without competition for land, cannibalism stopped even as the voyages between Polynesia and Hawai'i continued for hundreds of years. Life was good in paradise.

Then, the Tahitians arrived. Ready to do battle and conquer, they struck out for Hawai'i in the 12th century. According to oral histories, Pa'ao, a Tahitian priest, decided the chiefs in Hawai'i had weak gods. He erected a *heiau* at Waha'ula on the Big Island and introduced Kū (a war god) and the rigid *kapu* system that worked against the locals as the religious and social systems of the Tahitians subsumed their own. The most powerful deity to emerge was Pele, who appeared with every volcanic eruption or ooze. With the emergence of this goddess and others, the locals even lost their language, customs, and legends to the Tahitians, who, for about 100 years, kept refreshing their culture with voyages back to Tahiti. Bishop Museum researchers have shown that these open-sea voyages were more than legends; they have determined that the source rock for an adze found in the Tuamotus in the 1930s came from Kaho'olawe, the Hawaiian Island best known to most non-Hawaiians for its use as a weapons-testing ground and for protests against the weapons testing.

Contact Ceases

There's no reason given in the oral histories why the trips from Tahiti to Hawai'i stopped, but they did, and even the Polynesians forgot about the Hawaiian Islands. During the next four centuries of isolation, a highly stratified society developed. There was a strict demarcation of castes. The *ali'i* or chiefs ruled over the people and the land. *Kahuna*, respected and sometimes feared, were expert in key areas such as healing, medicine, canoe building, and religious rituals. *Maka'ainana*, the commoners, built houses and fishponds, raised crops, fished, and paid taxes to the paramount chief and the chiefs below him. The lowest caste, *kauwā*, were slaves or outcasts.

Many Hawaiians lived in villages, fishing in coastal waters; harvesting shellfish, seaweed, and salt along the shore; and farming the crops grown from seeds, roots, and saplings brought from long-forgotten Polynesia. The communities were roughly pie-shaped. Called *ahupua'a*, each ranged from the shore to the mountains, which meant every staple needed for life—fresh water, fish, verdant lowland soil, and lumber was available. Men pounded *kalo* into poi, a staple food. Women made *kapa*, a bark cloth, from paper mulberry, or *wauke*. Their *oli* (chants), *mele* (songs), and hula (dance) preserved a rich history, one forever intertwined with the lives of the *akua* (gods) and *'aumakua* (guardians).

A legal system, *kānāwai*, maintained the social order. Certain aspects of life—times, places, people, and things—were forbidden because they were sacred. Men and women ate apart. Certain foods, such as pork, coconuts, and bananas, were reserved for men. That meant they were *kapu* for women. The *kapu* system governed fishing, planting, and

Steam vents blur the edge of the caldera at Hawai'i Volcanoes National Park.

harvesting. Breaking *kapu* threatened the overall social system and was punishable by death.

Europeans Arrive

Captain James Cook arrived in 1778, a time of political uneasiness in Hawai'i. He went ashore on stone-age Kaua'i. The islands were a detour on his third attempt to find the Northwest Passage, and he encountered people without a written language or metal tools. For Hawaiians, Cook was the first contact with the white outsiders who would from then on influence the political, economic, cultural, and social evolution of Hawai'i.

Cook, famous in Britain for exploring much of the South Pacific, catapulted Hawai'i into the Iron Age. The Hawaiians, quickly aware of the material's capabilities, took whatever metal objects they could from Cook's ships and crew, particularly nails. The crew members took whichever women they could, spreading venereal disease. Cook noted in his diary that the Hawaiians looked like people he had encountered elsewhere in the Pacific. He also recorded that they were strong swimmers and well mannered. Then, after stocking up on fresh water, possibly in exchange for nails, he sailed away.

Cook returned to Hawai'i, which he called the Sandwich Islands after one of his patrons, the Earl of Sandwich, about a year later after he had failed to find the Northwest Passage in Alaska. He anchored the *Discovery* and the *Resolution* in Kealakekua Bay on the Big Island's Kona Coast. The expedition's chronicler and artist recorded the strange coincidences that led to the tragedy of Cook's return.

When the expedition dropped anchor on January 16, 1779, they stumbled into a period celebrating Lono, the fertility god depicted as a small wooden figure perched on a tall crossbeam festooned with long trails of white *kapa* cloth. According to legend, Lono was expected to return to earth—someday. As part of the celebration of Lono, normal *kapu* days had been suspended, which meant that people were free to dance, eat, and make love with abandon. It was a *makahiki* time of rejoicing, and to celebrants, it didn't take much to see Cook's tall ships as Lono's floating *heiau*; after all, Kealakekua Bay was Lono's own sacred harbor.

The Hawaiians took Cook ashore and treated him well while replenishing the ships' provisions. Sailors joined in all aspects of the celebrations. Then one of Cook's men died, blowing the sailors' cover as gods. His fellow crew members buried William Watman at Hiki-au Heiau. The Hawaiians began stealing from the crew, and the Englishmen broke many local laws. Relations became strained, and on February 4, 1779, when the ships sailed away, it was probably with the relief everyone feels when a celebration that's gone on too late finally winds down.

Then, like a party guest who returns to report his windshield smashed, Cook returned to Kealakekua Bay on February 13. Heavy weather broke the *Resolution*'s foremast. To the Hawaiians, this further proved the mortality of Cook's expedition, and they stoned the ships. As the confrontations increased, the crew captured an *ali'i* with a group that had stolen a small boat, and reportedly smacked him with a paddle. The Hawaiians attacked the sailors. Next they stole a cutter from the *Discovery,* angering Cook, who ordered men to stop any canoes trying to leave Kealakekua Bay.

Cook went ashore with armed men and persuaded King Kalani'opu'u to come back to the *Discovery* to remain there until the cutter was returned. The queen persuaded the king

Grass, shrubs and trees are reclaiming what was once a lava flow.

Rushing streams are one of the sights on the Old Māmalahoa Highway on the Hāmākua Coast.

to remain on the beach, and sailors fired on a canoe attempting to leave the bay, killing a lesser chief. A vast crowd gathered around the king and Cook. In the ensuing violence, Cook and his men killed several Hawaiians, then fled back to their ships. Cook, who could not swim, was killed in shallow water.

On February 16, the Hawaiians returned some of the remains of Cook's body to the expedition. The next day, Hawaiians displayed Cook's hat as they canoed past the English ships. That did it. The expedition turned its cannons on the shore, wounding Kamehameha the Great and a handful of *ali'i*, and killing about two dozen commoners. On February 21, the Hawaiians returned many of Cook's bones, including his skull, which were buried at sea. The expedition sailed away the next morning.

A Time of War

Cook's uneasy second sojourn coincided with a period of war among the three kingdoms of Hawai'i. By the 1780s, Kalani'opu'u ruled Hawai'i and Maui's Hana district. Kahekili ruled the rest of Maui, Kaho'olawe, Lana'i, and latterly, O'ahu. Kahekili's brother Kaeo ruled Kaua'i. It took King Kamehameha to unify the islands.

Kamehameha was born in the Kohala district of the Big Island in the early 1750s, near the *heiau* of the war god Kuka'ilimoku, or Kū the Destroyer. His father was Keoua Kupua-paikalaninui, the Kohala chief. His mother was a chieftess from Kaua'i, Kekuiapoiwa. Before his birth, a priest predicted that the child would grow up to be a "killer of chiefs," so when his mother gave birth secretly at the royal birthing stones near Mo'okini Heiau, she gave the baby to a trusted servant to raise him on the rugged coast around Kapa'au. Kalani'opu'u trained Kamehameha in things military, and he earned the reputation as a fearless warrior. As Kalani'opu'u neared death, he gave his kingdom to his son Kiwala'o and made Kamehameha keeper of the family's war god, Kū the Destroyer. After the old king died, Kamehameha fought Kiwala'o and his brother Keoua for nine years for control of the Big Island. Kamehameha killed Kiwala'o in battle at Moku'ōhai and reached a truce soon after with Keoua.

In 1790, the *haoles* returned, this time aboard two American ships, the *Eleanora* and the *Fair American*. Simon Metcalfe captained the first, his son, Thomas, commanded the second, smaller vessel. Looking for a harbor after sailing from the Pacific Northwest, they anchored east of Lahaina on Maui. A Hawaiian stealing a small boat killed one of the elder Metcalfe's crew. He invited Hawaiians to come aboard, luring them with offers of trade. As they approached, he took his revenge. His guns and cannons killed more than 100. Metcalfe then sailed off for Kealakekua Bay. Kameiamoku, a ruling chief stung by an unrelated incident, vowed to kill the next *haole*, or white, crew he encountered.

That crew was the younger Metcalfe and the *Fair American*. Kameiamoku overran the ship, which he turned over to Kamehameha, at about the same time the senior Metcalfe, anchored in Kealakekua Bay, sent John Young as an envoy to the ruler. Kamehameha prevented Young from returning, and Metcalfe, fed up and unaware of his son's fate, sailed for China. Isaac Davis, a *Fair American* survivor, joined Young when Kameiamoku gave him to Kamehameha, who realized that two *haoles* and the *Fair American*'s cannons might be useful.

With David and Young his advisors, both given the rank of chief, Kamehameha invaded Maui with the cannons rattling along on carts. Maui fell. But the other islands didn't follow like dominoes. Keoua set out to conquer the Big Island, and it looked bad for Kamehameha as he also faced Kahekili there. He defeated Kahekili at Waimanu; the cannons backed a fleet of war canoes. Kahekili accepted Kamahameha as the king of Maui. Still, Keoua remained.

Plants emerge from hardened lava left by the latest eruption.

But as he and the army traversed the slopes of Kīlauea, Pele, the fire goddess, spat poison-ous gas and ash into the air, instantly killing the troops, whose footprints remain in the hardened ash in a Pompeii-like memorial. Keoua saw this as a bad sign. Kamehameha and Keoua met at a temple to Kū that had just been completed by Kamehameha. Keoua knew he would die there. Kamehameha's men killed him as he arrived in Kawaihae.

Kamehameha next faced Kaeo of Kauaʻi and Niʻihau, and Kalanikupule of Oʻahu. They had received their islands from their father, Kahikili. Kalanikupule had captured a ship that anchored in Honolulu and decided to use it to attack Kamehameha on the Big Island. But the crew overtook their keepers and sailed on to warn Kamehameha. He raised an army, sailed for Maui, conquered it and Molokaʻi, then headed for Oʻahu. As his warriors overtook the island, they found the hiding Kalanikupule and killed him. In 1796, Kame-hameha quashed an uprising on the Big Island. Kauaʻi surrendered to the inevitable rather than endure a bloody war. For the first time in Hawaiian history, the islands were united, and Kamehameha ruled in peace until his death on May 8, 1819.

He moved the court to Lahaina,on Maui, where he built the Brick Palace in 1803. A benevolent tyrant, he wrote laws to protect commoners. He also participated in the sandal-wood trade, coming in greater contact with white traders who sold it for him in China.

Kamehameha returned to the Kona Coast of the Big Island, where he died in 1819, the year missionaries set out from New England for the islands and the year the *kapu* was cast aside. His bones were buried in a still-secret tomb after the flesh was baked from them. His kingdom passed to his son, Liholiho, with his first wife, Keopuolani, but power re-mained with his beloved Kaʻahumanu, the third of his 21 wives.

Born in Maui's Hana district, Kaʻahumanu had the people's respect. So when she and Keopuolani persuaded Liholiho to break two sacred *kapu* by eating with women and allow-ing women to eat bananas less than a year after Kamehameha died, Hawaiians knew the old ways, the old laws, and the old gods were finished. This defining change came just as the missionaries arrived, determined to convert the Hawaiians and civilize the wild seafarers who had settled in the islands they saw as their paradise.

Greater Contact

Cook's adventures put Hawaiʻi on the navigational charts, and as more seafarers discovered the islands' pleasures, they became a more frequent provisioning and recreational stop for whalers and China traders. Change was not always good for the islands.

In exchange for aloha, the sailors, starting with Cook's crews, left behind common colds, venereal disease, and other ailments that devastated the Hawaiians, who lacked immunities to these foreign bugs. When Cook arrived in 1778, he estimated the population to be 300,000. By the 1850s, there were barely 60,000 Native Hawaiians, a decline that was not offset by growth in the number of *hapa haole* children, the offspring of Hawaiians and white seamen. In one example of change, the American sea captain John Kendrick took aboard a cargo of sandalwood and sailed for China, where it was highly valued. That was in 1791. By 1825, the islands were stripped of sandalwood, opening the land to invasive species in the first environmental catastrophe wrought by visitors.

But change wasn't always bad, either. Two years after Kendrick set sail, an Englishman, George Vancouver, who had first visited Hawaiʻi with Cook, left cows and sheep on the Big Island. To control them, King Kamehameha I sent to Mexico and Spain for cowboys, begin-ning the *paniolo* tradition that continues today throughout the islands but is especially strong on the Big Island.

Missionaries Arrive

The biggest changes came with the missionaries fresh from the revival that "burned over" western New England and much of upstate New York in the early 19th century. Single men and women volunteered for missionary duty in the heathen Sandwich Islands, answering a call from the American Board of Commissioners for Foreign Missions, the first organized missionary society in the United States. The organization publicized the godless condition of Hawaiians after hearing stories from returning sailors and a few Hawaiians who ventured to New England. Among them was Henry Opukaha'ia, an orphan from Nāpō'opo'o on the Big Island, who had been befriended by a Yankee captain. Opukaha'ia learned to read and write, then embraced Christianity. He wanted nothing more than to return home to spread the word, but he caught pneumonia and died in 1819 before he could.

On October 23, 1819, the brig *Thaddeus* set sail from Boston carrying newly married couples on their honeymoon voyage to Hawai'i. After 157 days at sea, they landed in Kailua Bay on the Big Island on April 4, 1820. King Liholiho granted them a one-year trial period for their work, which was met with great hostility from the seafarers and traders who greatly enjoyed life among the uncivilized pagans, particularly the female heathens. One upset captain fired his ship's cannons on a church on Maui. Nonetheless, the missionaries burrowed in on the Big Island and O'ahu. New Englanders to the core, they believed in education and enterprise as well as the "fiery god" of the 18th-century Calvinist Jonathan Edwards. They soon had Hawaiians wearing more clothing and even shoes. They adapted the Roman alphabet to Hawaiian and started recording Hawaiian history in writing and documenting plants and animals, fish, and birds. They were determined to succeed, and within four years of their arrival Keopoulani climbed Kīlauea and defied Pele by eating forbidden *'ohelo* berries and proclaiming "Jehovah is my God." She inspired other *ali'i* to

At Pu'uhonua O Hōnaunau, two images, called ki'i , overlook Keone'ele Cove.

embrace Christianity. When she died in 1824, she received a Christian burial. In her, the missionaries had a powerful ally for their condemnation of all things true to the old Hawaiian ways, and once Ka'ahumanu died in 1835, it wasn't until David Kalakaua took the throne in 1874 that a ruler stepped up to promote Hawaiian culture.

Fast-Paced Change

By the time Kalakaua was elected, missionary children had become political and business leaders. They did well. In 1848, King Kamehameha III proclaimed the Great Mahele, a division of land that allowed commoners and eventually foreigners to own crown land. That first year, almost 250 *ali'i* entered their claims on land. In 1850, commoners received title in fee simple for the land they occupied as tenant farmers; commoners without land were allowed to buy small farms from the government for 50 cents an acre, and foreigners were allowed to buy land in fee simple. The foreigners had more money; they bought more land. As their holdings grew, life in Hawai'i changed. Within two generations of the Great Mahele, white foreigners owned 80 percent of the land.

Elias Bond started the first sugar plantation on the Big Island in the mid-19th century, several years after Koloa Sugar Plantation successfully refined sugar on Kaua'i in 1835. By the early 1870s, the Kohala Plantation was making a profit, and the enterprise there continued until 1975.

Operating a plantation required labor, more than could be provided by just Hawaiians. The first imported laborers were brought in from China in 1852, but they left the fields as soon as possible to set up shops and small businesses. Next came Japanese laborers in 1885. The planters, mostly New Englanders, sought labor wherever they could recruit it cheaply. Puerto Rico, Germany, Korea, Portugal, Russia, and the Philippines were all sources for workers, the ones with the lightest skin usually working as overseers.

Kalakaua, known as "the Merrie Monarch," began his reign as this stew of cultures—each with its own beliefs, foods, and practices—began to thicken. As the foreigners intermarried with each other and with Hawaiians and shared their cultures, Kalakaua lifted missionary imposed prohibitions on hula and other Hawaiian arts. He also gave Pearl Harbor to the United States in exchange for passage of the 1875 Reciprocity Act, which exempted Hawaiian sugar from import duty.

Hawai'i Is a Rainbow

In 2003, the Big Island had 163,000 residents.

They were:

Caucasian	28.2%
Japanese	15.1%
Filipino	8.2%
Chinese	0.8%
Black	sample too small
Korean	sample too small
Samoan/Tongan	0.2%
Mixed (ex-Hawaiian)	18%
Hawaiian/part	28.9%

The summit of Mauna Kea casts a sunset shadow over a nearby peak.

His enthusiasm for closer ties with the United States didn't sit well with his sister, Lydia Lili'uokalani, who became queen upon Kalakaua's death in 1891. Among the *haole* nations with designs on Hawai'i, she favored England. Most of the planters saw her as an impediment to greater profits, and some 30 of them, led by Lorrin Thurston and backed by supporters in the U.S. Congress, overthrew her with a coup. U.S. Marines anchored in Honolulu harbor came ashore to save American lives in the chaos. One of the insurgents wounded a Hawaiian policeman. The monarchy fell on January 17, 1893, and Sanford Dole became president of the Hawaiian Republic. The former queen surrendered to the U.S. ambassador because she believed the U.S. government would be outraged by the *haoles'* shenanigans and opposed to annexation. But she was up against prominent citizens who wanted to join the United States, and when her counterrevolution failed in January 1895, she was forced to abdicate, then swear allegiance to the island republic. She remained queen to most Hawaiians until her death in 1917. She wrote *Hawai'i's Story* and the beloved farewell ballad "Aloha 'Oe."

Becoming American

Most Hawaiians, like Lili'uokalani, opposed annexation, but when the time came to decide on the matter, they discovered they failed to meet the property and income requirements for voting set out by the republic. Hawai'i became an American territory in 1898 with Dole in charge. He and his cronies controlled every element of economic life on the islands, and under their rule, Hawai'i entered the 20th century unalterably changed from the islands of 100 years earlier. Most of the few native Hawaiians who remained struggled to survive in remote isolation. Plantation ways strongly influenced by imported Asian workers dominated the local culture. A white elite ruled.

Yet once again, change was in the air. Beginning in 1935, the Webley Edwards weekly radio show *Hawai'i Calls* sent the sounds of paradise to listeners throughout the United States, Canada, and Australia (you can listen to the program at www.hularecords.com/radio/). In 1936, Pan American Airlines launched flying boat service from San Francisco to Honolulu. The flight took 21 hours to make the crossing that steamers covered in four or five days. But Pam Am scheduled daily flights, and an increasing number of passengers, many humming tunes from *Hawai'i Calls,* made the $360 one-way flight until December 6, 1941.

It took the Japanese attack on Pearl Harbor on December 7, 1941, to truly solidify the notion that Hawai'i was part of the United States. Statehood first came up in the 1850s, but it wasn't discussed seriously in Congress until the overthrow of the monarchy. Until World War II, opposition continued for economic reasons and a fear of admitting a state without a white majority. By the war's end, feelings had changed. Hawai'i's 100th Battalion was the most decorated U.S. unit in all of World War II, making it difficult to question the loyalty of nonwhites. GIs from the mainland who had spent time in Hawai'i during the war appreciated its exoticism but saw how much life, particularly in the bigger cities of O'ahu and Hawai'i, resembled that back home. The statehood movement in Hawai'i grew, and the eventual vote was 132,000 for and 7,800 against. The islands officially became a state on August 21, 1959.

That year saw the first jet airliners arrive from the mainland. In 2006, 7,561,311 visitors arrived in the state of Hawai'i; all but 100,012 came by air.

In Hilo, the Lili'uokalani Gardens feature Asian landscaping

2

Transportation

Getting Here, Getting Around

For most people, flying to the Big Island means touching down at Honolulu International Airport, then catching an interisland flight to either Kailua-Kona or Hilo. The interisland fares can vary wildly from startlingly high to unbelievably low. In both cases, fares can change by the day, so familiarize yourself with the airlines flying to Hawai'i and the range of prices they offer before making a booking. This will also give you a chance to evaluate packages of flights and hotel lodgings available from mainland and Hawai'i-based carriers as well as tour companies and consolidators.

In the past, most flights to the Big Island landed at Hilo International Airport because it is the state's second-largest city and close to Hawai'i Volcanoes National Park. As development surged on the island's other side, the state recognized the need for expanding a local airstrip in 1947. Kona International Airport, which opened at Keāhole in 1970, is where most flights arrive today. Both airports have the capacity to handle the jumbo jets used on long-haul direct flights from the East Coast or Asia. The availability of direct flights to the Big Island depends on your departure airport and the time of year.

Animal Quarantine
Hawai'i is not the vacation destination for your pets. The state has strict animal quarantine regulations, but guide dogs and other service dogs are exempt. For more information, go to the Department of Agriculture Animal Quarantine Web site at http://hawaii.gov/hdoa/ai/aqs/info or call 808-483-7151.

Agricultural Inspection
Hawai'i's ecosystem is varied and delicate. As your first introduction to how seriously protection is taken, you'll be asked to complete a "Plant and Animals Declaration Form" on your flight to Hawai'i. It is collected before you touch down. If you are carrying any of the items, which include fruits, vegetables, seeds, plants, soil, live insects, and snakes, they will be inspected by the state's agricultural team at the airport. The full list of prohibited items is available at http://hawaii.gov/hdoa.

As you leave, your bags will be inspected again. Usually, this is a quick and simple procedure. Some items, like papayas, must be treated before you take them home. Others, such as some plants, can't leave the island. Many growers offer items prepacked and certified. If you have questions about plants that you want to take to the mainland, call the U.S. Department of Agriculture at 808-326-1252.

Plants sprout from trees in a path near the village of Volcano.

Due to the volume of visitor traffic at Honolulu International Airport, the procedure for landing, then transferring to an interisland flight, is relatively easy. Once you disembark, there are signs directing you to the Wiki-Wiki shuttle bus, or you can stretch your legs with a quick walk along a sidewalk kept nice and smooth for wheeled luggage. The interisland terminal has a restaurant, fast food, and a gift shop with magazines and books, so there are distractions while you wait for your connection.

Once you're on the Big Island, a car is almost a necessity unless you plan to take a taxi from an airport, check into one place, and stay there for your entire visit, an honorable option for the exhausted, the romantics who can't see beyond each other, or those on family reunions seeking maximum togetherness. Otherwise, when you think of distances on the island of Hawai'i, focus on why it is called the Big Island and keep that first word in mind. Population centers, historic sites, and areas of great beauty are miles apart, many of them on secondary roads. In fact, this is a destination where it makes sense to rent a sport utility vehicle or a pickup truck. Not only will you get the height needed to see over barrier railings (where there are such things), it's swell to have the clearance that allows you to pull off the road onto a lava rock under the trees and park for a picnic feet from tide pools or crashing waves or overlooking a pasture surrounded by extinct volcanoes and filled with sleek cows staring back at you. SUVs and pickups will get you through mud, over gravel, and across pastures, all of which you can encounter on the driveway to your vacation cabin with an ocean view.

Another reason for renting a car, even if you are planning to stay at a self-contained resort, is that the Big Island has some world-class drives. Stretches of the main highway are glorious, and many of the secondary roads, such as the Kohala Mountain Rd.–Akoni Pule Hwy. circuit through North Kohala, have breathtaking views.

Getting around the Big Island is confusingly simple. The Hawai'i Belt Rd. that circles the island is also known as the Māmalahoa Hwy. and it has different route numbers in different parts of the island. It goes by HI 11 when connecting Kailua-Kona to Hilo around the southern end of the island and is called HI 190 when going north from Kailua-Kona to Waimea, where it becomes HI 19 to Hilo. Although it's possible to drive around the island in one day, why would you? The 225-mile trip takes some seven hours, and that's without exploring anything off the main road, let alone hitting many of the highlights.

GETTING TO THE BIG ISLAND

By Air

If you fly to the Big Island, and most people do, you'll land at one of two airports. **Kona International Airport** at

Hibiscus bloom everywhere. Pick one to tuck behind your ear.

Keāhole, on the west side, serves Kailua-Kona, Keauhou, and the Kohala Coast. **Hilo International Airport** is a better choice for those going to the east side of the island or to Volcanoes National Park. It is a long drive from one side of the island to the other. If you don't want to do it after a long flight, a taxi will cost between $200 and $250.

Both airports have ATMs, car rental stands, restaurants, gift shops, newsstands, family and accessible restrooms, porter services, and TTY devices for the hearing impaired. Accessible parking spaces are in the public parking lot directly across the street of the terminal near the crosswalks. Accessible loading and unloading zones are available curbside in front of the terminals.

Waimea-Kohala Airport, called Kamuela Airport by residents, is used primarily for interisland commuting and private aviation.

United Airlines (800-225-5825; www.ual.com). United Airlines has the most frequent service from the U.S. mainland, offering flights to Honolulu and Kailua-Kona.

American Airlines (800-433-7300; www.aa.com). AA offers flights from Dallas, Chicago, and elsewhere to Honolulu.

Continental Airlines (800-231-0856; www.continental.com). Continental Airlines flies directly from the New York City area to Hawai'i, leaving from Newark International Airport in New Jersey for Honolulu.

Delta Airlines (800-221-1212; www.delta.com). Delta Airlines flies nonstop from the West Coast and Houston to Honolulu.

Hawaiian Airlines (800-367-5320; www.hawaiianair.com). Hawaiian Airlines has non-stop service from many West Coast cities to Honolulu and Kailua-Kona.

Northwest Airlines (800-225-2525; www.nwa.com). Northwest Airlines flies to Honolulu from hubs in Minneapolis and Detroit with stops along the way.

All-inclusive packages are available from many of the airlines. Some travel agencies offer all-inclusive packages as well:

American Express Travel (800-297-6898; www.americanexpress.com)

Costco Travel (www.costco.com)

Cheap Tickets (www.cheaptickets.com). Cheap Tickets started as an interisland discounter in Honolulu and grew.

Liberty Travel (888-271-1584; www.libertytravel.com).

Pleasant Hawaiian Holidays (800-242-9244). Pleasant Hawaiian Holidays offers packages in every price range.

TravelZoo (www.travelzoo.com). TravelZoo often has attractively priced packages.

Interisland Flights

Hawaiian Airlines (800-367-5320; www.hawaiianair.com). Hawaiian Airlines offer flights from Honolulu, and other islands, to both Big Island air-

Not everyone has left the Kalanpana area near the current lava flow.

Another day, another stone seal sporting flowers and pearls near Keauhou.

ports throughout the day. Ticket prices vary by time of day. It does not cost more to fly into one airport and out the other. The first and last flights of the day are usually the least expensive. There are several smaller airlines, but Hawaiian has been around the longest and is unlikely to go out of business suddenly, as has happened with other airlines in the past.

GETTING AROUND

By Bus
The County of Hawai'i operates a public transit system, the **Hele-On** bus. It does not go to either airport. The routes will take you from one side of the island to the other with stops along the way. There is wheelchair access. If you're in a hurry, don't take the bus. For a full schedule and route map, go to www.co.hawaii.hi.us/mass_transit/heleonbus.html or call 808-961-8744.

By Taxi or Shuttle
There are taxi companies serving the airport at Hilo and Kona. Neither has a public transit link. Taxi fares are regulated. The approximate taxi rate is $3 to start, plus $.30 every ⅛ mile, with surcharges for waiting time at $.30 per minute and $1 per bag. From Hilo International to downtown costs about $12, to the Banyan Drive hotels, expect to pay about $13. From Kona International Airport south to Ali'i Drive hotels and condos, fares range from $25 to $35. Heading north, fares can be as much as $75 to the Mauna Kea Resort.

A well-protected driveway in the Puna jungle.

If you don't rent a car, taxis are available for private tours, but this can be very expensive. In Hilo call:
A-1 Taxi (808-959-4800).
Hilo Harry's (808-935-7091).
In Kailu Kana
Speedishuttle (808-329-5433, 877-242-5777; www.speedishuttle.com). Speedishuttle operates at the Kona airport from 7 AM to 10 PM daily. It uses multipassenger vans, so your fare is cheaper, but the ride to your destination may be longer. You can make a reservation for airport or hotel pickup.

By Rented Car

Reserve a vehicle in advance. There's a limited supply of vehicles, and if there's a big conference or festival on one side of the island, the extras are sent over to meet the demand.

Be sure to read the rental contract carefully. You may be prohibited from driving off all paved roads.

Do consider renting an SUV or a pickup, because you're after clearance, height, and comfort. You need a four-wheel-drive vehicle for the Mauna Kea and Mauna Loa summit roads, and the South Point roads. Do NOT drive into the Waipi'o Valley. The grade is very steep, the road narrow, and the potential for a serious, if not deadly, accident high.

Only **Harper's Car and Truck Rental,** a local outfit with competitive rates and offices at both airports, allows you to drive its vehicles across the Saddle Rd., a beautiful, big-sky shortcut across the island from Hilo to Waimea. If you want to make the drive and can't rent from Harper's, know exactly what your personal automobile insurance policy covers. It is worth calling your agent. Tow charges and repair costs can be unpleasant.

Ask for a child seat or installation of controls for handicapped drivers when booking your vehicle.

It is possible to rent a car at the Hilo Airport and drop it off in Kona. Most companies charge extra for this, but it often is a worthwhile convenience.

While deals exist, expect taxes and fees to be at least a 25 percent add-on to the daily rate.

Gas is costly on the Big Island. Keep an eye on your tank, because fuel can be shockingly European in price if you pump at one of the little general stores up-country.

The best map is the *Map of Hawai'i* prepared by James A. Bier and published by the University of Hawai'i Press. It has a useful index and shows a detailed network of secondary roads, hiking trails, parks, beaches, natural features, and points of cultural and historic interest. It is available at www.uhpress.hawaii.edu and costs $4.95. It is also on the island at bookstores and newsstands and online at Amazon.com.

Almost all the major car rental agencies operate at the two airports. They all accept all major credit cards.

Alamo (800-327-9633; www.goalamo.com).

Avis (800-321-3712; www.avis.com).

Budget (800-527-0700; www.budget.com).

Dollar (800-800-4000; www.dollar.com).

Enterprise (800-325-8007; www.enterprise.com).

Harper's (800-852-9993; www.harpershawaii.com).

Hertz (800-654-3011; www.hertz.com).

National (800-227-7368; www.nationalcar.com).

Thrifty (800-367-3277; www.thrifty.com).

Even with affinity group, credit card, or loyalty program discounts offered by the national agencies, it is often tough to beat the rates at **Discount Hawaii Car Rental** (888-292-3307; www.discounthawaiicarrental.com). They're pleasant and efficient.

By Motorcycle

Big Island Motorcycle Rentals (808-326-9887, www.konaharleydavidson.com, 5615 Luhia St., Kailua-Kona; 808-934-9090, 200 Kanoelehua Ave. #106, Hilo).

Driving Tips

Wear a seat belt at all times. Police will pull you over and issue a ticket if you're not.

All infants and toddlers must be in child seats according to state law. Bring one from home or rent one from your car rental agency.

Speed limits are enforced by air and radar. There are long stretches of open road on the Big Island, and the temptation is great to open up. Leave it to the locals.

There are yellow, solar-powered emergency call boxes along the main roads. Calls from these telephones go to the local emergency response center.

A GPS device is not necessary, but it is handy to have in Hilo and Kailua-Kona if your map-reading skills are rusty or if you feel daunted by unfamiliar street names.

Pay attention to landmarks and mile markers. You will receive directions to look for landmarks or to turn based on these numbers at the side of main and some secondary roads. The mile markers are small, but reflective.

Remember that many of the people on the road are visitors just like you and aren't sure of where they're going, so drive defensively. If you're on back roads or going slowly on a main road, pull over to let local residents pass.

If a sign says a road requires four-wheel drive, believe it. Just because it looks fine at the sign doesn't mean it isn't a muddy nightmare a mile ahead.

If signs say DO NOT ENTER or PRIVATE PROPERTY, KEEP OUT, or KAPU, stay off the road. Cane roads are on private property, so stay off them even if the carload of folks in front of you turns and speeds into one.

Avoid driving in rush hour on the Kailua-Kona side of the island from north of the resorts to south of the turnoffs for Captain Cook. The morning rush, or rather, the morning slow, gets under way before 6 AM and lasts until close to 9 AM. In the afternoon, expect delays from 3 until 6. Traffic can also be heavier during these times in Waimea, and going into Hilo from Kea'au and Pāhoa.

A quiet South Kona road leads down to the Pacific Ocean.

Onward through the jungle on a Harley. Riding on the Big Island is how it should be. Expect to pay about $150 for a Harley-Davidson for a day that begins at 8:30 AM and ends at 5:30 PM. Twenty-four-hour rentals are also available, as are half-day and seven-day rentals. Helmets and rain gear are available. You must have a motorcycle license.

By Bicycle

Circling the island by bike isn't usually the main attraction, even though main roads on the Big Island are well paved and most of the grades are easy with a few notable exceptions. Most people pick an area and explore it on their own bicycle or one they rent on the island from a local shop. Beyond rentals, almost all offer repairs, equipment, and the latest updates on conditions and locally organized rides. For a complete listing of bicycling options, see chapter 7, Recreation.

At the Parker Ranch Center, they're serious about making sure all traffic stops.

Driving Times

Kailua-Kona to Hilo via HI 19: 2 hours, 30 min. (north)

Kailua-Kona to Hilo via HI 11: 3 hours, 15 min. (south)

Kailua-Kona to Hilo via Saddle Rd: 2 hours, 15 min

Kailua-Kona to Hawai'i Volcanoes National Park via HI 11: 2 hours, 30 min.

Kailua-Kona to Waimea via HI 19: 50 min.

Kailua-Kona to Hāwī via HI 19 and 279: 1 hour, 15 min.

Kailua-Kona to Kohala: 45 min.

Hilo to Hawai'i Volcanoes National Park: 50 min.

Hilo to Waimea: 90 min.

Hilo to Kohala via HI 19: 2 hours.

Kona International Airport to Kailua-Kona: 30 min.

Kona International Airport to Kohala: 25 min.

Hilo Airport to downtown Hilo: 10 min.

Hilo Airport to Banyan Dr. hotels: 10 min.

Never underestimate the time it will take you to get someplace. Distances are long and roads are narrow and often twisting. Construction or a fender bender can slow traffic to a crawl. More times and distance are available at: www.bigisland.org/maps-regions/525/driving-times-distances.

When a road's name contains the word "Old" expect twists, turns and views.

Honolulu Overnight

There's a case to be made for spending the night in Honolulu even if your flight from the mainland arrives in plenty of time to connect to an interisland flight to the Big Island. Here's why:

No matter where you come from, the flight to Hawai'i is long and there's a time change, a five-hour gain from the East Coast, for example. Because you can purchase a separate round-trip interisland ticket, there's no extra fee for stopping over. Once you land in Honolulu, most flights from the mainland arrive in the afternoon, so you have time to catch some sun and have a swim, both good ways to overcome **jetlag**. After dinner and a good sleep, you can fly to the Big Island, after spending the morning at the **Bishop Museum**. Charles Reed Bishop founded the museum in 1889 in memory of his late wife, Princess Bernice Pauahi Bishop, the last royal descendant of the Kamehameha line. It houses her extensive collection of Hawaiian artifacts and royal family heirlooms and has expanded to include millions of artifacts, documents, and photographs about Hawai'i and other Pacific island cultures. It is a **crash course in the history of Hawai'i,** a series of exhibits so well thought out and so informative there's a danger of lingering too long. The benefit to this educational jaunt is that the knowledge you absorb will inform almost everything you see or do on the Big Island.

The ins and outs of how to overnight are easy. **Reserve a room** at one of these three hotels on the **quiet beach** in a ritzy, residential neighborhood **beyond Waikiki**: Diamond Head Beach Hotel, the New Otani Kaimana Beach Hotel, or W Honolulu–Diamond Head. At the same time make a **dinner** reservation at **Hau Tree Lanai** in the Kaimana Beach Hotel. Of all the beachfront restaurants in the state, this is among the closest to the sand and waves. Dinner is moderately priced, and breakfast is inexpensive. Don't miss it.

Book a car at Hertz or Avis because they have stalls inside Honolulu Airport. Once you collect your luggage, you walk mere yards to collect your keys and go. The drive to Waikiki is well marked. Take the Nimitz Hwy., HI 92. Follow the Nimitz until it merges with Ala Moana Blvd. Keep driving on Ala Moana Blvd. Merge right onto Kalākaua Ave. Continue traveling on Kalākaua Ave for about 2 miles. You're in the right neighborhood when you see a traffic circle with a gushing water fountain.

Check into your room. Change, **slather on sunscreen, and hit the beach.** There's a white-sand beach, the Sans Souci Beach, in front of the New Otani Kaimana Beach Hotel that you can use if you stay at the other hotels. Look for signs that say: BEACH ACCESS. Swim out far enough to flip on your back and use your toes to frame a view of the low-scale hotels and condos.

Have dinner, then walk west on Kalākaua Ave. and explore the heart of Waikiki. Bed. An early rise. A **walk along the lava seawall** is a good way to start the day. For access, enter the Diamond Head Beach Hotel, pass the check-in lobby, step up onto the low wall when you reach the ocean, and turn left. Walk to the end. Jump down onto the sand. If you've made a thermos of coffee or tea in your room, here's where to drink it. Turn around and head back the same way, or you can take any of the walkways through to the street and turn left.

The Bishop Museum opens at 9 AM every day but Christmas. Plan to be there when it opens. It's all good. Don't miss the volcano exhibit at the Hall of Science. If you're hungry, try the **tasting plate of Hawaiian foods** in the open-air café. It's an inexpensive lunch, and you can eat outside under the trees. Museum admission is $15.95 for adults, $12.95 for seniors 65 and older and children 4 to 12. Children under 3 are free.

It's a quick drive back to the airport, where you can leave your car and check in for your interisland flight.

Lodging

Diamond Head Beach Hotel

808-922-1928; www.dhbh.com

2947 Kalākaua Ave., Honolulu, HI 96815

Price: Moderate

For the location, location, location, this is a bargain. There is no restaurant, but the rooms have microwaves and refrigerators, and there's a convenience shop half a block away where you can get the basics and even the extras needed for a sunset cocktail hour. The decor can vary, as many of the units are individually owned condo units that are rented out part of the year. Spend extra for an oceanfront room. If you don't, be sure to go down to the lava wall for sunset. You'll know without a doubt you're in Hawai'i, and you're getting a dose of light needed to help set your body in a new time zone.

New Otani Kaimana Beach Hotel

808-923-1555; 800-356-8264; www.kaimana.com

2863 Kalākaua Ave., Honolulu, HI 96815

Price: Moderate–Very Expensive

All major credit cards accepted

A welcoming offshoot of Tokyo's New Otani Hotel, the Kaimana Beach Hotel exudes the tropical wonderland vibe you need after a long flight. Trade winds fill the open-air lobby filled with orchids that don't distract from views of brilliant blue-green waves just beyond the tiled floor and bar. The rooms are cozy but feel expansive if you spring for an oceanfront view, even on the lower floors. The staff provides exceptional service.

W Honolulu–Diamond Head

866-716-8111; www.starwoodhotels.com

2885 Kalākaua Ave., Honolulu, HI 96815

Price: Very Expensive

Part of a deeply cool chain of boutique hotels, the Honolulu W grades its rooms from "Wonderful," which are on floors 3–7, to "Extreme Wow Suite," with "Spectacular" and "Fabulous" in between. They're all plush and lovely, with 350-thread-count linens, waffle robes, down pillows, and amenities from Bliss. There are only 48 rooms, and the square footage, floor, and view account for the differences. The spa offers Hawaiian *lomi-lomi* massage as well as other treatments; there's gourmet dining at the Diamond Head Grill for breakfast, lunch, and dinner; and the bar scene is lively. In short, it's a W hotel.

Dining

New Otani Kaimana Beach Hotel

808-921-7066

www.kaimana.com

2863 Kalākaua Ave., Honolulu, HI 96815

All major credit cards accepted

Breakfast Daily: 7:00–10:45

Dinner Daily: 5:30–9:00

Price: Moderate–Expensive

Handicapped Access: Yes

Special Features: Entertainment Tues. through Sat. nights

Hau Tree Lanai

On a white-sand beach in a setting praised by author Robert Louis Stevenson a century ago, this is a delightful place for dinner or breakfast. For dinner, I prefer local food prepared in ways inspired by local kitchens, which means I invariably order the catch of the day. It never disappoints.In the morning, I like the Asian Breakfast, a feast of longanisa sausage, garlic fried rice, eggs, green papaya salad, and sliced Japanese cucumber. It can be shared. Less exotic and lighter fare is available. The pancakes and waffles made with poi are good.

The Bishop Museum

808-847-3511

1525 Bernice St., Honolulu, HI 96817

Open: 9–5 every day except Christmas. There is ample free parking. Admission is $15.95 for adults; $12.95 for children ages 4–12 and seniors 65 and older; children under 3 free.

Driving directions from Diamond Head area:

Follow signs for HI 1 West

Take the ramp onto I-HI W

Take exit 20A to merge onto HI 63 N/Likelike Hwy.

Turn right at Bernice St.

Avis (800-321-3712; www.avis.com)

Hertz (800-654-3011; www.hertz.com)

Builders laid lava walls and tie bamboo by hand at Tara Cottage.

3

LODGING

Not Just for Sleeping

Built in 1866, the first hotel on Hawaiʻi was the Volcano House, which overlooks the Kīlauea Crater. It was built near where the chiefess Kapiolani built a grass shack in 1824 when she came to the crater to denounce Pele, the volcano goddess, and declare her conversion to Christianity. That episode didn't stop people, Hawaiian and others, from visiting the powerful site, and in 1846, Benjamin Pittman Sr. built another grass shack he called Volcano House to accommodate crater visitors who traveled from as far away as Europe. By 1866, *ʻōhiʻa* wood poles had been added to the grass structure, and the Volcano House became a permanent fixture. Mark Twain, who stayed in the Volcano House that same year, described it as "neat, roomy, well furnished, and a well-kept hotel. The surprise of finding a good hotel at such an outlandish spot startled me, considerably more than the volcano did."

The place continued to grow in response to the increasing numbers of tourists, and by 1877, it was an all-wood building with a dining room, six rooms, and a parlor with a fireplace in which a fire has burned continuously ever since. A long, low-slung building, the hotel offered accommodations and sustenance for travelers and their horses, with a bathhouse out back. Purchased by George Lycurgus in 1895, the place burned down 45 years later, and he rebuilt the hotel, right at the edge of the crater.

Today, you may not be surprised to find a hotel near a volcano, but you will be taken aback at the range of accommodations available on the Big Island. From camping near the beach to booking into one of many resorts consistently rated among the best in the world, the Big Island offers more options for Morpheus than a Sleep Number bed. There are historic business hotels, many of them started by Japanese immigrants. There are bargain condos and ultraluxe condos and every price in between. You can rent a home by the week or for months. Bed-and-breakfasts span the range of known accommodation: tree houses, Victorian mansions that feel like English country homes elegantly infused with aloha, hillside cottages with upland views, and hillside cottages with ocean sunset views. You want jungle, no problem. Dry heat, ditto.

If you prefer a recognizable chain, international, national, and Hawaiian hoteliers are well represented. However, like everything else on the Big Island, figuring out where you want to stay requires a series of choices: the actual location, the kind of place, the price, and then deciding which of the options fulfills your dream of what the Big Island should be.

In this chapter, we describe and review lodging options. The list covers the spectrum. In evaluating them, we've considered many factors, including service, friendliness, atmosphere, and convenience as well as price. Whenever you can afford it, opt for accommodations with the best view, which is usually oceanfront rather than oceanview. You've come a long way. Hear the surf at night. Wake up and see the ocean.

BIG ISLAND LODGING NOTES

The prime tourist seasons for the island of Hawai'i start in mid-December and last through early May—prime whale-watching season—and pick up again in early June until the end of August. Expect prices to be higher, if not doubled, during the Christmas and New Year's holiday season and accommodations to be heavily, if not fully, booked because many visitors reserve for the next year as they're checking out. Japan's Golden Week, when there are four national holidays in a seven-day span, can make for crowds starting on April 29. Japanese tourists are also a significant presence during Obon, a week in mid-August traditionally set aside for commemorating one's ancestors, but now often used as a time for travel. It is worth checking the up-to-date calendar of events at www.bigisland.org, so you don't pay extra when room rates go up due to the demands of a convention, a festival, or a sporting event such as the Iron Man Triathlon.

If you're planning to visit during a busy time, book flights early and arrive on the island with hotel and car reservations already in place.

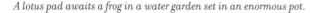

A lotus pad awaits a frog in a water garden set in an enormous pot.

As all the Hawaiian Islands become more of a year-round vacation destination, there are fewer off-season times than there were in the past. You can expect fewer people and lower prices at some times of the year, particularly two or three weeks after Thanksgiving. It never hurts to ask if there is an off-season rate, and on many online reservation pages for home rentals or B&Bs you'll see how the prices dip in the off-seasons. Price codes in this chapter are based on a per-room rate, double occupancy, during the high season.

Lodging Price Codes

Inexpensive	Up to $100
Moderate	$100–225
Expensive	$225–350
Very Expensive	Over $350

Credit Cards

AE: American Express
CB: Carte Blanche
D: Discover Card
DC: Diners Club
MC: MasterCard
V: Visa

Minimum Stay

Many B&Bs and vacation home rentals, including condo units, require a minimum stay of two or three nights throughout the year. While this may be negotiable during slower periods, your best option for a single night's lodging or if you want some spontaneity in your visit is to stay in a hotel.

Deposits/Cancellations

You will often be asked to make a deposit when you reserve accommodations. The deposit can be the price of one night, although more is often required if you will be staying several nights. Don't be surprised if you are asked for the total cost in advance if you are making reservations for the holiday season or during a big event. If you must cancel a reservation, you'll usually get your deposit back if you are canceling within the policy of your lodging. These vary widely and can require as much as a month's notice for a full refund, so check the cancellation policies when you make a reservation. Some establishments deduct a service fee from the refund. Some will issue a refund only if your room is rented. In which case, expend a bit of effort to call late in the evenings on the dates you were booked, ask if your room was rented, identify yourself, and ask for a transaction number for the refund to your credit card. Many places will not give a refund for cancellations at peak times or during events.

Once you have checked in, ask if there are add-on fees for things like the newspaper delivered to your door each morning or for storing your own food and drinks in the minibar. If you're staying at a B&B, there may be a cleaning fee levied at the end of your visit. If you're unclear, ask for your bill to be subtotaled each day and question unfamiliar charges.

Be aware of the no-smoking policy if it applies to your room. If you smoke, the housekeeping will sniff out the infraction, and you'll find a hefty cleaning fee on your bill.

Handicapped Access

The information blocks for each lodging list handicapped access in one of three categories: none, partial, or number of rooms with full access. Full access includes wide doors, grab bars, and other amenities. Partial access means that there has been some effort made to accommodate disabled visitors, usually ramps and access to common areas, and that one or more rooms are accessible by wheelchair. To be safe, call ahead and talk with a staff member. Access Aloha Travel, www.accessalohatravel.com, specializes in assisting travelers with disabilities. They are a treasure chest of information and can book lodging, transportation, tours, or anything else you might need. Their services are free, so consider making a generous donation to keep them in business.

Gay and Lesbian Travelers

Hawai'i is well known for accepting gays and lesbians, and it is the rare property that fails to accept gay and lesbian couples as they would any other travelers. The Big Island's Puna district is developing a reputation as a haven akin to a tropical Provincetown. For lodgings that cater specifically to gays and lesbians, check the listings on www.outinhawaii.com.

Other Options

For information on camping on the Big Island, see "Camping" in chapter 7, Recreation.

CONDOMINIUMS AND SHORT-TERM VACATION HOME RENTALS

If you want to get a sense of living like a local in a house or a condominium, there are many options on the Big Island. Homes are available throughout the island, and condominium rentals are clustered on the Kona side. In both cases, single nights are almost never available. Often there is a three-night minimum, with many offering weekly or monthly options. Rental prices vary widely. Maid service may be provided or available for an extra charge. Renting a home is an appealing option for a large group; there are properties that can accommodate as many as 15 people. The agencies are good places to call if you need lodging at the last minute.

Rental Owners, Agents, and Agencies

Black Bamboo Hawaii

808-328-9607, 800-527-7789; www.blackbamboohawaii.com
michael@blackbamboohawaii.com

Michael Sisk manages properties throughout the island. His talent is hearing what you want and need, even when you may not be clear on this yourself. Trust him. As a first step, go to the Web site, then e-mail him. If your first choice isn't available, Michael invariably knows a place that's not pictured that's just as nice or perhaps even nicer. Prices are moderate to very expensive, yet all the properties he represents have a special ambience that makes them uniquely Big Island.

Hawaii Island B&B Association

www.stayhawaii.com

The association's members offer an assortment of properties throughout the island listed by district, which is helpful when you're planning a trip. Hosts are knowledgeable about things local, and there's a wide range of prices.

Kohala Pacific Realty
808-889-5181; www.kohalapacificrealty.com

A small realty office that specializes in North Kohala vacation homes for sale and for rent. Properties for rent are expensive to very expensive.

2Papayas
808-896-0732; www.2papayas.com
mary@2papayas.com

Mary Fox began her Big Island career in guest services at the top-flight Mauana Lani Hotel. She specializes in managing properties available for rent in Puakō, a quiet beach enclave with many older cottages and bungalows that is undergoing rapid gentrification to include elegant and very modern beachfront properties. Mary offers the full range of options, but I must report that the vintage beach cottage gets rave reviews for location, decor, and value. She also features places on Waialea Bay and in Waimea. Prices are moderate to very expensive, and they all offer lots of bang for your bucks.

KAILUA-KONA

C. J. Kimberly Realtors
808-329-7000, 888-780-7000; www.cjkimberlyrealtors.com

These Realtors specialize in renting select ocean-view and oceanfront properties in the Kailua-Kona area. The prices are expensive to very expensive.

MacArthur & Company
808-885-8875, 877-885-8285; www.letsgohawaii.com

With an office in Waimea, this company offers rental properties in a variety of price ranges. They do not accept credit cards.

Property Network
808-329-7977, 800-358-7977; www.hawaii-kona.com

This agency rents a range of condos and a few homes, mostly moderately priced.

South Kohala Management
808-883-8500, 800-822-4252; www.southkohala.com

This agency handles very expensive premium condos, town houses, and private homes at the resort complexes along the Kohala Coast.

SunQuest Vacations
808-329-6438, 800-367-5168; www.sunquest-hawaii.com

Managing over 200 condo units in 30 properties, this agency can also arrange car rentals and recreational activities. The condos are moderate to expensive in price.

Many of the agencies rent properties at the same condo complexes. Prices vary within the complex based on the floor, views, and updates as well as size.

Vacation Rental By Owner
www.vrbo.com

Vacation Rental By Owner offers a variety of lodgings, grouped by geographic location. Properties on the site change frequently but almost always feature pictures; detailed descriptions of what is available in terms of kitchen equipment, recreation equipment, and linens; and easy-to-use booking calendars. The properties offer a variety of payment options, including credit cards. A caution: No matter how many pictures an owner may provide, you never know what you'll find upon arrival. However, I've had good luck renting cottages, or *ohana* units that are on a larger property where the owner lives. Even off-island owners are very willing to answer questions and can provide information on things like driving times to the nearest grocery store and local attractions. Be certain you understand the cancellation policies. If you are curious about living off the grid and operating entirely on alternative power, there are often several such options in the listings. Be sure to ask what is available in terms of modern electrical conveniences and water. Hawai'i is a good place to experiment with going green, but it is best if you know there's somebody nearby who can help if something goes awry.

West Hawaii Property Services Inc.
808-322-6696, 800-799-5662; www.konarentals.com

The offerings here range from inexpensive condos to very expensive oceanfront properties in Kailua-Kona and Waikoloa. They also have long-term rentals with a 30-night minimum.

THE KOHALA COAST

Resorts

Resorts are the hallmark of the Kohala Coast, a region that encompasses areas of the North Kona and South Kohala districts. Less a political area than an attitude with a strong sense of place, these resorts are among the best of the best available anywhere on the planet with prices to match. Each is somebody's vision of heaven, with white-sand beaches, spas, restaurants with big-name chefs and cuisines of many lands, golf courses, manicured lawns and gardens, and, if you ask, program options that span the human cycle from bachelor(ette) parties to family reunions. These are the places to go when you want to be pampered, or to be supremely lazy in the shade with an umbrella drink, moving only to track the sun for the length of your stay. If you want to ramp up a bit within the resort area, you can play golf at courses up and down the coast, or, in many cases, explore historical, cultural, or anthropological sites on the grounds of your resort, preserved as part of an ancient trail the chiefs and their entourages used as they traveled the island. If you want to make a break for it, and you mustn't feel obligated to, the resorts offer recreational bookings for activities throughout the island from skiing to wild-game hunting. Most of the outdoor hiking and adventure companies offer pickups at the resorts.

There are four clusters of resorts on the coast north of Kailua-Kona and the Kona International Airport at Keāhole. To some extent, they function as independent fiefdoms, as they offer not only resort rooms but also longer-term rentals in condominiums or time-shares as well as private homes with access to small shopping centers and services. All these communities are off HI 19; some are bisected by it.

Linked by Kūki'o Beach and a private, gated community with a golf course, the Four Seasons Resort at Hualālai and the Kona Village Resort are in North Kona. The Kona Village is the oldest resort on the Kohala Coast, the Four Seasons the newest.

The Waikoloa Resort is the next cluster, officially in South Kohala. It is the biggest and busiest, with the Waikoloa Beach Marriott, the Hilton Waikoloa Village, hives of luxury condominiums, time-shares, and private oceanfront estates. There are two golf courses, many tennis courts, the King's Shops, petroglyphs, a white-sand beach, a commercial heliport, and the free Waikoloa shuttle bus connecting all the dots.

The Mauna Lani Resort anchors the next resort cluster, which consists of two hotels, an ever-expanding colony of condominiums, two golf courses, two tennis centers, small beaches, historic fishponds, petroglyphs, and a shopping center. The Fairmont Orchid is next door, another outpost of hotel luxury just off Mauna Lani Dr.

At the northern coastal tip of South Kona, the intimate Mauna Kea Resort consists of the Mauna Kea Beach Hotel and the newer Hāpuna Beach Prince Hotel. It is farthest from the diversions of Kailua-Kona, which means you're closer to Waimea's gourmet row. Golf is a big draw, as are the two beaches, which many locals call the finest on the coast.

Which resort you choose depends on everything from recreational options for teens to where your favorite aunt had a great time on her 50th wedding anniversary. The resorts know word-of-mouth recommendations mean business, and each place tries to outdo the other with service and aloha. I've listed them in geographical order, south to north, rather than alphabetically. It just makes more sense.

Four Seasons Resort Hualālai

Manager: Robert Whitfield
808-325-8000, 800-819-5053
www.fourseasons.com/find_a_hotel.html, click on "Hawaii, Hualalai" link in menu
100 Ka'ūpūlehu Dr., Kailua-Kona, HI 96745
The Four Seasons is the first major resort once you turn left upon leaving Kona International Airport onto HI 19, also known as Queen Ka'ahumanu Hwy. The entrance, about 2 miles from the airport, requires a left turn across traffic. If you are going south, it is the last cluster of resorts before you turn off to the airport. In both directions, the entrance is well marked.
Price: Very Expensive
Credit Cards: AE, D, DC, MC, V
Handicapped Access: Yes

The beautiful views and lush landscaping suggest that this resort, built in 1996, was designed to bring out the best in its surroundings. Located on lava flows from the Hualālai volcano, the resort has a well-considered collection of Hawaiian art. The Ka'ūpūlehu Cultural Center offers an introduction and insights into Hawaiian culture. The accommodations, suites and rooms, are split into 36 two-story bungalows in four groups that front onto a half-mile-long ribbon of beach and natural lagoons. Each group has its own swimming pool or pond to make up for the skinny-mini beach, and one of them, the King's Pond, offers good snorkeling as it is stocked with colorful, local fish. There's also an infinity pool that lives up to its name looking out to the ocean's horizon. The rooms, featuring natural toned hardwoods, stone, and slate softened by fine linens and luxurious amenities, manage to be both large and cozy, each opening onto a private lanai, garden, or patio. Most have ocean views, although a few look out onto the golf course. Ground-floor rooms have outdoor showers, always a plus. The resort has three restaurants and two bars. Despite a sophisticated, adult sensibility, the resort offers activities for children and teens. Only resort guests can use the eight courts at the Hualālai Tennis Club, which is next to a sports club and spa. It has sand volleyball and basketball courts as well as the classes and machines you would expect of a state-of-the-art fitness endeavor. The Hualālai Golf Club offers play on 18 holes along the ocean; this course hosts the PGA seniors. If you have been comfortable staying in other Four Seasons properties, you won't be disappointed with the Hualālai resort.

Kona Village Resort
Manager: Ulrich Krauer
808-325-5555, 800-367-5290
www.konavillage.com
1 Kahuwai Bay Dr., Kailua-Kona, HI 96745
The is the second major resort once you turn left upon leaving Kona International Airport onto HI 19, also known as Queen Ka'ahumanu Hwy. The entrance, about 2 miles from the airport, requires a left turn across traffic. If you are coming south, it is the last cluster of resorts before you turn off to the airport. In both directions, the entrance is well marked.
Price: Very Expensive; rates include all meals
Credit Cards: AE, D, DC, MC, V
Handicapped Access: Yes

The most Hawaiian in feel of the Kohala Coast resorts, this is where you turn off every connectivity device and retreat. There are no TVs, radios, phones, or clocks, and the only Internet access is in the concierge office. Thus it is the perfect place to get away from everything, and everybody, tucked into your own private thatched-roof *hale,* or house, near the beach. Place a coconut at your front door, and you will not be disturbed. There are hammocks scattered throughout the grounds for first-come-first-served naps. The place overflows with references to cultures of the South Seas, and the resort's ocean program reflects this. There's scuba diving and a certification program, traditional and deep-sea fishing, kayaking, and special expeditions by boat for snorkeling. Golf and horseback riding are available nearby, and the Royal rooms have private hot tubs—and they, like even the less-expensive bungalows facing the lagoon, include every amenity you could need to make your stay perfect. There are 125 hideaways, two pools, two restaurants, three tennis courts, a beach, and programs for children ages 6 to 12 except during May and September. The hotel offers customized family reunion packages, and the lūʻau on Wed. and Fri. evenings is exceptional.

Hilton Waikoloa Village
Manager: Dieter Seeger
808-886-1234, 800-445-8667
www.hiltonwaikoloavillage.com
9-424 Waikoloa Beach Dr., Waikoloa, HI 96738
This is the middle cluster of resorts on HI 19. The entrance requires a left turn across traffic, but it is well marked in both directions.
Price: Expensive–Very Expensive

Credit Cards: AE, D, DC, MC, V
Handicapped Access: Yes

Hawai'i is a playground, and that is nowhere as true as at this Hilton, a fantasy that may meet your wildest dreams if your nighttime imagination features a monorail and boats to shuttle you around the 62-acre grounds, illuminated waterfalls, a half-acre swimming pool, an epic water slide, and a man-made beach surrounding a 4-acre saltwater lagoon. (There's a coastal trail to 'Anaeho'omalu Bay, one of the island's nicest for the irregularities of nature. Most guests seem content on campus.) If you make reservations in advance, this is where you and your children can swim with dolphins and five other people in the on-site Dolphin Quest Program. There is Camp Menehune for children, a Robert Trent Jones Jr.–designed golf course, and one designed by Tom Weiskopf/Jay Morrish. Both are set in lava fields. Robin Nelson designed the putting course, which includes waterfalls and koi ponds. Each room has a private lanai, and they're all similar aside from the number of beds and the view.

Waikoloa Beach Marriott Resort

Manager: Rodney Ito
808-886-6789, 800-922-5533
www.marriott.com.
69-275 Waikoloa Beach Dr., Waikoloa, HI 96738
Price: Moderate–Expensive
Credit Cards: AE, D, DC, MC, V
Handicapped Access: Yes

Newly and elegantly refurbished in an Asian-Hawai'i style, this hotel continues to offer value amid the Kohala Coast glitter. On land once claimed by King Kamehamea, there's a wealth of historical and cultural information on discreet signs throughout the 15-acre resort that spans petroglyph fields and ancient fishponds. Bordering the white sands of 'Anaeho'omalu Bay, the hotel features a range of ocean activities, including wedding-renewal vows aboard a catamaran, windsurfing, whale-watching, snorkeling, and sunset cruises. The Cabana, separate from the six-story Ka'ahumanu and Kamehameha towers, has slightly larger rooms with ocean views, and special concierge services. If you're planning a family gathering or a getaway for bridesmaids or groomsmen, this would be where you'd want to be in this resort for privacy. The on-site Mandara Spa (808-886-8191; www.mandaraspa.com) looks as if it were lifted from Bali, and its signature "La Therapie Hydralift Facial" will erase traces of the real world. Book it for your first day. There are 533 rooms and 22 suites, and poolside and more formal, yet still relaxed, dining at the Hawai'i Calls restaurant and lounge. The all-inclusive Wednesday- and Sunday-night lū'au, set against the sunset over 'Anaeho'omalu Bay, is a good value with a Hawaiian feel.

The Mauna Lani Resort

General Manager: Brian Butterworth
808-885-6622, 800-367-2323
www.maunalani.com
68-1400 Mauna Lani Dr., Kohala Coast, HI 96743
From Kailua-Kona International Airport, turn left at the exit and go north on HI 19 for 19.5 miles. Turn left on Mauna Lani Dr. The entrance is well marked.

The pool at the Marriott Waikoloa Beach Resort is steps from the ocean.

Price: Very Expensive
Credit Cards: AE, D, MC, V
Handicapped Access: Yes

Things get dreamy immediately at the Mauna Lani. Maybe it's the open-air lobby with that
constant, fragrant breeze. Or the extreme luxury offset by a staff that makes you feel as if
you've just come home. The resort features 29 oceanfront acres and 3 miles of ocean
shoreline. It is rich in historical and cultural sites preserved with pride, guided by Danny
"Kaniela" Akaka, the resort's multitalented cultural historian. If you can, arrange your stay
to coincide with a full moon, when he conducts a special program of storytelling and
entertainment. It's special and may launch you on a deeper exploration of Hawaiian culture. The resort includes the 343-room hotel, where almost every room has an ocean view,
and secluded bungalows, each with private staff and access to a private area of the beach.
The spa offers a variety of traditional lomi lomi massage treatments. The Francis H. I'i
Brown Golf North and South Courses, a total of 36 holes carved from lava fields along the
Pacific Ocean, have been named among America's best golf courses every year since 1988.
They are also two of the most beautiful. There are five restaurants, a fitness center, tennis
courts, a children's program, water activities that include swimming in a protected cove,
and an extensive collection of Hawaiian art and artifacts. The restaurants are reliably good,
particularly the seafood. Yes, this is an expensive option, but I always feel I've gotten more
than my money's worth.

The Fairmont Orchid
Manager: Ian Pullan
808-885-2000, 800-257-7544
www.fairmont.com/orchid
1 North Kaniku Dr., Kohala Coast, HI 96743
Price: Expensive–Very Expensive
Credit Cards: AE, D, MC, V
Handicapped Access: Yes

After starting life as a Ritz-Carlton, the Fairmont is now part of the Starwood family of
hotels, and the adoptive parents have done themselves proud. Friendly and relaxed, with
just enough formality in the design to remind you it is special and you are lucky, even the
least expensive of the 540 rooms and suites are indulgent. The Spa Without Walls offers
massages sometimes enlivened with a hint of Pacific spray, an unforgettable experience.
The expansive beach encourages long walks. Activities include surfing classes, yoga
classes, and snorkeling that often includes a glimpse of green sea turtles. There are children's activities, and the staff can arrange special activities for multigenerational family
reunions. There's a special "Hula Girl Getaway" package for bridesmaids or pals. The nine
restaurants include Brown's Beach House, consistently rated one of the island's best.

Mauna Kea Beach Hotel
Front Office Manager: Alvin Oshiro
808-882-7222, 800-882-6060
www.princeresortshawaii.com
62-100 Mauna Kea Beach Dr., Kamuela, HI 96743

Turn left at the exit from Kaila-Kona International Airport and continue on HI 1 for 26 miles. Turn left on Mauna Kea Beach Dr. From Waimea/Kamuela, head northeast on Māmalahoa Hwy., turn left at Lindsey Rd., then a slight left at Kawaihae Rd. Continue for almost 10 miles; make a left on HI 19. The well-marked entrance is just over a mile on the left at Mauna Kea Beach Dr.

Closed on December 1, 2006, after an earthquake on October 15, the legendary and beloved resort is scheduled to reopen in December 2008 after a $150 million restoration of the buildings and golf course. Skidmore, Owings and Merrill of San Francisco designed the 1965 hotel, which was recognized in 2007 by the American Institute of Architects as one of the best works of architecture in the United States. During the renovations, only the interiors will be changed. The room count will be reduced, and the rooms enlarged and decorated in a contemporary island style. Rees Jones, son of the course's original architect, Robert Trent Jones Sr., is redesigning the 18-hole, par-72, 7,165-yard Mauna Kea Golf Course that opened in 1964 and quickly became known for its oceanfront Number 3 hole.

Hāpuna Beach Prince Hotel
Manager: Kevin Kim
808-880-1111, 888-977-4623
www.princeresortshawaii.com
62-100 Kauna'oa Dr., Kamuela, HI 96743
About 25 miles north of the Kailua-Kona International Airport on HI 19, turn left at Hāpuna Beach Rd., then right at Old Puakō Rd. You'll make a U-turn to turn left on Old Puakō Rd., then a left onto Kaunao Dr. It is clearly marked.
Price: Very Expensive
Credit Cards: AE, D, MC, V
Handicapped Access: Yes

Opened in 1994, the hotel shares over a thousand acres with Laurence Rockefeller's legendary Mauna Kea Resort. Consider it the Mauna Kea's hip young cousin who really likes golf. Nestled into the bluffs, the low-rise building sits on what many locals consider the island's best beach, perfect for relaxing after a round of golf. While you're waiting for your tee time, the resort also offers tennis, water sports that include deep-sea fishing, and sailing, but limited shopping other than a fully equipped pro shop. It serves an Arnold Palmer/Ed Seay–designed 18-hole championship course that follows the shoreline and features spectacular views of Mauna Kea. Nongolfers are treated as exquisitely as golfers. There are four restaurants and two bars, with a shuttle bus connection to other dining options at the Mauna Kea Beach Hotel. The 350 guest rooms, including 36 oceanfront suites, are luxuriously and thoughtfully appointed. All have ocean-facing views and a private lanai.

Condos
Mauna Lani Point
Front Office Manager: Lei Kihara
808-885-5022, 800-842-6284
www.maunalanipoint.com
68-1050 Mauna Lani Point Dr., Kohala Coast, HI 96743
Price: Expensive

Credit Cards: AE, DC, MC, V
Handicapped Access: Partial

Part of the Mauna Lani Resort, these units are luxury one-, two-, and three-bedroom suites with kitchens, making this resort a good option for families. The beautifully furnished and maintained accommodations are wrapped around the resort's famed Francis H. I'i Brown South Golf Course. You have access to all the resort's facilities, which are within walking distance even though a shuttle is available. The Point has its own beach.

The Shores at Waikoloa

Manager: Jerry Jamieson
808-886-5001, 877-997-6667
69-1035 Keana Pl., Waikoloa, HI 96738
Off HI-19
Price: Moderate–Expensive
Credit Cards: AE, CB, CD, D, MC, V
Handicapped Access: Partial

Surrounded by the Waikoloa Beach Golf Course, this complex has 11 low-rise buildings set amid a necklace of lagoons. Most of the buildings face the ocean, which makes for lovely sunset views rather than full-on waves. Although the rental units are privately owned, they're comfortably furnished and have fully equipped kitchens (handy because there are no restaurants in the complex), washer-dryers, and large furnished lanais with wet bars. They range from one-bedroom, one-bath to three-bedroom, two-bath villas. Most have picture windows overlooking the greens. Daily maid service is included. In-room high-speed Internet access is not. The Shores has tennis courts and a pool. It is about a five-minute drive from the beach, and you must arrange all your own activities, such as golf or spa outings. The complex is gated, and free parking stalls are located just outside each unit. Check the Web site for exclusive pricing on units and air-inclusive packages.

Beyond the Gold Coast

Kohala

Kohala Vista Inn

Hosts: Jerry and Audrey Maluo
808-962-0100, 800-262-9912
www.blackbamboohawaii.com
Kohala Ranch Rd., Kawaihae, HI 96743
Off HI 270, north of Kawaihae.
Price: Moderate
Credit Cards: MC, V
Handicapped Access: Partial

The guest wing of secluded property on the exclusive Kohala Ranch features jaw-dropping, million-dollar views and a serene setting. I had a died-and-gone-to-heaven moment upon arrival at what must be one of the best values on the island. There are two comfortably appointed bedrooms, both with queen beds and private baths. The second bedroom is

At the Kohala Vista bed & breakfast, the views go on forever.

offered only to additional guests in the same party, assuring complete privacy. The master suite opens directly to the pool and Jacuzzi. A generous breakfast, assorted snacks, and free wireless access are included with the rooms. I didn't want to leave.

Puakō Bed and Breakfast
Host: Punahele Andrade
808-882-1331, 800-910-13315
Puakō Beach Dr., Kamuela, HI 96743
From HI 19, turn toward the ocean at Puakō Beach Dr. North of the resort area.
Price: Moderate
Credit Cards: MC, V
Handicapped Access: Partial

The host is a *kumu hula,* or hula teacher, who exudes the spirit of aloha even when he's not dancing at one of the nearby resorts. There are four guest rooms, two of which have a shared bath. A lovely place with easy beach access, this is a good option for group of friends traveling together. Breakfast is provided; there's no smoking; all rooms have TVs and can be air-conditioned.

IN AND AROUND KAILUA-KONA

The center of Kailua-Kona can feel frantic with visitors eager to pack 26 hours into every day. If you want a quieter option, staying the Keauhou area might be the answer. You're not far from the sights, shops, and restaurants, yet the vibe is more laid-back.

Hōlualoa Inn
Manager: Chella Cook
808-324-1121, 800-392-1812
www.holualoainn.com
76-5932 Māmalahoa Hwy., Hōlualoa, HI 96725
Price: Expensive
Credit Cards: AE, D, DC, MC, V
Handicapped Access: Partial

The town of Hōlualoa is an up-country artists' enclave, perched above Kailua-Kona in the cooler coffee belt. The inn hints as its past as an art collector's private home, and the views west over the Pacific extend beyond to forever. The rooftop gazebo promotes quiet reflection, and the pool insists that you relax. You're a quick drive from downtown Kailua-Kona and the beaches, yet you're tucked into a 30-acre spread. The two suites and four rooms, all with either a king- or queen-size bed, ceiling fans, private bathrooms, and touches like luxury linens, are each decorated differently, playing up views of the ocean or gardens. They're elegant and serene. Breakfast, served in the dining room, looks wonderful and tastes better. Distractions such as a comforting fireplace, a billiards table, and a telescope occupy a living room accessible to all. A TV, refrigerator, and a microwave are in a common room on the low level. For a small group traveling together, the inn operates the nearby yet secluded Lako Hale Estate, which sleeps four in two suites at either end of the house. It has a fully equipped kitchen, fruit trees galore, and, at the right time of year, you can brew a cup of coffee grown on the estate while watching pickers harvest the next crop.

King Kamehameha Kona Beach Hotel
Manager: Jak Hu
808-329-2911, 800-367-6060
www.konabeachhotel.com
75-5660 Palani Rd., Kailua-Kona, HI 96740
In the center of town, on the water.
Price: Moderate–Expensive
Credit Cards: AE, CB, D, DC, MC, V
Handicapped Access: Yes

A local landmark known as the King Kam, this 460-room hotel stands on the grounds where King Kamehameha once resided, giving it a historical significance that includes the Ahu'ena Heiau, dedicated to Lono, the god of peace, that Kamehameha constructed in the early 1800s. The hotel features a small kid-friendly white-sand beach alongside the pier. A renovation is planned, but the hotel will remain open. There are two restaurants, a pool, a launderette, and the popular Island Breeze Lu'au Sun. and Tues. nights. Ask about packages and insist on a fifth- or sixth-floor room. If you're a light sleeper, opt for an oceanfront room or suite.

Kona Seaside Hotel
Manager: Rochelle Kagawa
808-329-2455, 800-560-5558
www.seasidehotelshawaii.com
75-5646 Palani Rd., Kailua-Kona, HI 96740
Price: Inexpensive–Moderate
Credit Cards: AE, DC, MC, V
Handicapped Access: Yes

Recently renovated, this is a good option if you don't need lavish amenities or a large room and want to be downtown, across the street from the beach. Tanti's Restaurant and Paleo's Bar and Grille on-site, a shopping mall, and two pools. The least-expensive rooms are poolside, which is close to the street. Internet access is available by the hour, day, or week.

Kona Tiki Hotel
Manager: Mark Matlock
808-329-1425
www.konatiki.com
75-5968 Ali'i Dr., Kailua-Kona, HI 96740
About a mile south of town.
Price: Inexpensive
Credit Cards: No
Handicapped Access: No

Book early or be disappointed—particularly in the winter high season—at this friendly operation. Ocean breezes and fans cool each of 15 rooms. With either twin or queen beds, the rooms are modest but comfortable with ocean-facing lanais. There's no beach, but the pool is right above the crashing waves, which makes for a great way to wake up, as this is where the continental buffet breakfast is served. Away from the hubbub, it is one of the best deals around. No room phones.

Uncle Billy's Kona Bay Hotel
Manager: Tracy Kimi
808-961-5818, 800-367-5102
www.unclebilly.com
75-5739 Ali'i Dr., Kailua-Kona, HI 96740
Across the street from the ocean.
Price: Inexpensive–Moderate
Credit Cards: AE, MC, V
Handicapped Access: Partial

Centrally located downtown with a pool and a slightly kitschy Polynesian atmosphere in the public spaces, this is an institution among locals visiting from other islands. Each somewhat utilitarian room has a mini-fridge. Parties can spill into the halls or sound as if they are; this might be a problem for light sleepers.

KEAUHOU AREA OF KAILUA-KONA

Outrigger Keauhou Beach Resort
Manager: Paul Korner
808-322-3441, 800-462-6262
www.keauhoubeachresort-hawaii.com
78-6740 Ali'i Dr., Kailua-Kona, HI 96740
Price: Moderate–Expensive
Credit Cards: AE, D, DC, MC, V
Handicapped Access: Yes

After renovating all 309 rooms and 3 suites, which now include free wireless access, as does the lobby, this hotel is due some respect for the true value it delivers. The rooms are decorated in a low-key island style, and the open-air lobby and restaurants reflect a local, casual sensibility. In a great location next to Kahalu'u Bay Beach Park, a premier snorkeling spot, the grounds are rich in archaeological treasures easily explored on marked walking trails. The oceanfront rooms and ocean-view rooms overlook tidal pools, letting you observe marine life without getting your feet wet, although that's encouraged. The garden-view rooms have private lanais as well. There's a pool in case you don't feel like walking over to the beach. Although the restaurant gets lots of local groups, you may want to explore other options if you're staying for several days. There's also a waterfront cocktail

---

Easy Riding
There's a free, open-air trolley connecting the Keauhou resort area with the Kailua Pier area. It stops at the Keauhou Bay, Sheraton Keauhou Bay Resort & Spa, Kona Country Club, Keauhou Shopping Center, Outrigger Keauhou Beach Resort, and Kahalu'u Beach Park. For information, contact concierges at either the Sheraton Keauhou Bay Resort & Spa (808-930-4900) or the Outrigger Keauhou Beach Hotel (808-322-3411), or download the schedule from either resort's Web site before you leave home.

lounge and a takeout grill near the pool and the beach. Check the Web site for packages and special rates. If you can, reserve an oceanfront room on an upper floor. Leave the blinds open, let the breeze flow through the screens to sleep, and wake to the gentle sounds of the surf.

Sheraton Keauhou Bay Resort & Spa

Manager: Scott Brooks
808-930-4900, 866-716-8109
www.sheratonkeauhou.com
78-128 'Ehukai St., Kailua-Kona, HI 96740
Price: Expensive–Very Expensive
Credit Cards: AE, D, DC, MC, V
Handicapped Access:

About 15 minutes south of downtown, this hotel has four restaurants and lounges (try Kai for breakfast even if you usually skip it), tennis courts, an on-site wedding chapel and reception garden, a children's activity program, an oceanfront spa, the Ho'ola, and the respected Kamaho Luau Monday and Friday nights. It has adopted a local *hula halau,* or school, Halau Kala'akeakauikawekiu, which allows guests to watch classes and rehearsals. There's a program for a nighttime snorkel or scuba with manta rays. What this resort doesn't have is a beach; it's perched atop a lava field. To compensate, the water slide into the multilevel freshwater pool is 200 feet long and the kiddie pool has a sandy bottom. The 511 rooms and 10 suites are airy, comfortable, and equipped with data ports and Wi-Fi. Many have good bay views, but a mountain view is nothing to weep about. If you're reserving online, there's a function that lets you compare two rooms. Also check the Web site for special packages.

Condos

KAILUA-KONA

To equip your rented condo, head to the Crossroads Shopping Center with its well-stocked Safeway that is close to the complexes along Ali'i Dr. However, if you're coming from the airport, or from the north, and you belong to Costco, there's a warehouse with a pharmacy set above the airport. Gas prices are excellent, and the pumps are the closest ones to the airport—good to know when returning a rental car.

Costco

808-331-4833
73-5600 Maiau St., Kailua-Kona, HI 96740
Open: Mon. through Fri. 10–8:30; Sat. 9:30–6; Sun. 10–6.

Safeway

808-329-2207
75-1027 Henry St., Kailua-Kona, HI 96740
Open: 24 hours every day

Casa de Emdeko

808-329-2160
www.casadeemdeko.org

75-6082 Ali'i Dr., Kailua-Kona HI 96740
Price: Moderate
Credit Cards: Unit by unit
Handicapped Access: Partial in public areas

Casa de Emdeko is an oceanfront complex with an on-site convenience store and two pools, one freshwater and the other salt. The condos are privately owned, and some owners offer units for rent on the Web site with rates and contact information. Be sure to check the photographs of units you're considering as each is different, although they all have a lanai with either a garden or ocean view. Payment, check-in, and almost everything else is handled between you and the unit owners, although the on-site staff can help out in a pinch.

Kanaloa at Kona
Manager: Charles Okazaki
808-322-9625, 800-688-7444
www.outrigger.com
78-261 Manukai St., Kailua-Kona, HI 96740
Price: Expensive–Very Expensive
Credit Cards: AE, DC, MC, V
Handicapped Access: Yes

A gated community, Kanaloa at Kona is surrounded by Keauhou Bay on one side and the Kona Country Club/Ocean Golf Course on the other side. There are three pools, one oceanside. In smartly designed, low-rise buildings, the spacious units are individually owned, thoughtfully equipped, and often professionally decorated. There are one- and two-bedroom units; some can sleep as many as eight people. All have a washer-dryer, a lanai with a wet bar, cable TV, and daily maid service. The vibe is casual, elegant, and in-the-know. Although there is shoreline access, there is no beach. In exchange, you get value-rich top-flight resort accommodations and amenities.

Royal Sea Cliff Resort
Manager: Carol Hanna
808-329-8021, 800-688-7444
www.outrigger.com
75-6040 Ali'i Dr., Kailua-Kona, HI 96740
Price: Moderate–Very Expensive
Credit Cards: AE, DC, MC, V
Handicapped Access: Yes

A mile south of downtown, the sun-bleached Royal Sea Cliff stands atop a lava shoreline. The studio, one-bedroom, and two-bedroom units feel private even though the multi-leveled family-friendly property is big. There is a washer-dryer in each unit, the kitchens are well equipped, and the furnishings are comfortable but not luxurious. There's daily maid service. Do opt for oceanfront accommodations. There are often special offers and packages on the Web site.

Bed-and-Breakfasts

Kyoto House
Host: Michael Sisk
808-328-9607, 800-527-7789
michael@blackbamboohawaii.com
www.blackbamboohawaii.com
Price: Expensive
Credit Cards: MC, V
Handicapped Access: No

Kyoto House is on 3 secluded acres overlooking the Kona Coast, just 10 minutes from the heart of downtown Kailua-Kona. In the Japanese style, there are pavilions enclosing an interior courtyard. The pool and hot tub complex faces the ocean and features stunning views of the Kona coastline. There are extensive decks, covered and uncovered, where you can sunbathe, relax, or dine. The sleeping pavilion provides three bedrooms and three baths. There is a comfortably furnished living room with futon-style couches and a state-of-the-art entertainment center, a fully equipped kitchen, and a pleasant dining room. It sleeps up to eight. For safety reasons, children under five are strongly discouraged.

SOUTH OF KAILUA-KONA

Aloha Guest House
Managers: Greg Garriss and Johann Timmermann
808-328-8955, 800-897-3188
www.alohaguesthouse.com
4-4780 Māmalahoa Hwy., Captain Cook, HI 96704
Price: Moderate
Credit Cards: AE, D, MC, V
Handicapped Access: Yes

About an hour south of the Kailua-Kona airport, high above Kealakekua Bay, the Aloha Guest House lives up to its name. Although you really need a high-clearance vehicle or SUV to get up the challenging mile-long access road, once you're here, take refuge in the views and organic breakfasts with seasonally adjusted menus in the dining room. Other shared spaces include a kitchen and living area with an extensive media center. This is a good base for outdoor and cultural activities in the Captain Cook area, a quick drive from the City of Refuge and Kealakekua Bay. The Honu Room is more like an apartment than the other five units; all have private baths. The Honu Room is the one you want if you're avoiding stairs or have other mobility issues. While the breakfast buffet is up a flight, Greg willingly swoops downstairs with a delivery to any room if requested. Just when you think you're cut off from the world, you discover there's Internet access. Preserve the mood—don't sign on.

Cedar House Coffee Farm B&B
Hosts: Fred and Laura Keener
808-328-8829, 866-328-8829
www.cedarhouse-hawaii.com
Captain Cook, HI 96704

Price: Moderate
Credit Cards: MC, V
Handicapped Access: Partial

The big draw here for families, or folks seeking privacy, is the two-bedroom Coffee Cottage and the two-story Hibiscus Suite. Both are equipped with full kitchens, and the Keeners deliver hearty island breakfasts. Like the other rooms, these have ocean or farm views (or both), a private entrance, cable TV, king- or queen-size beds, and private baths. Each room, and the cottage, is simply but thoughtfully decorated and has either a private lanai or garden. There's free Internet access, which may not be your preferred activity while staying at a working 2,500-tree coffee farm. If you want to be in on the harvest, the picking season starts around the end of October. Watching the work that goes into your cup of Kona will make you appreciate it even more.

Hale Hualālai

Host: Lonn Armour
808-326-2909
www.hale-hualalai.com
74-4968 Māmalohoa Hwy., Hōlualoa, HI 96725
Price: Moderate–Expensive
Credit Cards: MC, V
Handicapped Access: Partial

About a 15-minute drive from Kailua-Kona, near the junction of CR 180 and HI 190, the Hale Hualālai harbors two almost identical, spacious suites in lush coffee country. They are at opposite ends of the main house. Each has a private entry, exposed beams, hardwood floors polished to a glow, free Internet access, a Jacuzzi bathtub, and a king-size bed. There's no hint of kitsch or cute, but there are views. You face due west, into the sunset, and it is a glorious way to begin an evening. Breakfasts give the sunsets a run for their money. Lonn cultivates about 500 coffee trees, the source of your morning cup. A pound or two makes a fine souvenir. You can call and reorder when you get home.

Horizon Guest House

Host: Clem Classen
808-328-2540, 888-328-8301
www.purpleroofs.com/horizongh-hi/horizongh-hi3.html
Māmalahoa Hwy. between mile markers 101 and 100, Hōnaunau, HI 96726
Price: Expensive
Credit Cards: MC, V
Handicapped Access: Yes

Surrounded by 15,000 acres of the McCandless Ranch, the Horizon Guest House opens to the outdoors and sits in elegant isolation at 1,200 feet elevation but is only a 10-minute downhill drive to the beach. You may not want to make the drive; basking in the infinity pool encourages inertia. The rooms each have a private entrance and are placed to be very private. All have panoramic views of the Keauhou-Kona coast. The Hawaiian quilts are handmade, and the decor includes a touch of Asia among the antiques. Clem, who designed the house to accommodate wheelchairs, makes a healthy, hearty breakfast buffet.

There's a well-equipped barbeque area, so you can cook rather than go out—each room has a refrigerator and coffeemaker—and a media room well stocked with books, music, and movies. The wing ends with a laundry and utility room for the use of guests.

Ka'awa Loa Plantation

Hosts: Michael Martinage and Greg Nunn
808-323-2686
www.kaawaloaplantation.com
82-5990 Nāpō'opo'o Rd. (1.1 miles off Māmalahoa Hwy.), Kealakekua, HI 96704
Price: Moderate
Credit Cards: MC, V
Handicapped Access: Partial

Here are your options: standard rooms, a luxurious suite, or a guest cottage. Pick one and you're virtually guaranteed an ocean view. There's an outdoor hot tub, a wrap-around lanai that may be too comfortable, a common room with a fireplace, and a fully equipped gas grill. The plantation orchards yield oranges, tangerines, grapefruit, lemons, limes, star fruit, lychee, breadfruit, and jaboticaba. Vanilla and cocoa plantings are in the planning stages. Don't forget to take home a jar or two of Greg's curried lime pickles. It's a health food, really, because of the tumeric. The plantation participates in the B&B&B triple play program with the folks at two other B&Bs, Waianuhea and Kalaekilohana.

Manago Hotel

Managers: Dwight and Cheryl Manago
808-323-2642
www.managohotel.com
HI 11, Captain Cook, HI 96704
Price: Inexpensive
Credit Cards: D, MC, V
Handicapped Access: Partial

The Manago Hotel started in 1917 with two cots and some futons. The helpful and delight-fully welcoming family now oversees 64 full rooms, with a new wing overlooking Kealake-kua Bay in the distance. There are 42 rooms with private baths and 22 rooms with shared baths. They're not fancy, so book a room with a private bath on an upper floor (be aware that smoking is permitted on the first floor). There's also a traditional Japanese tatami room with a *furo,* or deep soaking bath. The Manago reminds me of *minshuku,* rural inns scattered throughout Japan. It's not for you if you want luxury, but it is a good, local value. The big draw here, even if you're not a hotel guest, is the simple restaurant known far and near for its pork chops. They live up to the hype. Be sure to eat your veggies, because the Managos grow most of them.

Nancy's Hideaway

Host: Nancy Matthews
808-325-3132, 866-325-3132
www.nancyshideaway.com
73-1530 Uanani Pl., Kailua-Kona, HI 96740
Price: Moderate

Credit Cards: MC, V
Handicapped Access: Partial

Nancy's one of the lucky ones, living in paradise, and she's sharing a country cottage and a cozy studio, so you can experience the place for a while. Although both options on this 3-acre spread near the Palani Junction include high-speed Internet, treat these accommodations as a peaceful country retreat. Each has its own entrance, a lanai, a wet bar, a small refrigerator, a toaster oven, and a microwave. Breakfast is delivered to your door each morning. Expect locally grown coffee and fruit, juice, and an assortment of baked goods. Don't be daunted by Nancy's detailed directions. Following them off HI 190 is easy, and suddenly, just like she promises, there's the white mailbox on the pink post.

Ocean Song
Host: Michael Sisk
808-962-0100, 800-262-9912
www.blackbamboohawaii.com
Captain Cook, HI 96726
Price: Expensive
Credit Cards: MC, V
Handicapped Access: Partial

On a private cove of Kealakekua Bay, this three-bedroom, two-bath house has everything you need, including a pool, on pesticide-free grounds. Shushing surf, sunsets, swaying palm trees, sun—baby, you and up to five others have arrived. There's a secluded sandy beach nearby and even closer to the house, bay access (be careful at first), so you can snorkel or kayak with the occupants: turtles, inquisitive dolphins, and a array of camera-ready fish. Being this close means you can be in the water before the crowd arrives or get wet again after they've gone. It's a haunting place just after dawn. While all this sounds like tropical perfection, the shoreline is rough lava, so it isn't suitable for families with children seven or younger.

South Kona Hideaway
Hosts: Lou D'Angelo and Erik Hinshaw
808-328-0160, 877-632-0999
www.southkonahideaway.com
Captain Cook, HI 96704
Price: Moderate
Credit Cards: Call
Handicapped Access: Partial

If the thought of staring at strangers over the strudel every morning is what keeps you from staying at a B&B, you have soulmates in Lou and Erik. Which means a full breakfast in bed, or at least breakfast in your room, is the only option here. It's a sassy repast—homemade preserves, incredible baked goods, and of course, everything's as local and organic as possible. They're new to the B&B game, but old hands at service. Both did time at some of San Francisco's top restaurants and food purveyors—Zuni Café and Fran Gage's Patisserie Francaise, for example—before opening their own café, D'Angelo Bread in Santa Barbara, a place known for the finer things. They have two private ocean-view suites (one with an en

At the South Kona Hideaway, you may be served truffles made with Big Island-grown chocolate.

suite kitchen and a smaller bedroom suitable for children or young adults), and a romantic bungalow tucked amid the coffee and banana trees. Yes, this would be dandy place for a multigenerational family vacation. Or a happy solo you. (Ask nicely and you might get the recipe for their truffles made with Big Island–grown chocolate.)

Tara Cottage
Host: Michael Sisk
808-962-0100, 800-262-9912
www.blackbamboohawaii.com
Hōnauau, HI 96726
Price: Moderate–Expensive
Credit Cards: AE, MC, V
Handicapped Access: No

Does the mention of an octagonal main room make you think hippie-dippy chic? Let go of that notion and enter one of the sweetest, most exquisitely thought out properties on the island. It's romantic. It's inspirational. It's the hideaway, complete with an outdoor shower and lush tropical landscaping, you won't want to leave. Maybe it's homegrown coffee at breakfast. Or the sweet white organic pineapples waiting to be picked at perfection. There's an efficient kitchen with a full-size refrigerator, microwave, and halogen cooktop, as well as an outdoor grill, so you can stock up and hunker down. The decor features original work by local artists and Indonesian wood carvings. An extensive library of books and movies reflects an intriguing mind at work. The two-level lanai has views of the extensive gardens and the ocean below. Michael leaves you alone but is there if you need him, if only for a chat or some local tips. This an indulgent option for one, a delight for two, but it tops out with three. Older children only.

Ka'u or South Point Area

Bougainvillea B & B
Innkeepers: Martie and Don Nitsche
808-929-7089, 800-688-1763
www.bougainvilleabedandbreakfast.com
Ocean View, HI 96737
Three blocks off HI 11.
Price: Inexpensive

Halfway between Kailua-Kona and Hilo, Martie and Don perched on a seemingly inhospitable lava flow, then created a bougainvillea-marked oasis. Their four guest rooms each have a private entrance and bath, and there's a small communal kitchen area. Breakfast is served either on the outside lanai or in the dining room. It is a fine, friendly meal. Either setting provides a good way to the start the day's exploration of an often-overlooked part of the Big Island, unless the pool beckons. Save the hot tub for the evening. A soak under the stars is revelatory because of the clear, clear skies.

Colony One at Sea Mountain
Manager: David Baglow
808-939-7368
www.thelandoffice.com
95-789 Ninole Loop Rd., Punalu'u, HI 96472
Price: Inexpensive–Moderate
Credit Cards: MC, V
Handicapped Access: Yes

At one time, this condo development overlooking the windblown Sea Mountain Golf Course and the beautifully rugged Ka'u coast seemed like the land of the lost boys. But the grounds at the southernmost condo development in the United States have been upgraded to remove that forlorn feeling, and I find it an intriguing option. There are 15 studios, one- and two-bedroom units, and a guest house that sleeps eight available in the rental pool, all fully equipped and comfortably furnished. That said, it is quite isolated. You must plan ahead, or you'll be driving to Pāhala, Nā'ālehu, or Volcano to dine.

The Hobbit House
Hosts: Bill and Darline Whaling
808-929-9755
www.hi-hobbit.com
Wai'ōhinu, HI 96772
Price: Moderate
Credit Cards: No
Handicapped Access: No

The Big Island has its share of unusual lodging options, and Bill and Darline's hand-carved house ranks high among them. He's a skilled woodworker. She's no slouch with stained glass. Together they've created a four-room gem, suitable for one couple. The apartment with a private entrance is wind and solar powered. The spare, simple furnishings highlight the couple's handiwork. (Bill carved crossbeams for the windows from tree branches, then highlighted them with Darline's glasswork.) An antique queen four-poster bed fits as if made for the bedroom, with its private lanai lush with ferns and palms. The bathroom has a two-person tub. It faces the ocean. The living room is spacious and the kitchen fully equipped. An undulating roof that suggests thatch tops the structure. It sits half a mile up from HI 11 on a recently paved road on what locals call The Hill, overlooking Wai'ōhinu village. And while you might think from looking at a map that this is the end of the world, it doesn't feel that way at all. Bill and Darline are there, making things cozy and helping you explore the area with a local's knowledge, preferably in a four-wheel-drive vehicle.

Kalaekilohana
Hosts: Kenny Joyce and Kilohana Domingo
808-939-8052
www.kau-hawaii.com
94-2152 South Point Rd., Nā'ālehu, HI 96772
Price: Moderate
Credit Cards: MC, V
Handicapped Access: Partial

It's impossible to ignore the richness of Hawaiian culture when you're at Kalaekilohana. Since opening in 2006, Kilohana and Kenny have often used their big yellow plantation-style house for classes in traditional arts such as lei making. This is the real deal: Kilohana's skill at making fresh and feather leis has earned him a Smithsonian Institute fellowship. His work is on display at the Museum of Arts and Design in New York. He's a member of Hula Halau Na Kamalei and holds a degree in Hawaiian Studies from the University of Hawai'i. Kenny, on the other hand, keeps it real. He's the cook and prepares a full hot breakfast. (He'll also pack a bento, or picnic box, for lunch.) Their home is on the road to South Point, the last bit of the United States before Antarctica. The four spacious rooms, each with a private back, feature beautifully restored hardwood floors and lovely island-style furnishings with either Cal king– or queen-size beds. Kilohana and Kenny know their surroundings well and provide thoughtful itineraries for exploring an area filled with surprises and empty of tourists.Be sure to ask about theB&B&B program.

Pāhala Plantation Cottages
Manager: Julia Neal
808-928-9811
www.pahala-hawaii.com
Pāhala, HI 96777
Price: Moderate
Credit Cards: AE, MC, V
Handicapped Access: Partial

More than an hour's drive from Hilo, and more than two hours from Kailua-Kona, Pāhala is a glimpse into Hawai'i's past. A plantation town, it was the hub for the northeastern

Kaʻu. Big sugar pulled out, but the plantation manager's home and some workers' housing have been restored. The Maile House, Paniolo Cabin, Hale Macadamia, and the elegant Pāhala Plantation House are available individually or as a cluster for a large family reunion or other group gathering. The decor evokes the plantation's past, although there's Internet access and cable television. All the cottages have fully equipped kitchens, and the main house kitchen can handle cooking for a big crowd. The grounds are landscaped with tall palms, fruit trees, and flowers. It's an easy stroll to a pool with private showers, tennis courts, and a modest commercial area with a grocery, a bakery, a bank, and a post office. I found it appealing, like time travel with modern conveniences, but others might find the rural ambience too, well, rural. You must plan ahead for supplies and entertainment.

South Point Banyan Tree House

Host: Jaime Sessler
715-302-8180
www.southpointbth.com
Pinao St. and Māmalahoa Hwy., Waiʻōhinu, HI 96772
Price: Moderate
Credit Cards: MC, V
Handicapped Access: No

About 15 miles north of Ka Lae or South Point, in the Kaʻu District distance, Jaime Sessler, and her helpful dad, Greg, who lives next door, operate a getaway nestled in a huge Chinese banyan tree. When you ascend, the place is often open, the keys left on the table. Inside the cheerful and compact white structure with red trim, you can lie back and see the

The Wood Valley Temple has hosted the Dalai Lama.

leaves through the transparent roof. There's one queen-size bed and a sofa, a well-equipped kitchen, an outdoor grill, a hot tub, and masses of birds. The surrounding area is really rural, so even though there are shops nearby, the selection is limited, and most dining options require a drive. Plan accordingly. Nonetheless, it can be magical on a moonlit night, and it's easy to understand why romantics on their honeymoon or special anniversary getaway are the single biggest group of Jaime's guests.

Wood Valley Temple Retreat and Guest House
Manager: Marya Schwabe
808-928-8539
www.nechung.org
Off HI 11, left at the end of Pikake St., Pāhala, HI 96777
Price: Inexpensive–Moderate
Credit Cards: MC, V
Handicapped Access: No

Even when the peacocks scream, this Tibetan Buddhist retreat in a clearing surrounded by eucalyptus exudes serenity. Dedicated by His Holiness the Dalai Lama in 1980, 13 years after its founding, the center offers guests a chance to meditate in solitude or join an organized retreat. I've found even short stays of several hours here can be a transformative, exceptional experience. The spirit from the land is strong, and an almost magical tranquility soothes you if you're open to it. Rooms are simple, with Asian touches. You're expected to help maintain shared public spaces. Teas and coffee are provided. You can cook in the full kitchen or rely on the dining options in Pāhala, Nāʻālehu, or Volcano.

VOLCANO

Aloha Cottage
Host: Nancy Matthews
808-325-3132, 866-325-3132
www.nancyshideaway.com
Volcano, HI 96785
Price: Moderate
Credit Cards: MC, V
Handicapped Access: Partial

Simply furnished for two with a king-size bed and room for one more on a full-size futon sofa in the living area, this comfy option sits amid the fern forest typical of the area. There's a full bath, and the kitchen is well equipped and roomy. Both the lanai and the carpet are covered, pluses in Volcano because it can be foggy, if not drippy, in the early morning.

Hale ʻŌhiʻa Cottages
Host: Michael Tuttle
808-967-7986, 800-455-3803
www.haleohia.com
11-3068 Hale ʻŌhiʻa Rd., Volcano, HI 96785

Price: Moderate–Expensive
Credit Cards: MC, V
Handicapped Access:

Come for the volcano, stay for the cosseting. Singled out by *Condé Nast Traveler* as the place to stay in Volcano, the Hale ʻŌhiʻa Cottages are rich in history and even richer in charm. The main building, built in 1931, is a shingled beauty crowned with red turrets. It anchors a compound invisible from the road that includes guest cottages, a gardener's residence, and various outbuildings set in noteworthy Japanese gardens. The two-room master suite in the main house has a private entrance, a queen-size bed set into a bay window, and an oversize tub. Ihilani Cottage is one of the most private options and predates the main house. The antique leaded windows give a real sense of the past, and a fireplace keeps the present pleasant. With a queen-size bed, it's a romantic getaway. In contrast, Hale ʻŌhiʻa Cottage, the gardener's residence, offers room for a family. It sleeps five easily, and there's an outdoor barbeque area. Another family or group option is the two-story Cottage in the Woods. No matter which of the nine accommodations you select, you can return after a day exploring Hawaiʻi Volcanoes National Park and settle in for delight.

Kīlauea Lodge

Owners: Lorna and Albert Jeyte
808-967-7366
www.kilauealodge.com
Old Volcano Rd., Volcano, HI 96785
Price: Moderate–Expensive
Credit Cards: AE, MC, V
Handicapped Access: Partial

Every so often I think I could live in Volcano Village, but I'm really thinking this updated 1930s YMCA lodge and surrounding spread. And while I appreciate the effort that went into making the dozen or so cozy rooms—many with fireplaces—feel homey, Hawaiian style, it is the staff who get to me every time. One evening, arriving well after the expected check-in due to flight delays and a harrowing drive from Hilo through torrential rain, I was tucked into the sofa in the lodge, close to the fire, the better to scan international mementos set into the stonework of the massive fireplace. The paperwork arrived with a warming whiskey and an apology that the kitchen, one of the island's best, was closed. Moments later, out came a plate of toast and tidbits. After that, to retreat to one of the quiet second-floor rooms to dream under a handmade Hawaiian quilt—bliss. That room was in Hale Aloha, a yellow building the Jeytes added to the compound in 1991. Designed in the traditional style, it has five centrally heated rooms, each with either a queen-size bed or two twins, private bath, garden views, and decorated with Hawaiian touches. A common room on the ground floor has a fireplace, games, a library, and a TV. There are more rooms on the second floor of the lodge itself. They each have private baths, wood-burning fireplaces, and queen or twin beds. There's also a suite suitable for honeymoons or other romantic celebrations, and Tutu's Place, a 1920s cottage a short walk from the lodge. Of course, there's a full breakfast in the dining room included with the room price. It will stand you in good stead as you explore the volcanic attractions nearby.

The fire in the Volcano House lobby has burned continuously for decades.

Volcano House Hotel
Owner: The Ken Fujiyama family
808-967-7321
www.volcanohousehotel.com
Crater Rim Dr., Hawai'i Volcanoes National Park, HI 96718
Price: Moderate–Expensive
Credit Cards: AE, CD, MC, V
Handicapped Access: Yes

The views are the attraction here. If you want to stay in the most accessible parts of the park, this is the best option aside from the Namakani Paio Cabins, a 3-mile hike away. Both are rich in unrealized potential. If you opt for the hotel, insist on a second-floor crater-view room as far from the uninspired dining room as possible. (It does have beautiful views, however.) The cabins are set in a potholed gravel-covered site. A high-clearance SUV would be smart. You'll need to bring your own firewood, sleeping pad, and sleeping bag. The bathhouse is shared, and there are grills for cooking.

Volcano Places
Host: Kate Grout
808-967-7990, 877-967-7990
www.volcanoplaces.com
Volcano, HI 96785
Price: Moderate–Expensive
Credit Cards: MC, V
Handicapped Access: Partial

Kate Grout's cottage enterprise consists of four delightful lodging options. Kahi Malu is a two-bedroom, one-bath cottage with koa floors, in a private setting among tree ferns and flowers. It sleeps five or six. Kate's Volcano Cottage is a spacious studio with a king-size bed, full-size futon couch, fully equipped kitchen, bathroom, and private covered deck. While suitable for a couple or single traveler, it sleeps three or four adults. The Bungalow, another studio cottage, blends into its forested setting with a shingled exterior. It sleeps up to five adults. The pièce de résistance is Nohea, a shining example of the craft of wood-working. It is extremely private, it is utterly indulgent (there's a spa room), and state-of-the-art media options include an Internet connection (with a foot massager under the desk). If you book online, Kate offers the option of selecting a cottage.

Volcano Teapot
Hosts: Ann and Bill Bullough
808-967-7112
www.volcanoteapot.com
19-4041 Kilauea St., Volcano, HI 96758
Price: Moderate
Credit Cards: AE, MC, V
Handicapped Access: Partial

It's not short, it's not stout, it's a perfect confection. Built early in the last century by a Hilo family as a summer retreat in cooler elevations (it's above 3,500 feet), the plantation-style home has been restored by the Bulloughs as they tap into their passions: his, woodworking, hers, afternoon tea. The result is a retreat furnished with restored antiques—the master suite features a four-poster bed with flannel sheets and a claw-footed tub in the bathroom. The other bedroom has a set of twin beds. Warming the living room in the evenings, a gas fireplace all but demands you snuggle up in front with your sweetie while waiting for a gourmet dinner to be delivered to the homey dining room by a local chef. (Yes, the Bulloughs have thought of everything. They can arrange for a masseuse to make a teapot call.) However, if you feel inspired, the kitchen is fully equipped. It's also stocked with breakfast treats, all locally made. There's an assortment of local coffees, and, of course, an assortment of teas.

In and around Puna

Coconut Cottage
Hosts: Jerry Cooksey and Todd Horton
808-965-0973, 866-204-7444
www.coconutcottagehawaii.com
3-1139 Leilani Ave., Pāhoa, HI 96778
Price: Moderate
Credit Cards: AE, MC, V
Handicapped Access: Yes

If I were planning a family reunion or a gathering of friends, Coconut Cottage is a place I'd consider. It's large enough—the Garden Bungalow sleeps four, the Bali Spirit Suite accommodates two, and the Grand Pineapple Suite, which sleeps four, accommodates children—yet there's plenty of privacy for each of the rooms. It's near the live lava flow, the black sands of Kehena Beach, and thermal pools as well, so there are plenty of nearby off-site diversions to amuse subgroups who might not want to make the 30- to 45-minute drive to Hawai'i Volcanoes National Park or Hilo. There's a soaking spa on-site, so go all the way and ask for a visit from a local masseuse.

Kalani Oceanside Retreat
Director: Richard Koob
808-965-7828, 800-800-6886
HI 137, Pāhoa, HI 96778
Price: Inexpensive–Moderate
Credit Cards: AE, D, MC, V
Handicapped Access: Partial

Kalani is all things to all people if you are the right sort of person. The accommodations range from a campsite to cabins, with tree houses in the mix. There's an extensive menu of yoga, tai chi, Pilates, *kuk sool won* (a Korean martial-arts system), meditation, bodywork, Hawaiian cultural programs, and hula and other dance activities. There are workshops and certification courses in a variety of bodywork and wellness techniques. Some programs are geared to gay men, others to lesbians. Bathing suits are optional at the Kalani pool and at the nearby beach. There are off-campus tours to Hawai'is Volcanoes National Park and scuba and snorkeling expeditions. The grounds are beautiful, your cell phone probably

Pohakunani is a vacation rental that has been featured in two design books.

won't work, kids are welcome (but there's no child care), and the three healthy buffet-style meals served each day cost extra.

Pohakunani
Host: Robert Trickey
808-965-7710
www.vrbo.com/30871
Kehena Beach, HI 96778
Off HI 137.
Price: Inexpensive–Moderate
Credit Cards: MC, V
Handicapped Access: Partial

Driven by design? Then pull up at Pohakunani, described by the *New York Times* as a "modernist house floating ethereally on a 1955 lava field." Designed by San Franciscan Craig Steely, Pohaakunani is a "sleek structure of glass and steel . . . an elegant object framing the lava." It's all that and more. This home, which has been featured in two books, *Island Living* by Linda Leigh Paul and *Minimalist Houses* by Simone Schleifer, may transform your perception of a lava landscape and Hawai'i. There's a self-contained studio and three guest rooms (which share a kitchen) in the main house. They can be booked separately or in any combination you need. Reserve the entire place, bring friends—it sleeps as many as 12— and challenge everyone to add modernism and minimalism to their Hawaiian vocabulary.

Ramashala
Manager: Chuck Creel
808-965-0068, 801-583-1077
www.ramashala.com
12-7208 Kapoho-Kalapana Beach Rd.
Pāhoa, HI 96778
On HI 137, mile marker
Price: Moderate
Credit Cards: MC, V
Handicapped Access: Partial

Ramashala is a compound just off the coastal road that operates as an inn and a spiritual and wellness retreat. The yoga instruction can be personalized, and there are trainers to customize a fitness program. The bodywork options are extensive and include *watsu*, massage with movement that occurs in a temple pool. The namesake building houses a yoga studio and four guest rooms—two on the second floor with queen-size beds, private baths, and lanais, and two singles on the first floor that share a bath. The second building, Prana, is completely private. Upstairs it has two king-size beds, a small loft accessible by ladder, a full bath, a living room area, and a kitchen, which staff will stock prior to arrival if you ask. There's a yoga studio and a second bath downstairs. Both buildings and their furnishings are the in the Balinese style. Asian, Indian, Island, Ayurvedic, and Italian meals are available, as is raw food for cleansing regimes.

The upside of daily showers are the rainbows that appear over Hilo Bay.

HILO

Bay House Bed and Breakfast
Host: Christine Jimenez
808-961-6311, 888-235-8195
www.bayhousehawaii.com
42 Pukihae St., Hilo, HI 96720
Price: Moderate
Credit Cards: MC, V
Handicapped Access: Partial

At this quiet B&B within a short walk of downtown Hilo (you'll cross the famous Singing Bridge), the guest rooms are all about the views. Comfortably furnished and featuring handcrafted Hawaiian quilts, they each look out onto Hilo Bay. You'll always see cruise ships steaming by, and you may see whales from your private lanai. It's a relaxed, and relaxing, place, even more so if you reserve the end room.

Dolphin Bay Hotel
Manager: John Alexander
808-935-1466, 877-935-1466
www.dolphinbayhotel.com
333 'Iliahi St., Hilo, HI 96720
Price: Moderate
Credit Cards: MC, V
Handicapped Access: Yes

A low-rise cinder-block motel in a lush, tropical setting in a quiet residential area, this is one of the nicest places to stay in Hilo. John and his staff make it special. They're kind, fun, and filled with information about Hilo and Hawai'is Volcanoes National Park. I am positive it's their personalities that encourage guests, many of them Europeans, to gather informally to swap tips and tales, or share a bottle of wine after a day's exploring. A few blocks from Hilo Bay and downtown, the rooms are nothing remarkable, but from the standard studio to the one-bedroom suites, they're eat-off-the-floor clean and comfortable. Each room has a ceiling fan and louvered windows that allow you to control the breezes. I think the second-floor rooms are a better bet; they're away from the parking lot and have higher ceilings, so they feel bigger. The continental breakfast consists of papayas, bananas, baked goods, and coffee, all of it local. There's enough fruit that I confess I always snag an extra papaya for later in the day. The only downside is the very vocal presence of nonnative coqui frogs that have invaded the state. Look in the medicine cabinet. You'll find earplugs and sleep like a babe.

Emerald View Bed and Breakfast
Hosts: Kenneth Richard and Antonio Garcia
808-962-0100, 800-262-9912
www.emeraldview.com
272 Kalulani St., Hilo, HI 96720
Price: Moderate

Credit Cards: MC, V
Handicapped Access: Partial

This guest house, with two rooms available, sits atop a cliff overlooking the Wailuku River, within a quick drive of downtown Hilo. It's a quiet place on a cul-de-sac, and because you must walk over an old wooden bridge to gain access, it feels a bit enchanted. The house has been newly renovated and is now as green as possible. The verandas, a gazebo, and a foyer are of renewable Douglas fir. Landscaping includes a palm garden, an orchid garden, and a Japanese rock garden, again designed to be ecologically sensitive. The Orchid Falls room has a king-size bed covered with a blue and white Hawaiian quilt, and the Ginger Falls Room has a full- and a queen-size bed. Both have views of waterfalls, and the furnishings point to Asia's enduring influence on this island. The polished chests are Japanese, the wooden chairs Chinese.

Hilo Hawaiian Hotel
Manager: Daryle Kitamori
808-935-9361, 800-272-5275
71 Banyan Dr., Hilo, HI 96720
Price: Moderate
Credit Cards: AE, D, DC, MC, V
Handicapped Access: Partial

The Hilo Hawaiian has a friendly, helpful staff with a can-do attitude, even though the building could use some sprucing up. Each comfortable room has a refrigerator, a coffeemaker, and a private lanai. It is well worth the extra cost to get an ocean-view room in the middle, or the right wing of a high floor. (If you go too far in the other direction, you may hear noise from the parking lot.) I love looking down and seeing fish jump in the waters surrounding Coconut Island. Even better is leaving the curtains open to wake as dawn spreads a pink glow across the slopes of Mauna Kea. It's a magical setting as early-morning crew teams practice rowing or kayakers cut across the bay. I usually make coffee in the room and head out for a stroll along Banyan Dr. to Lili'uokalani Park. Beware the local residents on their morning constitutionals. Pull over to let them speed-walk on by unless you want to keep up as part of your fitness regime.

Hilo Seaside Hotel
Manager: Rochelle Kagawa
808-935-0821, 800-560-5557
www.seasidehotelshawaii.com
126 Banyan Way, Hilo, HI 96720
Price: Inexpensive–Moderate
Credit Cards: AE, D, MC, V
Handicapped Access: Partial

Parking's an issue, the rooms are small, and noise from the nearby airport can sometimes be a problem, but if you get an upper-floor superior room overlooking the lagoon, this can be a good value for the money. Check the Web site for room and car rental packages.

Naniloa Volcanoes Resort

Owner: Ken Fujiyama
Manager: Mitch Green
808-969-3333
www.volcanohousehotel.com/naniloa_volcanoes_resort.htm
93 Banyan Dr., Hilo, HI 96720
Price: Inexpensive–Moderate
Credit Cards: AE, D, MC, V
Handicapped Access: Yes

The Naniloa experience varies wildly, depending on who's telling the story and when they stayed there. I have fond memories of it, but for a time it fell into disrepair. The place, with 383 rooms and suites in two towers, is undergoing extensive upgrades scheduled for completion in 2009. However, it will take time to rebuild the reputation of a once-lovely oceanfront property. Be sure to ask for a renovated room.

Shipman House Bed and Breakfast

Owners: Barbara Ann and Gary Anderson
808-934-8002, 800-627-8447
www.shipmanhouse.com
131 Ka'iulani St., Hilo, HI 96720
Price: Expensive
Credit Cards: AE, MC, V
Handicapped Access: Partial

If you want an experience that is more like staying in a grand home than hunkering down at a B&B, Shipman House is for you. On the National Register of Historic Places, the residence was designed by Henry Livingstone Kerr and offers a gracious reminder of life in Old Hawai'i, a sense highlighted by the period furniture, some of it antique koa. Every piece has a story, and Barbara, a direct descendent of the original owner, W. H. Shipman, who bought the house in 1901 as a surprise for his wife, Mary Kahiwaaiali'i Johnson Shipman, is happy to share them. Hawai'i's last queen, Lili'uokulani, visited often; she was a friend of the Shipman family and enjoyed a cigar as she played the Steinway. Jack London bunked in for a monthlong stay. No wonder. All five guest bedrooms have private baths, and they are furnished with the same slightly formal grace as the public parlor, dining room, and library. There are three rooms in the main house, Flossie's (where Jack stayed), within earshot of Wai-ka-pū Stream; Aunt Clara's Shell Room, which has a claw-foot tub and a knockout Hilo Bay view; and Auntie Carrie's Room, carved out of the original ballroom. (Is that a waltz in my dream?) There are two larger rooms, Mauka and Makai, in an adjacent guest house. These are more private than the rooms in the main house, but all the rooms are delightful. Breakfast is divine. No children because of the nearby gulch.

Uncle Billy's Hilo Bay Hotel

Manager: Sandy Yokomizo
808-961-5818, 800-367-5102
www.unclebilly.com
87 Banyan Dr., Hilo, HI 96720
Price: Inexpensive–Moderate

Credit Cards: MC, V
Handicapped Access: Partial

It's on Hilo Bay, and that's why you'd stay here—as long as you're in an oceanfront room with a knockout view of Mauna Kea. Otherwise, it's noisy, and frankly, kind of funky bordering on dumpy, which doesn't make it any less popular with folks visiting from other islands. But if you're after a room only for sleeping, with a few moments carved out to bask in the view, then this is a money-saving option for exploring the area. Check the Web site for rental car packages that go a long way to countering the tired tiki kitsch.

HĀMĀKUA COAST

Cliff House
Hosts: Richard and Li Zhu Mastronardo
808-328-9607, 800-527-7789
www.cliffhousehawaii.com
Kukuihaele, HI 96727
Price: Moderate
Credit Cards: AE, MC, V
Handicapped Access: Partial

Friends stayed here on their honeymoon, and whenever they show the photos, conversation stops. The seclusion that comes with being on a 40-acre spread is evident from the breathtaking, unobstructed coastal views of green cliffs embracing nearby Waipi'o Valley. It's a wonderful, inspirational spot for getting away. From late December to late February, you can see whales from the lanai, and on clear days, you can see Maui.

Kālōpa Cabins
808-974-6200
www.bigisland.org/parks/315/kalopa-state-recreation-area
About 6 miles south of Honoka'a, 3 miles inland (and upland) at the end of Kalōpā Rd.

The two simply furnished cabins at the Kālōpa State Recreation Area each sleep eight people bunkhouse style. Each has a shower and a bathroom. The shared kitchen is in a separate building. Bedding is provided. You can't stay here without a permit. (See chapter 7, Recreation, on how to obtain one.) This is an untouristed spot, and when I was last here midweek, there was nobody else around. Even if you don't plan on staying overnight, the drive to the park is pleasant, and the easy nature trail, a 0.7-mile loop through an 'ōhi'a forest, helps walk off a picnic. Tables provided.

Luana Ola Cottages
Hosts: Marsha and Ray Tokareff
808-775-1150, 800-357-7727
www.island-hawaii.com
5-3474 Kawila St., Honoka'a, HI 96727
Price: Moderate
Credit Cards: MC, V
Handicapped Access: Partial

These off-the-beaten-path plantation-style cottages are furnished in rattan and wicker; each features a kitchenette (you'll find breakfast fixings there when you wake) and sleeps up to four. Both have ocean views. A gulch typical of the coast borders one side of the property. It is filled with a vast assortment of tropical plants, including several varieties of ginger and orchids. There's also an intermittent waterfall, so for once on a vacation rain is a good thing, because rain makes the waterfall do its thing. Although secluded, the cottages are within easy reach of Honoka'a.

The Palms Cliff House Inn
Hosts: John and Michele Gamble
866-963-6076
www.palmscliffhouse.com
Honomū, HI 96728
Price: Very Expensive
Credit Cards: AE, DC, MC, V
Handicapped Access: Partial

Year after year, the Palms Cliff House wins awards from judges as disparate as the WeddingChannel.com—there are special wedding packages that include assistance in obtaining a license—and *Outside* magazine. It has such a special place in local history that it's been celebrated in hula at the Merrie Monarch Festival. The hosts offer far more services and amenities than a traditional B&B, and it is absolutely worth the splurge. All the luxuriously appointed rooms overlook the ocean and Pohakumanu Bay; each features a king-size bed, private bath, and a private lanai. The four corner suites have fireplaces and in-room oversized Jacuzzi tubs tucked in a round alcove overlooking the ocean. A generous and delicious breakfast is served on a veranda overlooking the coastal cliffs. Dinner is available upon request, and you should take advantage of this opportunity.

Waianuhea
Hosts: Carol Salisbury, owner; Ginger and Bruce Mosher, managers
808-775-1118, 888-775-2577
www.waianuhea.com
45-3503 Kahana Dr., Honoka'a, HI 96727
Off HI 19, near mile marker 43 between Waimea and Hilo.; located in Āhualoa above Honoka'a.
Price: Expensive–Very Expensive
Credit Cards: AE, MC, V
Handicapped Access: Partial

Waianuhea proves that remote or rural does not mean rugged. In a spectacular part of the world, this is a spectacular place to stay. It is solar powered, and Internet and TV come via satellite. The five bedrooms, including two queen-bed rooms, two large king-bed rooms, and one full suite, are plush and pampering (there are large soaking tubs in the rooms with king beds). A gas stove or woodstove warms the three larger rooms. The decor is simple but sophisticated. Breakfast may be thinly sliced Canadian bacon shaped into bowls with poached eggs in the middle. For later in the day, snacks and meals are available. There's a large selection of reading material and an extensive DVD library. Views of the summit of

Mauna Kea above and Pacific Ocean below are included. This would be a memorable place for a family or business gathering, if only because it can easily be a destination in and of itself. As is true of the best resorts, there's really no need to leave during your stay. Be sure to ask about the B&B&B triple play they coodinate with two other upscale Big Island lodgings. One call books nine nights for a "drive less, see more" experience.

Waipi'o Wayside Bed and Breakfast

Host: Jacqueline Horne
808-775-0275, 800-833-8849
www.waipiowayside.com
Waipi'o Valley Rd., Honoka'a, HI 96272
Price: Moderate
Credit Cards: MC, V
Handicapped Access: Partial

Time and again when I hear people talking about the Big Island, Jackie's place gets praised. While it's in a perfect location for exploring the Waipi'o Valley and the artsy town of Honoka'a, the white picket fence comes in for comments, as do the views and the organic breakfasts tailored to dietary needs when necessary. She really goes all out; she's even thought about the reading lights in the five rooms—halogen to minimize strain. So, as you would imagine, the rooms rock. The second-floor Birds Eye Room, the largest, is the de facto honeymoon hideaway with warm wood-paneled walls, its own bath, and lots of privacy. The views are memorable. The other upstairs offering, the Library Room, also has a great view, but that might not be the main attraction for the bibliophile; the room is stocked to the sloping ceilings with books. On the first floor, the Chinese Room has the best views. The other two rooms have garden views.

WAIMEA

Ahhh, the Views

Hosts: Derek and Erika Stuart
808-885-3455, 866-885-3455
www.aaahtheviews.com
66-1773 Alaneao St.
Off Akulani, past mile marker 60 on HI 19, Waimea, HI 96743
Price: Moderate
Credit Cards: MC, V
Handicapped Access: Partial

Designed as a healing retreat, this streamside refuge is a tranquil place disturbed only by birdsong and the sound of water. Derek and Ericka have professional training in massage and yoga. That conscious sensibility pervades the four guest rooms, all with large windows —the name Ahhh, the Views is based in reality—and tasteful, light-colored decor. The Dream Room, actually an apartment with a king-size bed and a daybed set in a windowed alcove above the stream, has a dozen windows and absolute privacy. A garden cottage with a kitchen sleeps two downstairs and two in a loft. Two other rooms can be combined into a suite for up to eight. All rooms have private baths and kitchens.

Jacaranda Inn
Manager: Mary Ellen Revana
808-885-8813
www.jacarandainn.com
65-1444 Kawaihae Rd., Waimea, HI 96743
Price: Moderate
Credit Cards: MC, V
Handicapped Access: Partial

The ridgeline of the hills behind the Jacaranda Inn always floats to my mind's eye when I think about Waimea. The rounded crests exude Waimea's sense of place. Built in 1897, the Jacaranda Inn was once home to the Parker Ranch manager, a personage of note. Another worthy, Laurence Rockefeller, who then owned the luxurious Mauna Kea Beach Hotel down the hill, acquired it in the early 1960s. He hosted Jacqueline Kennedy at this up-country retreat. Now it is one of the best values on the Big Island. There are eight rooms and suites, suitable for a maximum of 22 people. All the accommodations are separate from the main house but connected to it via covered walkways. One of them, the Begonia, is actually a private bungalow. Modest plantation-style exteriors hide deluxe interiors that are very, very different in style, so be sure to ask questions when you make a reservation. The person who delights in the Anthurium room with its ambience of a cowboy's mountain house might find the whimsical Hibiscus room with its peach palette a tad discomfiting. Aside from personal aesthetic preferences, you cannot make a wrong choice. Each room has a sitting area and a spacious bathroom. A full hot breakfast is served daily from 8 to 8:30 each morning in the garden room of the main house, which includes a living room with fireplace, several dining rooms, a koa-wood-paneled library with a billiard table, and a bar with trellised lanai. The Cottage is a three-bedroom, three-bath plantation-style home located streamside on the grounds, but away from other guest rooms. It sleeps six and suits families or groups.

Kamuela Inn
Manager: Carolyn Casvilla
808-885-4243, 800-555-8968
www.hawaii-bnb.com/kamuela.html
63-1300 Kawaihae Rd., Waimea, HI 96743
Price: Inexpensive–Moderate
Credit Cards: MC, V
Handicapped Access: Partial

This unpretentious motel-style lodging offers clean, basic rooms with private baths. Some suites have kitchens and lanais. It is quiet and popular with people who live in distant parts of the Big Island and work in the resort area in hospitality or construction.

Paniolo Cottage
Host: Sheila Cox
808-646-0346, 866-399-5842
www.vrbo.com/63899
Mana Rd., Waimea, HI 96743
Off Māmalahoa Hwy.

The Kohala Club Hotel started life as a place for the Big Island's business travelers.

Price: Moderate
Credit Cards: MC, V
Handicapped Access: Partial

I'd go back to this cozy cottage in a heartbeat. It is a tastefully converted outbuilding on a small farm with dogs, horses, and other livestock who take note of comings and goings. There's a queen-size sleigh bed in the bedroom with big windows looking out on a lawn to a corral. In the vaulted-ceiling living area with two walls of windows, there's a daybed that converts into two twin beds. The kitchenette has everything needed to make a light meal. Although I ate inside, there's a furnished lanai. The cottage, decorated by Sheila's deft hand, has cable TV, a DVD player, and wireless Internet access (none of which I used, preferring a book instead).

Waimea Gardens Cottage
Hosts: Barbara and Charlie Campbell
808-885-8550
www.waimeagardens.com
Off Māmalahoa Hwy., Kamuela, HI 96743
Price: Moderate
Credit Cards: No, personal checks only
Handicapped Access: Partial

Barbara and Charlie preserved parts of an old plantation home when they built their home. In 1982 they built the Kohala Cottage as a honeymoon retreat for their daughter, and renovated it in 1998 to add a whirlpool tub and double showerheads to the bathroom, which opens onto an enclosed garden. The cottage has a fully equipped kitchen and a queen-size bed. There's a twin bed in the entry room. Waimea Cottage, built in 1992, also has a queen and a twin sofa bed as well as a wood-burning fireplace and a kitchenette. The newest addition is the Garden Studio. Attached to the main house, it has a private entrance, a kitchen, a shower with glass doors that open to a private deck, and a king-size bed; it has "honeymoon" written all over it.

North Kohala

Kohala Club Hotel
Manager: Grant Wilson
808-889-6793
www.kohalaclubhotel.com
54-3793 Akoni Pule Hwy., Kapa'au, HI 96755
Price: Inexpensive
Credit Cards: No
Handicapped Access: Partial

This is an old business hotel with a cottage. Recently renovated and updated, the rooms are small, simple, and not without charm. There are single and double rooms in both buildings, and the club is convenient to the North Kohala historic sites as well as the restaurants and galleries of Hāwī and Kapa'au.

Kohala Village Inn
Manager: Leilani Scovel
808-889-0404
www.kohalavillageinn.com
55-514 Hāwī Rd., Hāwī, HI 96719
Price: Inexpensive–Moderate
Credit Cards: MC, V
Handicapped Access: Partial

This yellow plantation-style inn with a blue roof offers simple, rather pleasant accommodations located around a quiet, planted courtyard. There are five rooms for one or two guests and three suites that sleep three or four people. Each room or suite has a private bath. And while there's satellite TV and Internet access, the vibe is very old-time. Upgrade to a superior room. Noise may be an issue, even in sleepy Hāwī, so book a room away from the restaurant.

4

CULTURE

What to See, What to Do

It is undeniable that a good part of the Big Island's seductive power comes from the land, and the interwoven cultures on the island exert an equally appealing pull. No matter what the circumstances of their arrival, each group has contributed elements that would be sorely missed if removed. History erupts from each turn in the road. Cultural festivals throughout the year celebrate ethnic communities, art, agricultural products coffee and chocolate come to mind—theater, dance, and film. Take those and cross-pollinate them, for example hula performances at an annual cherry-blossom festival or a rodeo with flower-bedecked horses. Attend Sunday-morning services at a Buddhist temple, or at a Christian church where the choir sings hymns you know, but in Hawaiian. And remember, the first Christian church in Hawai'i was steps from the Ahu'ena Heiau.

That it is alive with investigation and innovations in astronomy, archeology, vulcanology, oceanography, ecology, renewable energy, and cold-seawater aquaculture makes the Big Island even more intriguing. These are not abstract or bookish pursuits. They are part of daily life. An evening spent at the Onizuka International Astronomy Visitor Center will change forever how you see the skies at your home. Considering a greener way of life? Visit the Hawai'i Gateway Energy Center, which uses innovative technologies to minimize its impact on a fragile environment, and get ideas for your next remodeling project.

To counter that green tech, look for New England–style architecture in Kailua-Kona at the Moku'aikaua Church. Add in a visit to the Hilton Waikoloa Village to see and experience its flamboyant interpretation of resort-style Hawai'i. The Lyman Museum features an interesting historical and anthropological collection. It is a New England–style house adapted to local conditions, a combination that suggests the missionaries' determination to carry on in Paradise in their usual way while being remarkably curious about their new home. The adapting and blending reaches full impact with C. W. Dickey's buildings throughout the state. Influenced by Spanish, Italian, Californian, and Hawaiian themes, the Hawaiian Telephone Building in Hilo is one of his most important efforts. Also in Hilo and evidence of its past as a thriving port, there's art deco splendor at the Kress Building and Palace Theater, a movie palace with a diverse schedule that includes musical and cinematic offerings. They include showings of films presented as part of the biggest festival in the United States for Asian and Pacific movies, an event filled with star power from both sides of the Pacific.

It is easy to drive by what was once the Jodo Temple in Laupāhoehoe.

CINEMA

The Palace (808-934-7777; www.hilopalace.com; 38 Haili St.) Built in the heyday of movie palaces, the Palace opened in 1925, when Hilo thrived as the commercial and administrative hub of the Big Island. It was part of a small chain of theaters owned by Adam C. Baker, the nephew of the last royal governor of the island. He built the theater entirely of redwood imported from the Pacific Northwest and had stadium seating to maximize a small space. It is on the National Register of Historic Places, and there is an active effort to restore it to its full glory. It is the home of the **Hawai'i Island Chinese Film Festival** held in conjunction with the Lunar New Year. The theater's original Robert Morton pipe organ is used to accompany silent movies. The theater plays first-run movies as well as special programming. For movie and event information, call the 24-hour recording at 808-934-7010. **Honoka'a People's Theater** (808-775-0000; Māmane St.) shows movies on the weekends.

Commercial Movie Houses

Commercial movie houses are only in the population centers. In **Kailua-Kona**, they include the **Makalapua Stadium Cinema** (808-327-0444) at 74-5469 Kamakaeha St. and the **Keauhou 7 Cinemas** (808-324-7200) in the Keauhou Shopping Center at 78-6831 Ali'i Dr. In **Hilo**, the **Kress Cinemas** (808-935-6777) are at 174 Kamehameha Ave., and the **Prince Kuhio Stadium Cinema** (808-296-1818) is in the Prince Kuhio Plaza at 111 E. Puainako St.

If your rental has a DVD player and you want to watch a movie, try **Blockbuster**: in **Kailua-Kona** (808-326-7694) in the Kona Coast Shopping Center, 74-5588 Palani Rd.; in **Hilo** (808-959-4977) at 111 East Puainako St.; in **Waimea** (808-887-1021) at 67-1185 Māmalahoa Hwy. Consider *Blue Hawaii* or *Picture Bride* or *Hawai'i*, the adaptation of the James Michener novel. All are set in Hawai'i.

The Palace Theater in downtown Hilo offers live music concerts, musicals and plays.

Festivals

Big Island Film Festival

www.bigislandfilmfestival.com

A growing festival that celebrates independent narrative films, it screens entries at three venues adjacent to each other in the Waikoloa resort area. *Movie-Maker* magazine selected the festival as one of 20 festivals worth the entry fee for filmmakers. While the focus has been on new works, the festival also shows movies set for distribution; however, only independent narrative films are eligible for the Golden Honu Awards. The festival runs for four days in May.

Louis Vuitton Hawai'i International Film Festival
www.hiff.org

Oh! The movies you'll see! Started at the East-West Center on the University of Hawai'i–Manoa campus in Honolulu in 1981, it screened seven films from six countries for an audience of 5,000 that first year. Now it is *the* primary U.S. source for the discovery and exhibition of Asian and Pacific feature films, documentaries, and videos. Big Island screenings are at the Palace in Hilo and elsewhere. The festival runs for about 10 days in October.

HISTORIC BUILDINGS AND SITES

KAILUA-KONA IN AND AROUND

Hulihe'e Palace
808-329-9555
www.daughtersofhawaii.org
75-5718 Ali'i Dr., Kailua-Kona, HI 96740
Open: Mon. through Fri. 9–4; Sat.–Sun. 10–4
Admission: $5 (guided tours by request)

Organic white pineapples are sweet, tangy and refreshing Big Island treats.

Built in 1838 by High Chief John Adams Kuakini, then governor of Hawai'i, this simple two-story building served as his own home. For the royal family, it was a retreat from the stress of O'ahu. After the overthrow of the monarchy, the Territory of Hawai'i purchased the property, and in 1927, the Daughters of Hawai'i saved it from demolition to make way for a waterfront resort. The graceful structure houses a noted collection of koa furniture and Hawaiian artifacts. Of note is a wardrobe commissioned by King Kalakaua. Made of koa and trimmed with the darker *kou,* the stunning example of a woodworker's skill was the Kingdom's entry in the Paris International Exhibition of 1889. Adorned with Greek muses, the King's crest, and traditional Chinese cranes—it was made by Chun Moke, a Chinese craftsman in Honolulu—the piece won a silver medal. The second-floor sitting room offers a provocative juxtaposition of traditional Victorian-style furniture—dark, heavy, stiff—with a pair of brightly feathered *kahili,* the royal standards. The palace suffered significant damage during the October 2006 earthquake, and only limited tours will be available until the completion of repairs and restoration. However, monthly concerts of Hawaiian music, singing, and hula will continue on the ocean lanai throughout restoration.

Moku'aikaua Church

808-329-0655
www.mokuaikaua.org
75-5713 Ali'i Dr., across the street from the palace, Kailua-Kona, HI 96740
Open: Daily during daylight hours
Admission: Free

On the National Register of Historic Places, Moku'aikaua Church is the oldest standing church in the state. King Liholiho gave the land to the first Christian missionaries who arrived on the shores of Kailua Bay in 1820. Thus the first Christian church in Hawai'i ended up being steps from Kamehameha's Ahu'ena Heiau. Large thatch-roofed churches built in 1820 and 1825 predated the current New England–style structure that was started in 1835 and completed in 1837. The exterior of the church, one of the tallest buildings in Kailua-Kona, was created using recycled lava rock from an ancient Hawaiian temple, while the interior was constructed using 'ōhi'a and koa wood. Like the palace across the street, it was constructed by foreign seamen visiting the islands. Sunday-morning services start at 8.

Carved elephants adorn the beams at the colorful Wood Valley Temple.

St. Michael's Church

808-326-7771
75-5769 Ali'i Dr., Kailua-Kona

This is the site of Kailua-Kona's first Catholic church. The current lava-rock building, erected in 1850, replaced a thatch-roofed structure. It was damaged extensively by the October 2006 earthquake and is closed for repairs. The bell, cast in Paris in 1853, is on display in front of the church.

St. Peter's Church
Ali'i Dr. in Keauhou area, Kailua-Kona
Open: Irregularly
Admission: Free

Also known as the Little Blue Church, this Catholic church is one of the most photographed buildings on the island and a popular wedding spot. Simple and profound, it floats amid hibiscus and bougainvillea, next to the ocean on what was once the site of a sacred Hawaiian temple, or *heiau*. The best time to visit is at sunset, when the final rays illuminate the interior; the turquoise trim and pews stand out against the lava rock foundation; and Kahalu'u Bay, a prime snorkeling spot, glistens. Look for the image of St. Peter.

SOUTH OF KAILUA-KONA

Captain Cook Monument
Kealakekua Bay

A 27-foot-tall white stone obelisk marks the site where Hawaiians killed Captain James Cook. Access to the monument was restricted after the October 2006 earthquake, when a nearby cliff face collapsed, but restrictions have eased. The shore adjacent to the monument is open, so you can beach a kayak, then visit the monument or access it via the 2-mile trail that starts on the ocean side of Nāpō'opo'o Rd. about 200 yards west of the HI 11 intersection. It is a steep trail and quite strenuous. It is not possible to drive to the monument.

St. Peter's Church on the water in Keauhou is a popular wedding spot.

Daifukuji Soto Zen Mission

808-322-3524
www.daifukuji.org
79-7241 Māmalahoa Hwy., Kealakekua
Open: Every day
Admission: None required, but there is a box for donations.

For many people, the red-and-white Daifukuji Soto Zen Mission is a landmark to indicate they're heading into the mountain region of Kona. Yet as one of the oldest buildings in the areas, it is a significant example of early-20th-century Buddhist temple architecture that blends construction techniques from the local plantation tradition with Japanese temple design. The result is strikingly eclectic. While once a preserve of Japanese immigrants eager to retain their culture and beliefs in a new land, the mission is now multiethnic, multicultural, and imbued with a calmness that may persuade you to pause on your travels. I find it a comforting place to visit. I leave feeling renewed. Morning zazen is at 6, and evening zazen is at 7. Sun.-morning services start at 9:30, and there are Kannon (Kwan Yin) services on the third Wed. morning of every month at 10.

St. Benedict's Painted Church

808-328-2227
www.thepaintedchurch.org

The Daifukuji Soto Zen Mission is listed in the National Register of Historic Places.

84-5140 Painted Church Rd, Captain Cook, HI 96704
Open: Daily dawn to dusk
Admission: Free

Overlooking Kealakekua Bay, this masterpiece was created by Father John Velge, a Belgian priest, for his flock. A self-taught artist, he started to fill the small sanctuary with trompe l'oeil murals depicting Bible scenes in the first decade of the 20th century. His work covers almost every surface, from striped columns to the ceiling. Masses are Saturday night and Sunday morning.

Hilo

The old downtown lends itself to a self-guided walking tour of a cluster of early-20th-century buildings. Many merchants have a free map that lets you follow a route or wander, absorbing history while shopping.

First Hawaiian Bank Building

130 Kamehameha Ave.

Built in 1930 by C. W. Dickey, one of the state's leading architects, the concrete art deco building survived both the 1946 and 1960 tsunamis that swept through the low-lying bay-front neighborhood. Fittingly, it has been converted into the Pacific Tsunami Museum. (See Museums in this chapter.)

Murals decorate the interior of St. Benedict's Painted Church in South Kona.

Built in 1899, St. Benedict's Painted Church overlooks Kealakekua Bay.

Haili Congregational Church
808-935-4847
211 Haili St.
Open: Every day

Founded in 1824, the congregation settled at the current location some 30 years after occupying its first building—a grass canoe shed. The yellow and white landmark houses a well-known choir that sings in Hawaiian at Sun.-morning services.

Hawaiian Telephone Building
Kalakaua St. between Keawe and Kinoole

This 1929 building, a C. W. Dickey project, combines Polynesian, Asian, and European influences that work together in his signature style.

Honpa Hongwanji Hilo Betsuin
808-961-6677
www.hilobetsuin.org
398 Kilaua Ave.
Open: Mon. through Fri. 8–5; Sat. 8–4; Sun. 8–noon

Dedicated in 1926, this temple has its roots in a Jodo Shinshu Buddhist worship hall built in 1889, making it the oldest outpost of the sect in the West. Sunday-morning family service is at 9.

Koehnen's Interiors
76 Kamehameha Ave.
This furniture store has been in the same location since 1929, run by the same family who started the business as a jewelry store. While you may not be in the market for a sofa, peek in to see the koa walls and 'ōhi'a floors of their historic 1910 building with the soft blue exterior.

Kress Building
174 Kamehameha Ave.

A 1932 art deco delight, parts of which nobody seems quite able to figure out what to do with. The exterior façade is terra-cotta brownstone. Notice the floral embellishments and keep going to the rear, where there's a soda fountain serving local favorite Tropical Dreams ice cream, Kona coffee, and other snacks.

Palace Theatre
(See Cinema in this chapter.)

Post Office and Federal Building
154 Waiānuenue Ave.

Constructed in 1910 with two wings added in 1936, this is a prime example of neoclassical style as influenced by Spanish missions—a mélange typical of early-20th-century federal buildings in Hawai'i.

S. Hata Building
308 Kamehamea Ave.
Open: Every day during business hours

Built by the Hata family in 1912, the restoration has won state recognition for historical accuracy and adaptive reuse. A row of arched windows on the second floor makes it easy to identify from across the street. It now houses galleries, shops, and eateries as well as offices.

HĀMĀKUA COAST

Old Jodo Mission
Off HI 19 at mile marker 27 (signs are for Laupāhoehoe Beach Park), Laupāhoehoe

Now privately owned, the lovingly restored 1899 structure was closed in 2000, one of many Big Island Buddhist missions that closed as older members died and younger ones joined other organizations. Barely visible on the direct approach down to the beach park, it is surrounded by fruit trees and a good vibe. Look for it or you'll miss it.

WAIMEA (KAMUELA)

'Imiola Congregational Church
808-885-4987
Church Row, off Māmalahoa Hwy., Waimea

First Sunday of the month is Holy Communion with hymns in Hawaiian and English. The congregation was called in 1830, and the first church was made of grass.

Parker Ranch Homes
808-885-5433, 877-885-7999
www.parkerranch.com
Māmalahoa Hwy. at the yellow flags, Kamuela
Open: Mon. through Sat. 10–5 (last tour starts at 4)
Admission: $9, discounts for seniors and children
Gift shop

Tours are available of two homes on the Parker Ranch, Puuopelu and Mana Hale, "The House of the Spirit." Very different in style, they suggest the evolution of gracious living on the paradise frontier. John Palmer Parker replaced his traditional Hawaiian house with the Cape Cod–style Mana Hale in 1847. He built it with his sons from his marriage to the granddaughter of Kamehameha I, for whom he worked after jumping ship. Kamehameha awarded Parker the land for $10. The homes' interiors are noteworthy for the use of koa, the koa furniture, and the Hawaiian quilts. It was moved to this site—board by board—in the 1980s. John Palmer Parker II bought the larger home, Puuopelu, and it served as the main ranch house until the last Parker, Richard Palmer Smart, died and left the entire ranch in trust to benefit the community of Waimea.

NORTH KOHALA

Kalahikiola Congregational Church
53-540 Iole Rd., Kapa'au

Meaning "The Day Salvation Comes," Kalahikiola was consecrated in 1855 and overseen by the Reverend Elias Bond and his wife, Ellen. He learned to speak the Hawaiian language and opened a school for boys and teachers. She started the Kohala Girls School in 1874. (The New Moon Foundation, which has a Buddhist outlook, now uses it.) As immigrants arrived to work on the sugar plantations, Bond started churches for these language groups. By the mid-20th century, workers of Japanese, Chinese, Caucasian, Hawaiian, and Filipino ancestry had joined the original church. It was severely damaged in the October 2006 earthquake.

Tong Wo Society

Akoni Pule Hwy. (near mile marker 25, set back off the uphill side of the road), Halawa

The first waves of contract workers arrived on the Big Island throughout the mid-19th century, and by 1884, there were almost 1,300 Chinese residents, most of them initially plantation workers. In 1886, they established the Tong Wo Society. It was one of many mutual-aid societies founded in the islands to provide a social and religious focal point for single men far from home, one that ensured their bones would be returned home if they died in a foreign land. The building remains in use as a social center, and the grounds, including a cemetery, are immaculate.

HULA

Hula is more than a dance. For many dancers, it is a way of life, a chance to walk hand in hand with Hawaiian history.

An 2006 earthquake damaged the Kalahikiola Congregational Church in North Kohala.

Yes, there are gestures and movements, but they come from the dancers' deep knowledge of the stories they are telling. These form the cultural beliefs surrounding creation of the world and humans, gods and their exploits, humanity and its foibles, history and genealogy, relationships and the cycle of life.

It is this knowledge that informs the physical movements by giving the dancers the mental imagery they need to express the story. For the physical to resonate, the mental must be present.

The third part is spiritual, showing appreciation for life, the land, and all its gifts.

Little of this made sense to 19th-century missionaries, and they tried to ban public performances. In this, they had support from Queen Ka'ahumanu, the royal convert to Christianity. The ban managed to drive the dance into isolated areas, where it was kept alive, the knowledge transmitted in the traditional way of watching and listening to the teachers. King David Kalākaua revived it, famously saying, "Hula is the language of the heart, and therefore the heartbeat of the Hawaiian people."

After his death in 1891, however, hula again retreated. This time the traditional transmission of knowledge came under pressure from vaudeville, Broadway, and Hollywood, all eager to use those lovely hula hands to lure in more audiences, but the traditional ways continued quietly, persistently. Julia Keahi Luahine, one of the last court dancers of King Kalākaua and Queen Lili'uokalani, taught students like Mary Kawena Pukui, who, although best known for her scholarly work preserving and disseminating the Hawaiian language, was also a *kumu hula*. Widely translated as "teacher," *kumu* carries with it the sense of being the source, not just the imparter, of knowledge. It was, and continues to be, a title not easily earned or bestowed.

Pukui was a central figure in the start of the Hawaiian Renaissance in the late 1960s. Since then, musicians, chanters, language immersion programs, and traditional-crafts practitioners have flowered, breathing life into Hawaiian cultural practices. The result has been an upsurge in hula, meaning you are more likely to see authentic hula today than at any time since the missionaries arrived.

Keeping hula alive and expanding it is the responsibility of today's *kumu*. They impart their knowledge of the Hawaiian culture and dance in schools known as *halau*. The students, *haumana*, are expected to make a serious commitment and to learn how the implements they use, the movements they make, the lei they weave of certain flowers and leaves from specific places all help tell the stories that keep a culture flourishing.

To learn more, *Sacred Hula* by Amy K. Stillman (Bishop Museum Bulletins in Anthropology) is an excellent overview. To get a taste of hula, there are several venues offering regular *'auana* (modern) and *kahiko* (traditional) performances.

Scheduled Performances

Brown's Beach House, Fairmont Orchid (808-885-2000; www.fairmont.com/orchid) 1 North Kaniku Dr. Kohala Coast. Nightly with dinner.
Hulihee Palace 75-5718 Ali'i Dr., Kailua-Kona; the fourth Sun. of every month at 4. Free.
Kings' Shops Waikoloa Resort; Mon., Thurs., and Fri. evenings with classes on Wed. 12:30–1:30. Free.
Kona Inn Shopping Village 5-5744 Ali'i Dr.; every Fri. 12:30–1:30. Free.
Uncle Billy's (808-961-5818; www.unclebilly.com) 87 Banyan Dr., Hilo. Nightly with dinner.

Merrie Monarch Hula Festival
808-935-9168
www.merriemonarchfestival.org
Time: Mar. or Apr.
Location: Hilo
Fee: Tickets start at $15

Hawai'i's most celebrated hula celebration and competition began as an effort to attract more tourists to Hilo. Civic leaders and hula teacher George Na'ope kicked off the first festival in 1963. Tourists failed to flock.

The festival became a competition in 1971, adding to the excitement. That year, the nine *halaus* that participated were not merely performing in a show; they were showing their best. Fine, shrugged the tourists, who kept flocking elsewhere.

Then Hilo got lucky. With the revival of interest in hula as part of the Hawaiian Renaissance, a *kane* (men's division) was added, and the Merrie Monarch took off. The festival outgrew its birthplace in the Hilo Civic Auditorium and filled the Edith Kanaka'ole Stadium.

By 1980, every night of the event was televised statewide. *Halaus* worked hard to enter, their male and female troupes each dancing a traditional and modern hula. Dances spoke of the gods and goddesses, of myths and history. As the festival and the hula evolved, Na'ope exhorted the *kumu hula* to move forward. After all, in ancient times, *mele*, or songs for hula, were composed for every occasion: the arrival of visitors and babies, weddings, deaths, memorable natural events. "We shouldn't be writing about what happened 100 years ago," he told the *Honolulu Star-Bulletin* in 1999. "We weren't there. But we should write about today so that the children and grandchildren can see what the life was like before their time."

Today, dances can depict the joys and frustrations of trying to sleep as frogs croak or a day spent fishing, as well as the traditional myths and legends. Festival tickets have become so sought after, organizers dispense them through a lottery to keep things fair. Entries cannot be postmarked before December 26 and must be accompanied by money orders. If you win, tickets are mailed back in the envelope you provided. Several years ago there was an outcry when tickets appeared on eBay, selling for hundreds of dollars over their face value. Local newspapers wrote articles quoting people upset at the blatant scalping, saying profits like that violated the spirit of hula. Organizers vowed that eBay ticket sellers would never again get tickets. The next year, no tickets appeared online.

The festival is more than just hula, with a week of activities including exhibitions, music, and arts and crafts fairs as well as impromptu hula before the three-night competition with competitors from the mainland as well as Japan.

The gathering is a way of transmitting a respect for the hula, and respect for the gods and goddesses whose stories they tell. It is a reminder of the richness of those stories—flowers and leaves crushed in the dance release their perfumes, evoking places far from a tennis stadium—and the top Hawaiian musicians accompany the dancers. It is a cultural celebration for dancers and audiences alike.

Festivals

Na Mea Hawai'i Hula Kahiko
808-967-8222
www.volcanoartcenter.org

Time: Jan., May, June, and Aug.
Location: Hawai'i Volcanoes National Park
Fee: Free (park entrance fees of $10 per vehicle or $5 per person apply)

Traditional hula and chant are performed outdoors on the hula platform overlooking Kilauea Crater at Hawai'i Volcanoes National Park in the mornings from 10:30 to 11:30. There are Hawaiian crafts demonstrations at Volcano Art Center Gallery from 9:30 to 2.

George Na'ope Kane Hula Festival
808-969-3003
Time: Early June
Location: Hilo
Fee: Call

Each year the festival begins with a concert to honor the venerable hula master, teacher, and National Endowment for the Arts award winner George Na'ope on a Wednesday. It is followed by three days of competition for Hawai'i's male hula dancers, performing solo or in groups.

Moku o Keawe International Festival
808-886-1655
www.mokuokeawe.org
Time: 2nd week of Nov.
Location: The Waikoloa Resort area
Fee:

Competition by *hula halau* (troupes) from Hawai'i, Japan, and elsewhere competing in *kupuna* (senior), *'auana,* and *kahiko* hula divisions. Workshops and cultural classes take place throughout the event. The event attracts big names in Hawaiian music for the opening-night concert.

GALLERIES

Most Big Island galleries are focused on the selling of art (for listings, see chapter 8, Shopping). The following exhibition spaces present art for enjoyment or edification. The shows may include work from local children as well as juried artists.

The **East Hawai'i Cultural Center** (808-961-5711; www.ehcc.org; 141 Kalakaua St., Hilo) promotes local artists and craftspeople. The **Isaacs Art Center** (808-885-5884; 65-1692 Kohala Mountain Rd., Kamuela) features a permanent collection of rare books, paintings, furniture, and Hawaiiana and also operates as a gallery for local artists. Part of the Hawai'i Preparatory Academy, which was designed by the late architect **Vladimir Ossipoff**, it also accepts donations of art, which it sells to benefit the school. **Kahilu Theatre Gallery** (808-885-6017; Waimea) features work by members of the Hāmākua Artisans Guild and other local artists. There's an annual black-and-white photography competition and a yearly children's art show. The **Donkey Mill Art Center** (808-322-3362; www.donkeymill artcenter.org; 78-6670 Māmalahoa Hwy., Hōlualoa) features the work of local artists and works created in its classes and workshops in ceramics and printmaking. **Wailoa Center** (808-933-0416; Wailoa State Park, off Kamehameha Ave., Hilo), has monthly shows by local artists.

Libraries

For delving into Big Island history and lore, public libraries can be a good source. There are collections in Hilo, Hōlualoa, Honoka'a, Kailua-Kona, Kapa'au, Kealakekua, Kea'au, Laupāhoehoe, Mountain View Pāhala, Pāhoa, and Waimea.

The **Hilo Public Library** (808-933-8888; 300 Waianuenue Ave.) has a solid collection of material on Hawai'i, and you can purchase a visitor's borrowing card for a nominal fee with valid ID.

Lū'au

If you're thinking "let's party," let's get back to basics first.

Lū'au actually refers to the edible leaves of young taro plants, which are used to wrap food before it is cooked in the *imu,* an oven dug into the ground. The best place to experience this is at a gathering of friends or family where all the food comes from somebody in the group

The Tong Wo Society building in North Kohala is a reminder of early Chinese immigration.

celebrating a birthday, a graduation, an anniversary, or other significant event. But there's so much work involved—think Thanksgiving, Christmas, and Super Bowl meal prep combined—that even if you're a local resident, a lūʻau is an infrequent event, particularly since food is feeding more than the body, it is feeding the soul with an almost ritualistic gathering.

To experience something like it, plan ahead and set aside at least $65 per adult, because commercial lūʻaus are more than a meal, they're productions with a story line, dancers, musicians, and, of course, vast amounts of food.

The *imu* is central to any lūʻau. Many people are involved in digging it, firing the hot rocks lining it, and preparing and wrapping the pig and other food to be cooked for most of the day. Opening the *imu* is the magic moment. Extracting the pig, that's tense. Then unwrapping it to reveal meat ready to fall off the bone. There's usually chicken and fish, both steamed in *ti* leaves to the same buttery tenderness. Expect lomi lomi salmon and be sure to have it with poi, the paste made of pounded taro root. Poi is also good with pork, other fish, or chicken. It really needs something piquant to boost its inherent blandness in much the same way you add brown sugar, raisins, or maple syrup to oatmeal. Jazz up some poi, and you'll understand why Hawaiian groups on the mainland auction bags of fresh air-freighted poi at fund-raisers.

The following Big Island lūʻaus are well regarded, with the Kona Village Resort offering the best bet year after year. While all are held at resorts, they are open to nonguests. Reservations are required.

Gathering of the Kings
The Fairmont Orchid
808-885-2000, 808-326-4969
www.fairmont.com/orchid
1 North Kaniku Dr., Kohala Coast, HI 96743
When: Tues. and Sat. 4:30–8:30
Price: Adults $99, discounts for children

Island Breeze Lūʻau
King Kamehameha's Kona Beach Hotel
808-326-4969, 866-228-9009
www.konabeachhotel.com
75-5660 Palani Rd., Kailua-Kona, HI 96740
When: Sun., Tues.–Fri. 5–8:30
Price: Adults $69.95, discounts for children

Kamahaʻo "The Wondrous Myths of Hawaiʻi"
Sheraton Keauhou Resort
808-930-4900
www.sheratonkeauhou.com
78-128 Ehukai St., Kailua-Kona, HI 96740
When: Mon. and Fri. 5–8:30
Price: Adults from $79.95, discounts for children

Hula Mana and Savai'i, Origins of Polynesia
Kona Village Resort
808-325-5555, 800-367-5290
luau@konavillage.com
Queen Ka'ahumanu Hwy., Kohala Coast, HI 96740
When: Wed. and Fri. evening
Price: Adults and children older than 13, $98, discounts for children; group prices
available

"Legends of the Pacific"
Hilton Waikoloa Village
808-886-1234
www.hiltonwaikoloavillage.com
69-425 Waikoloa Beach Dr., Waikoloa, HI 96738
When: Tues. and Fri. 5:30–8:30
Price: Adults from $82

MUSEUMS

Hilo Art Museum
808-982-6006
www.hiloartmuseum.org
1266 Kamehameha Ave., Hilo, HI 96720
Open: Mon. through Sat. 10–6; Sat. 9–6
Admission: Free

Founded in 2007, the museum is just spreading its wings. It plans to open art centers
throughout the island to parcel out parts of its collection starting in 2008.

Kona Historical Society & Museum
808-323-3222
www.konahistorical.org
81-6551 Māmalahoa Hwy., between mile markers 111 and 112, Kealakekua, HI 96750
Open: H. N. Greenwell Store, Mon. through Fri. 9–3:30
Kona Coffee Living History Farm, Mon. through Fri. 9–2
Kailua Village Walking Tour by appointment
Admission: H. N. Greenwell Store, $4
Kona Coffee Living History Farm, $15
Kailua Village Walking Tour, $15
Gift shop

Started in 1976 by a handful of local residents, the society now maintains two historic sites
and a research archive (with over 50,000 photographs), and just can't seem to stop adding
new, interesting activities. The living history program includes a chance to take your shopping list to the historically accurate **H. N. Greenwell Store**. If you go into it wholeheart-
edly, it's fun. On Thursdays, volunteers and visitors **bake Portuguese sweet bread** in the
stone oven in the lower pasture of the **Kona Coffee Living History Farm**. Volunteers offer

A heaiu on the beach is visible from the road in Keauhou.

an hour-long tour of the early-20th-century 5.5-acre coffee farm through orchards, gardens, and a Japanese-style farmhouse. The **Kailua Village Walking Tour** is an hour-long stroll through historic Kailua-Kona that traces the political, social, and commercial development of what was the capital of Hawai'i for many years. It gives context to historic structures such as **Hulihe'e Palace**, **Moku'aikaua Church**, and **St. Michael's Catholic Church**. Be sure to book the walking tour. In fact, make a morning or an afternoon of it, and participate in all the society's activities.

Laupāhoehoe Train Museum

808-962-6300
www.thetrainmuseum.com
36-2377 Māmalahoa Hwy., near mile marker 25, Laupāhoehoe, HI 96764
Open: Mon.-Fri. 9–4:30; Sat.–Sun. 10–2
Admission: $3 adults
Gift shop

Created to entice tourists to a town ravaged by the sugar industry's failure, this small, community-run museum has videos, photos, and displays set up in the former station-master's 1928 home. The exhibits tell the story of sugar, plantation life, and the railroad that served them. A 1930 diesel switch engine rolls along 250 feet of track. An engine and a caboose are being restored. It's a good stop for kids and train buffs.

Lyman House Museum

808-935-5021
www.lymanmuseum.org
276 Haili St., Hilo, HI 96720
Open: Mon. through Sat. 9:30–4:30; guided tours at 11, 1, and 3
Closed: Sun. and major holidays
Admission: $10 adults; $8 seniors; $3 children 6–18
Gift shop

The 1839 home of missionaries Rev. David and Sarah Lyman, the museum houses Hawaiian and missionary artifacts, including the Lymans' collections of shells, flora and fauna, minerals, and Chinese art. The building is on the National Register of Historic Places, and the guided tour makes the place come alive. There are also special exhibitions and events.

Pacific Tsunami Museum

808-935-0926
www.tsunami.org
130 Kamehameha Ave., Hilo, HI 96721
Open: Mon. through Sat. 9–4
Admission: $7 adults; $6 seniors; $2 students 6–17
Gift shop

This is a well-curated presentation that focuses on personal accounts of local tsunami survivors while imparting vast amounts of scientific information on these giant, earthquake-generated waves. The exhibits include photographs, letters, oral histories, and art, which, combined, are a potent package. Don't miss the video screened in what was once a bank vault. The museum is in the former First Hawaiian Bank, a 1930 art deco building designed by renowned Hawaiʻi architect C. W. Dickey.

Parker Ranch Visitors Center and Museum
808-885-7655
www.parkerranch.com
Parker Ranch Shopping Center, Waimea, HI 96743
Open: Mon. through Sat. 9–5 (last ticket sold at 4)
Admission: $8
Gift shop

An interactive display on the history of the Parker Ranch, from houses made of grass and the evolution of *paniolo,* or Hawaiian cowboy culture. Founded by John Parker, who jumped ship on the Big Island rather than return to New England, the ranch was at one time the largest private ranch under single ownership in the United States.

MUSIC, THEATER, AND DANCE

Aloha Performing Arts Company
808-322-9924
www.apachehawii.org

In existence for more than 20 years, this community organization puts on musicals such as *Annie Get Your Gun* and serious dramas such as *Cat on a Hot Tin Roof*.

Aloha Sundays
2nd Sun. of each month
East Hawaiʻi Cultural Center
808-961-5711
www.ehcc.org
141 Kalakaua St., Hilo, HI 96720

Aloha Theatre and Performing Arts Center
808-322-2323
www.alohatheatre.com
79-7384 Māmalahoa Hwy., Kainaliu, HI 96750
Call for prices

The 320-seat Aloha Theatre opened in 1932 as a silent-movie house. While movies are still shown here, there's also an ambitious schedule of theater, music, and dance. Dinner is available before the show at the Aloha Angel Café. There are special packages for dinner and an event. Do catch a show if you can.

Hawaiʻiana Live
Wed. mornings
The Palace
808-934-7777

www.hilopalace.com
38 Haili Street, Hilo, HI 96720

Hawai'i Concert Society
808-935-5831
www.hawaiiconcertsociety.com
P.O. Box 233, Hilo, HI 96721
Season: Oct.–Apr.
Tickets: $15; season tickets available

For almost half a century, the society has been bringing outstanding classical musicians from all over the world to perform at the University of Hawai'i–Hilo Performing Arts Center.

Kahilu Theatre
808-885-6017, 808-885-6868 box office
www.kahilutheatre.org
P.O. Box 549, Kamuela, HI 96743
Season: Oct.–June
Call for prices

The theater opened in 1981, a project of the heart by Richard Smart, who became the sole heir of the Parker Ranch fortune when his parents died soon after his birth in 1913. Smart grew up with a love of theater, drama, and music, and as a young man left the Big Island for New York City, where he performed on Broadway for some 30 years. When he retired to the ranch, he hired a Honolulu firm to design a $1.5 million, 490-seat performing-arts center. Its name came from the first part of the Hawaiian middle name of his mother, Thelma Kahiluonapuaapiilani Parker. The theater opened with *Oh! Coward,* and the first season included the Honolulu Symphony, Little Consort of Amsterdam, Hawaiian entertainers Charles L. K. Davis and Nalani Olds, and a Kabuki drama. That eclectic variety continues.

Kamuela Philharmonic
www.kamuelaphil.com
P.O. Box 6682, Kamuela, HI 96743
Season: Oct.–April

Since its debut in 2004, the orchestra has grown from 12 strings to a full 44-piece symphonic orchestra. While concerts are free, don't be bashful about dropping a donation in the calabash that's always in the lobby.

Kīlauea Drama and Entertainment Network
www.kden.pajamaville.com
Volcano, HI 96785

The newest group on the scene, the season consists of a musical in the summer and mystery or comedy in February. They work with the Volcano Festival Chorus, and there's talk of mounting every Gilbert and Sullivan work over the next few years.

Kona Music Society
808-329-2646, 808-334-9880 box office
www.konamusicsociety.org
Season: Nov.–June
Check the Web site or call for prices and locales

The Kona Music Society includes the Kona Community Chorus, the Kona Youth Chorus and orchestra, a children's chorus, a teen chorus, and the Kona Symphony Orchestra.

University of Hawai'i–Hilo Performing Arts Center
808-974-7310
www.artscenter.uhh.hawaii.edu
200 W. Kawili St., Hilo, HI 96720
Season: Year-round
Call or check Web site for prices

The center produces, presents, or sponsors an extensive and diverse calendar of events by local, regional, national, and international artists. Dance, drama, music, mime, children's shows, special lectures, musicals, and now opera—it's all here.

Waimea Community Theatre
808-885-5818
www.waimeacommunitytheatre.org
P.O. Box 1660, Kamuela, HI 96743
Season: Year-round
Call or check Web site for prices

Since 1964, the Waimea Community Theatre has produced a steady stream of comedies, dramas, musicals, classical theater, staged readings, variety shows, one-acts, stand-up comedy, and choral concerts. A season may include Neil Simon, Molière, Shakespeare, Agatha Christie, and Oscar Wilde. The venue is the Parker School Theater, and standards are high.

NIGHTLIFE

Outside Kailua-Kona and the bars or lounges at the Kohala resorts (see chapter 3, Lodging), there isn't much on the Big Island that would pass for nightlife unless you're an astronomer. Most entertainment is either at home or hanging out somewhere with friends. Check the local newspaper listings for live music in coffeehouses or bars. Ask around to find out if there are other events like a school fund-raiser with a big name in Hawaiian music or a full-moon celebration in the Puna district. Here are some of the latest hot spots, which can, of course, change as quickly as hot styles on the catwalk.

Kailua-Kona

As the Big Island's tourist center, there are plenty of options for drinking and carrying on along Ali'i Dr. **Durty Jake's** (808-329-7366; Coconut Grove Marketplace, 75-5819 Ali'i Dr.) usually has dancing, often to live music. They serve dinner, but, really, you come here to dance off your drinks. **Hard Rock Café** (808-326-7267; Kona Marketplace, 75-5725 Ali'i

Dr.) features loud music, loud tourists, and a dynamite ocean view that distracts from the usual rock 'n' roll memorabilia plastered all over the place. **Huggo's** (808-329-1493; 5-5828 Kahakai Rd., off Ali'i Dr.) is about half a mile down the road from the tourist cluster. It's a local fixture, and the crowd starts to gather in time to watch the sunset, then stays on because the oceanside scene hops if you're of drinking age. There's usually live jazz or a piano bar inside, Hawaiian or dance music outside, and a bar menu with enough food to keep you going. **Lulu's** (808-331-2633; Coconut Grove Marketplace, 75-5819 Ali'i Dr.) is a sports bar with dancing. It's lively, but if you no longer feel the need to reveal your SAT scores, college, and GPA in initial conversations, you're probably too ancient to fit in except during playoffs or big games. **Sam's Hideaway** (808-326-7267; Kona Marketplace, 75-5725 Ali'i Dr.) is a karaoke bar.

Hilo

The Hilo scene is even quieter. **Emerald Orchid** (808-961-5400; 168A Keawe St.) is a live-music joint some nights, and on others there's a DJ and *pūpūs* (appetizers). As befits a pub-style place, there's a good selection of beers, and the bartenders are friendly. In the limited world of after-dark Hilo, it scores big points for staying open past 10. **Uncle Billy's** Hilo Bay Hotel (808-961-5818; 87 Banyan Dr.) is a local haunt with an evening hula show in the unremarkable restaurant. The bar stays open after the dancing ends, but it can be hard to get anything other than a beer or a glass of wine.

SCIENCE AND TECHNOLOGY

'Imiloa Astronomy Center
808-969-9700
www.imiloahawaii.org
600 'Imiloa Pl., Hilo, HI 96720
Open: 9–4
Closed: Mon., Christmas, Thanksgiving, and New Year's Day
Admission: Adults, $17.50; children 4–12, $9.50; under 4, free
Café, gift shop

The 'Imiloa planetarium's signature presentation, "Maunakea: Between Earth and Sky," showcases the connections between Hawaiian culture and the astronomical research under way at the Mauna Kea summit. It's worth seeing, and there's always an additional program going on that's stimulating. The architecturally significant center is designed around three titanium-covered cones, representing the Big Island volcanoes of Mauna Kea, Mauna Loa, and Hualālai. You can't miss it. Try to spend several hours here and time your visit around a late breakfast or lunch if you can; the center's café is good.

Mauna Kea and the Onizuka International Astronomy Visitor Center
808-961-2180, 808-969-3218 for road conditions
www.ifa.hawaii.edu
Off the Saddle Road—at mile marker 28, turn onto the road marked with a sign reading MAUNA KEA ACCESS ROAD. The visitor station is about 6 miles in.
Open: 10–10 every day
Gift shop

Ascending Mauna Kea is one of the things you *must* do while on the Big Island. The summit is one of the best places on earth for astronomical observations. The air is crystal clear and pollution free. There are almost no urban lights to interfere. (Notice the shielded street-lights used on the island as you explore.) It is near the equator. That's why the pros from more than 10 nations put a battery of telescopes up here, making it the world's largest observatory for optical, infrared, and submillimeter astronomy. Even with naked-eye astronomy, the stargazing is humbling in its crystal vastness.

Making this trip requires some planning. Schedule it early in your visit because bad weather can close the road, and you need some flexibility to adapt. In the 36 hours surrounding your trip, avoid dehydration by drinking plenty of liquid while avoiding liquor and coffee. Do not go scuba diving within 24 hours of making the ascent. The summit is 13,796 feet above sea level; you could get the bends. (Measured from its base on the ocean floor, the mountain is the world's tallest, over 33,000 feet.) If you smoke, don't for 48 hours before going up. Wear dark sunglasses and lots of sunscreen, right through sunset.

The visitor center, named for Ellison Onizuka, a Big Island native killed in the 1986 *Challenger* disaster, has telescopes for public use. During the daytime, there is a solar tele-scope equipped with protective filters. The stargazing program is conducted nightly from 6 to 10 regardless of weather conditions. Expect to see star clusters, double stars, nebulas, planets, galaxies, supernova remnants, supernovas, and various other objects. There is a special program at the center every Saturday night. On the third Saturday of each month there is a presentation on Hawaiian cultural beliefs about Mauna O Wakea before the

Mauna Kea Telescopes

OPTICAL/INFRARED

UH 0.6-m telescope	0.6m	University of Hawai'i	1968
UH 2.2-m telescope	2.2m	University of Hawai'i	1970
NASA Infrared Telescope Facility	3.0m	NASA	1979
Canada-France-Hawai'i Telescope	3.6m	Canada/France/UH	1979
United Kingdom Infrared Telescope	3.8m	U.K.	1979
W. M. Keck Observatory	10m	Caltech/University of California	1992
W. M. Keck Observatory	10m	Caltech/University of California	1996
Subaru Telescope	8.3m	Japan	1999
Gemini Northern Telescope	8.1m	USA/UK/Canada/Argentina/ Australia/Brazil/Chile	1999

SUBMILLIMETER

Caltech Submillimeter Observatory	10.4m	Caltech/NSF	1987
James Clerk Maxwell Telescope	15m	UK/Canada/Netherlands	1987
Submillimeter Array	8x6m	Smithsonian Astrophysical Observatory/Taiwan	2002

RADIO

Very Long Baseline Array	25m	NRAO/AUI/NSF	1992

Source: www.ifa.hawaii.edu/mko/telescope_table.htm

You need a warm parka to enjoy a visit to the Mauna Kea observatories.

stargazing. During events such the Perseid or Leonid meteor showers in August and November, respectively, the Visitor Information Station stays open late.

Every Saturday and Sunday, there is an escorted summit tour that starts at 1 PM. You must have your own four-wheel-drive vehicle for the 30-minute drive to the summit. The tour goes into at least one of the observatories and ends by 4:30. You can stay on the summit for the evening if you want. The tour is restricted to people who are at least 16 years old. Pregnant women are banned, and people who are extremely overweight, in poor health, or who have a history of heart or respiratory problems should check with their doctors before planning a summit trip. Emergency assistance is two hours away. Dress warmly, and be sure your vehicle has a full tank of gas before you visit the visitor center.

If you decide to go up to the summit on your own, take a 30-minute break at the visitor center to adjust to the altitude and drink some water. The final 6 miles will take 35 to 45 minutes, and you'll be in low gear going from about 9,000 feet to close to 14,000 feet.

If you achieve the summit in daylight, look for a footpath to a rock cairn. Climb it and you have a 360-degree view. If it's cloudy, you'll still see the summits of Mauna Loa and Maui's Haleakala. Lake Waiau, one of the highest lakes in the world, is just below the summit at 13,200 feet. You can't see it unless you hike in from a trail that starts at the hairpin turn just before you reach the observatories. It's easy to spot.

Call me a wimp, but I'm convinced tours—they last about eight hours—are the way to go if you want to spend time on the summit after dark. While you can do it on your own, you *must* have a four-wheel-drive vehicle that you can take on the Saddle Rd. Even then, above the visitor center, it is unpaved, rough, steep, and notable for hairpin turns. The ascent is daunting in daylight, and a white-knuckle event in the dark due to loose gravel. At times, you must drive directly into the sun, making it almost impossible to see oncoming traffic.

The altitude changes don't make it easier, and on top of this, at the summit you need a warm, wind-eating jacket that probably wasn't something you packed but is something the tours provide along with a tasty dinner, informed guides, and telescopes. **Hawai'i Forest & Trail**, 808-331-8505; www.hawaii-forest.com; 74-5035B Queen Ka'ahumanu Hwy., Kailua-Kona, HI 96740. $169. **Mauna Kea Summit Adventures**, 808-322-2366; www.maunakea.com; P.O. Box 9027, Kailua-Kona, HI 96745. $197.

Mokupapapa Discovery Center
808-933-8195
www.hawaiireef.noaa.gov.center
308 Kamehameha Ave., Hilo, HI 96720
Open: Tues.–Sat. 9–4

At first glance, this center seems like an odd addition to downtown Hilo. Devoted to the natural science, culture, and history of the northwestern Hawaiian Islands, it focuses on the Papahānaumokuākea Marine National Monument, which is the single largest conservation area in the United States and the largest marine conservation area in the world. But because the area regarded as sacred in Hawaiian tradition is so remote, the reserve comes to you via the Hilo center. There's a nifty 2,500-gallon seawater aquarium occupied by fish from the extensive coral reefs found in Papahānaumokuākea. You may pop in to escape one of Hilo's showers, but it's hard to escape quickly.

A strong wind can dislodge a frond or a coconut.

Natural Energy Laboratory of Hawai'i Authority
808-329-7341
www.nelha.org
73-4460 Queen Ka'ahumanu Hwy. #101, Kailua-Kona, HI 96740
Open: Weekdays 8–4

This ocean science and technology park is centered around pure cold water pumped from several thousand feet below sea level. It's enabled the development of aquaculture, alternative energy production, coldwater agriculture, marine biotechnology, low-cost cooling, and a wide range of research and development projects. Periodically odd sea creatures, like a red "octosquid," get caught in its 3,000-foot-deep pipelines, and scientists get excited. The visitor center is in the **Hawai'i Gateway Energy Center**, which was selected as one of the most environmentally sound new buildings in 2007. The center is a thermal chimney, moving outside air through the building at 10–15 air changes per hour without any mechanical assistance. The photovoltaic system provides all the energy needed, and collected condensation is used for flushing toilets and watering the deep-rooted landscaping. The self-guided tour is free. There are 40- to 60-minute presentations and a tour of the deep seawater intake site Tuesday, Wednesday, and Thursday mornings at 10. Admission is $8 per adult, $5 for students and seniors, and free for children age eight and under. Cash or traveler's check only.

SEASONAL EVENTS

Unless otherwise noted, admission is not charged for the following events. However, there may be fees for activities affiliated with the event. The most up-to-date listings can be found at www.bigisland.org/calendar.

February

Hawai'i Wood Guild Show
Various locations

A juried exhibition of work in furniture, turnings, and sculpture by members of the Hawai'i Woodworkers Guild. For dates and more information, contact the guild (808-882-1510: www.hawaiiwoodguild.com).

March

Annual Kona Chocolate Festival
Kailua-Kona

Top chefs, caterers, and bakers do their bit to showcase cacao farming on the Big Island, which has been going on since the 1800s. The Big Island is the only place in the United States where chocolate is made entirely from scratch, from growing the cacao trees and their pods, through processing the cacao nibs, to creating an all-Hawaiian chocolate bar. The gala dinner is a very (sugar) high-energy evening. For dates and more information, contact the festival (www.konachocolatefestival.com).

Hilo Chamber Music Festival
Hilo

For dates, programs, and ticket information, contact the festival (808-216-4722; www.orchid islemusic.com).

Prince Kūhiō Day
Various locations

The March 26 birthday of Prince Jonah Kūhiō Kalaniana'ole (1871–1922) is celebrated statewide, one of two holidays in the United States dedicated to royalty. (The other is King Kamehameha I Day.) Prince Kūhiō served as the delegate from the Territory of Hawai'i to the U.S. Congress and was instrumental in the passage of the Hawaiian Homes Commission Act, which was to provide homesteads for native Hawaiians. Signed into law by President Warren Harding in 1921, it continues to be controversial in Hawaiian politics.

April
Merrie Monarch Hula Festival
Hilo

The biggest hula festival in the state usually occurs in Hilo the week after Easter in April. (See Hula in this chapter.) There is a lottery for ordering tickets, and entries cannot be postmarked before Dec. 26 of the prior year. Book accommodations well in advance. At Hilo B&Bs and hotels, many people reserve for the next year as they're checking out. For dates and full details, contact the festival (808-935-9168; www.merriemonarch festival.org).

May
Lei Day
Various locations

Workers of the world may unite on May 1 elsewhere in the world, but in Hawai'i, folks make and wear lei, those garlands of flowers that range from a single strand of fragrant plumeria to multistrands of ginger, orchids, and exotic blue jade plants braided, woven, or knotted with vines. The tradition began in 1927 at the suggestion of two Honolulu newspaper columnists, Don Blanding and Grace Tower Warren. It is now a wonderful celebration of lei-making and other crafts. Check local newspapers for events.

June
King Kamehameha Day
Various locations
Time: June 11

Although this is a holiday honoring King Kamehameha I throughout Hawai'i, North Kohala may be the place to celebrate because local residents remain fiercely proud that he was born in the area and harbored here as an infant.

The festivities start with draping lei over the original King Kamehameha statue in Kapa'au off the Akoni Pule Hwy. (The Hawaiian legislature commissioned the statue in

1878, and the 9-foot bronze was cast in Paris only to be lost at sea near the Falkland Islands. A replacement bronze was cast and installed in Honolulu, but in 1912 the original was salvaged and installed near his birthplace. The extended saltwater bath corroded it, and local residents began painting it. The skin is brown, the feather cloak yellow, and the sash red. After restoration in 2001, the community voted to continue painting the statue rather than return it to the original bronze finish.)

There's a 2-mile-long route for a morning parade with floats, marching units, and *pa'u* riders followed by a day of music and food sales. This is small-town community togetherness at its best.

While all events are free, contributions are gladly accepted for the celebration or for maintaining the Kamehameha statue. Contact the Kohala Hawaiian Civic Club (808-884-5000; www.kamehamehadaycelebration.org).

Dolphin Days
Waikoloa resort area on the Kohala Coast

A four-day festival focused on the dolphins at the Hilton Waikoloa Village. The programs include a fun run and a golf tournament to benefit Hawai'i Shriners Hospital for Children and the Pacific Marine Life Foundation. Tickets are sold either for all events or for one day. Individual events require separate admissions; for example, the food, wine, and music extravaganza, which attracts top chefs and musicians. For more information, call 808-886-1234, ext. 2884, or long on to www.dolphindays.com or www.hiltonwaikoloa village.com.

July

Big Island Music Festival
Hilo

The stars of slack key, falsetto, steel guitar, and ukulele come out and attract fans from Japan, Europe, Mexico, and the U.S. mainland for a weekend of superb music. For more information and tickets, contact the East Hawai'i Cultural Center (808-961-5711; www.ehcc.org).

Leis arrived in Hawai'i with the early Polynesian voyagers. Today they're made from flowers, leaves, seeds, nuts, feathers, and shells or bones, and even wrapped candy or dollar bills. They are, perhaps, the symbol of Hawai'i to tourists.

A lei is usually given with a kiss, or at least that's the modern way. After all, it's a symbol of affection. On celebrations, such as graduations, people being honored will be up to their chins, if not their noses, in lei. They're also draped over statues, gravestones, and anything that deserves celebration.

Wear your lei draped over your shoulders, not hanging straight from your neck. Don't throw it away. Drape it over a lamp in your hotel room to scent your space as it dries. Then wrap it carefully and carry it home to hang on a mirror or along a door. The scent, while subtle, is an evocative souvenir.

If your visit to the Big Island coincides with a festival or a parade, you'll probably see beautiful women riding trim horses, both bedecked in flowers almost wherever they can be attached. These are *pā'u* riders, a contemporary manifestation of a historic love of horses. Hawaiian women, however, had no interest in riding sidesaddle. They rode astride, their dresses tucked around their legs to create floating petals of silk or white cotton. On special occasions, they made special costumes for themselves and for their horses. Today you'll see *pā'u* riders trailing yards and yards of fabric, sporting magnificent floral headpieces and dramatic matching lei, their horses bedecked similarly, with thick, elegant garlands attached to their tack, sometimes even on their legs or in their manes.

Usually a *pā'u* queen leads the procession, followed by princesses or ladies-in-waiting with a male *paniolo* outrider. All will wear the colors and flowers identifying their island: Red with *'ōhi'a lehua* represents the island of Hawai'i; pink with *lokelani* for Maui; gray or blue with *hinahina* for Kaho'olawe; orange with *kauna'oa* for Lana'i; green with *kukui* for Moloka'i; yellow with *'ilima* for O'ahu; purple with *mokihana* for Kauai; and white or brown with *pūpū o Ni'ihau* for the tiny Island of Ni'ihau.

Parker Ranch Independence Day Rodeo
Waimea

An action-packed day at the Parker Ranch track and rodeo grounds off HI 190. Expect horse races, branding, roping, and other cowpunching tests that can include a song contest. Of course there's food and special activities for children. There's a nominal admission

A pau rider greets the crowd watching the Merrie Monarch parade in Hilo.

fee; in 2007 it was $6 at the gate. For more information, call 808-885-2302 or visit www.parkerranch.com.

August

Admissions Day

A holiday on the third Friday in August to celebrate Hawai'i's 1959 admission to the United States. There aren't official celebrations unless you're a state worker who gets the day off.

Annual Hawaiian International Billfish Tournament
Kailua-Kona

The granddaddy of all big-game-fishing tournaments. Established in 1959, it now attracts an international array of teams to the warm, deep waters off Kona looking for the big one according to International Game Fish Association rules. For dates, rules, and other information, visit www.konabillfish.com.

Pu'ukohola Heiau Cultural Festival
808-882-7218
62-3601 Kawaihae Rd., Kawaihae, HI 96743
Time: Third week in August
Admission: Free

A weekend of cultural events featuring demonstrations of hula, lei making, and music at the National Historic Landmark, a temple constructed for ceremonies relating to the Hawaiian god of war and the place where Kamehameha's cousin was slain. The death had been prophesied and led to the conquest and consolidation of the islands under the rule of Kamehameha I.

September

Aloha Festival
Various locations
www.alohafestivals.com

Created in Honolulu in 1946 as a weeklong celebration of Hawaiian culture, it is now the largest statewide celebration in the United States. There are ceremonies at Hawai'i Volcanoes National Park, hula and storytelling events, a Miss Aloha Nui contest, parades, craft and music fairs, and even a *Poke* Recipe Contest. Once the winning recipe for this appetizer of raw fish is declared, there's lots to sample. For dates and locations, visit www.pokecontest.com.

Parker Ranch Rodeo
Waimea

A two-day Labor Day weekend event at the Parker Ranch Rodeo Arena in Waimea showcases all skills *paniolo* in a fund-raiser to provide scholarships for children of Parker Ranch employees. For more information, call 808-885-7655 or visit www.parkerranch.com.

October

Ford Ironman World Championship
Kailua-Kona

Physically fit or lunatic? You be the judge. It's a wild week of extreme athleticism and the people who cheer on the 1,700 participants who qualify each year. The main event is the grueling triathalon—a 2.4-mile ocean swim, a 112-mile bike ride, then a 26.2-mile run—but there are other attractions, such as the Underpants Race, a short in-town road race that began as a tribute to European Ironmen entrants who are given to wearing little more than their teeny Speedos around town. A recent race T-shirt, sold to benefit the Special Olympics, proclaimed: "I see England, I see France, no, it's your underpants." For race week dates and events, go to www.ironmanlive.com.

November

Kona Coffee Cultural Festival
Kailua-Kona and the coffee belt

There's lots of buzz surrounding this gathering, with a coffee-picking contest, a "cupping" workshop—like wine tasting for coffee fanatics—and other events that celebrate Kona's 600-plus coffee farms. Admission is charged, and some events have additional fees and require reservations. For dates and locations, call 808-326-7820 or visit www.konacoffeefestcom.

Ukulele & Slack Key Guitar Festival
Waimea
Admission: Per-class fees are $40 to $60

The focus is on master classes with musicians such as the father-son team of Dennis and David Kamakahi leading beginners, experts, and nonmusicians in workshops, master classes, and jam sessions. A master concert opens the event. For a full schedule and other details, call 808-885-6017 or visit www.kahilutheatre.org.

At Pu'uhonua O Hōnaunau, a carved wooden image looks out to sea.

5

SACRED SITES, ANCIENT RUINS, AND NATURAL WONDERS

Places of Revelation

Much of what is known about the early history of Hawai'i has come from sites on the Big Island. According to the state's Department of Land and Natural Resources' Historic Preservation Division, there are an estimated 11,500 archeological and historic sites on the island that have been identified. Only about 5 percent have been surveyed, however, and even fewer are open to the public or discernible to those who aren't in the know. Even experts admit there are more sites than they know about—the outside estimate is some 300,000 significant ones exist.

The richness of this heritage comes from the island having been settled by Polynesians starting as early as A.D. 300. From that culture sprang Hawaiian culture, and it is on this island that many of its most notable figures—Pa'ao, who set out from Kahiki, which was either Tahiti or Samoa, and a host of kings such as Liloa, Lonoikamakahiki, and Alapainui—held sway before Captain James Cook arrived in 1778. It was also the island called home by many figures significant in postcontact history: Kalaniopuu, Kamehameha, Kapi'olani. It is the home of the volcanic goddess Pele, a deity so compelling she is spoken of with respect today.

That the sacred and the merely ancient mingle easily and constantly on the Big Island only enhances its beauty for us quotidian souls who revel in the majestic spirit and topography of Wākea and Pāpā's firstborn. To begin to understand the interwoven nature of the sacred, the ancient, and the daily, carry with you *Place Names of Hawaii* by Mary Kawena Pukui, Samuel H. Elbert, and Esther T. Mookini. Look up street names you can't pronounce easily. Look up the names of hills or towns.

For example, here's part of what the authors say about the stunningly scenic village of Laupāhoehoe, where Kamehameha declared his law of the splintered paddle or *māmala hoe* law, which is probably the origin of the name of the belt road, Māmalahoa Hwy.: " . . . an ancient surfing area. . . . A man who came from Kahiki and thence to the canoe landing at Laupāhoehoe built a *heiau* he called Ule-ki'i (penis fetching). The man turned into a *pao'o* fish, and his sister into an 'a'awa fish. People who wanted to catch them were surprised to see them turn into human beings." At the beach park, notice the fresh flowers at the memorial for the 23 students and four teachers killed by the final and largest of three

The Creation Chant

The Kumulipo is the chanted record of the creation of Hawai'i from the dawn of time. Over two thousand lines long, it is a *meli oli*, or chant, that reveals the connections between the heavens and the earth, the earth and the oceans, the oceans and the land, the land and humans, humans and the gods. *Kahunas*, or priests, would memorize the entire epic and recite it at important festivals as a reminder of the origins of the Hawaiian people. It offers a point of view that recognizes the lunar cycle in relation to the ocean and planting. It acknowledges the sun and the rain for the nourishment they provide, and the wind, ocean currents, and rivers for the mobility they offer. The chant delivers sophisticated theories about the origin of life and of the cosmos. In the process, it reminds listeners of their relationship to each other and the earth. "At the time when the earth became hot, when the heavens turned inside out, when the light of the sun was weakened causing the moon to shine, the time of the rise of the Pleiades, the time of night darkness, the realm of Gods, the time of Po. . . ." The first half of the Kumulipo describes a world of spirits and a time when lower life-forms and eventually mammals are born. Then the time of Ao arrives, the subject of the second half of the Kumulipo. This is when the darkness gives birth to Kumulipo, the source of life, who is male, and Po'ele, night blackness, who is female. The darkness gives way to light, and the gods descend to earth. Wākea is the sky father, and Pāpā is the earth mother. From their union came the Hawaiian Islands. Hawai'i is born first, followed by Maui and Kaho'olawe, at which point Pāpā retreats to Tahiti and Wākea takes a second wife, who bears Lana'i. Wākea's third wife gives birth to Moloka'i. Pāpā, upon her return, retaliates by taking the young and virile Lua as her lover, giving birth to O'ahu soon after. But Wākea realizes his mistake, as does Pāpā. They reunite and give the world Kaua'i, Ni'ihau, Ka'ula, and Nihoa. All the *ali'i*, or rulers of Hawai'i, trace their roots to Wākea and Pāpā. It is a world of order, "a fixed whole in which all the parts were integral to the whole, including man himself," says Herb Kawainui Kane in the PBS series *The Hawaiians*. "Man was descended from the gods, but so were the rocks, so were the animals, so were the fish. Thus man had to regard the rocks, the fish, and the birds as his relatives. It's an ecological point of view which Western man is only now understanding." For a full translation, see *Kumulipo: A Hawaiian Creation Chant* by Martha Warren Beckwith, University of Hawai'i Press.

waves of April 1, 1946. Within yards, you've crossed the parallel universes of prehistory, the ancient, the recent, and today. Whatever your beliefs, this texture cannot be denied.

SACRED SITES AND ANCIENT RUINS

Think of many Big Island sites as akin to the prehistoric cave paintings of Lascaux in France or Itsukushima Shrine on Miyajima in Japan. They're mysterious, removed, and yet generous in the rewards they offer a visitor who pauses to be filled with awe. We've organized this section to follow a circle route of the island, starting in the northern, sacred area that includes the site of Kamehameha's birth.

North Kohala

The windswept Kawaihae Coast can be a desolate place even on a sunny day. It's you, wind, and cattle in a hot, dry landscape that has always been sparsely populated but rich in cultural and historic sites. There's one main road, the Akoni Pule Highway, around this knob on the Big Island's north edge. It is a full day's outing from the Kohala Coast, Kailua-Kona, or Waimea as there are restaurants, shops, and galleries in Kapaʻau and Hāwī, and beaches along the way.

Lapakahi State Historical Park
808-882-6207
Akoni Pule Hwy., 12.4 miles north of Kawaihae just before mile marker 14
Open: Daily, except state holidays, 8–4; last entry at 3:30
Fee: Free self-guided walking tour with a brochure takes at least an hour; guided tours for groups by reservation (call 808-889-7133)
Facilities: Restrooms, no drinking water

This 262-acre park is the site of an ancient Hawaiian fishing village that is a pick hit from December to April, when you can often see migrating whales close to shore. Which is not to say it isn't worth a stop other times during the year. It is.

With the annotated brochure as your guide, you walk a 1-mile trail laid out with wood chips past numbered points of interest that include a canoe longhouse and a shrine dedicated to Kuʻula, the deity for whom fishermen always reserved an offering from their catch. You'll also pass several house sites, and it helps to know that Hawaiians usually had several places to stay, depending on what they were doing—a shelter among cultivated mountain fields or beside a trail or a cave used when on a fishing trip.

One display shows how ancient fishermen used nets to catch *opelu*, a practice still in use. Another is a salt-making area showing the ancient technique of evaporating seawater by storing it in indentations carved into the rock, and then using the salt to preserve the

Views on the Onomea Bay Scenic Drive live up to the hype.

fish. There's also a game area that will interest children as well as adults who want to test their skills at Hawaiian games. There are instructions and game pieces available for *'o'oihe* (spear throwing), *konane* (Hawaiian checkers), and *'ulu maika* (bowling with stone disks). It's easy to really get into these, and that in turn helps you imagine ancient life. Such sneaky park rangers, turning games into a learning experience.

Kohala Historical Sites States Monument

Off Akoni Pule Hwy., at mile marker 20 turn *makai,* or seaward, into a paved single-lane road that bounces downhill to dead-end at the small and very quiet Upolu Point Airport. Look for a dirt road to the left. If it's been raining, it may not be passable, but if you have a four-wheel-drive vehicle with high clearance, it's a bumpy 1.6-mile drive that can test your mettle. During whale-watching season, pull over and watch for humpbacks. (You can park at the airport and hike in—it's about 45 minutes to an hour.)
Open: Daily, except Wed., 9–8
Fee: Free
Facilities: None—there may be brochures in a box next to the parking lot

This large monument set aside in 2005 includes the **Mo'okini Heiau and King Kame-hameha's birthplace.** Although these are places of extraordinary significance—both are on the National Register of Historic Places, and the *heiau* is one of the most sacred—their iso-lation guarantees that, for now, they are off the tourist trail. Treat them as you would any sacred building, do not enter roped-off areas, and remove nothing from the area. These are powerful sites, and you may see offerings of flowers at the *heiau*. You may, if you wish, bring flowers or a lei to leave to show your respect. The outer wall was built in 1981 by local people to protect the site and keep vehicles off the grounds.

The massive *heiau,* set next to the water with a view of Maui, is a lichen-covered mound of rocks once restricted to *ali'i nui,* high chiefs intent on purification, prayer, and human sacrifice. According to legends, the initial structure was built in A.D. 480,which means it was one of the first *heiau* built by the first groups of Polynesians. Pa'ao, the high priest from Kahiki, dedicated it to Ku, the god of war, when he enlarged it centuries later as he re-ordered the society he found when he arrived. According to legend, stones from the Pololu Valley were passed hand to hand by 18,000 *menehune,* or little people, during the one night it took them to build the rectangular enclosed space. It is routinely described as about the size of a football field, with walls as high as 30 feet and 15 feet thick in some places. Like other similar fitted-stone structures elsewhere on the island, it reveals the makers' great skill at laying walls. The large flat stone outside the wall is the sacrificial altar.

There's a thatched shelter in the southeast corner of the *heiau* still used for ceremonies. The Mo'okini family has provided the *kahuna nui,* or high priest, for generations according to oral histories, an unequaled cultural inheritance. Although the position is usually held by men, a number of women have filled the position at this *heiau.*

You can walk south on a dirt track along the coast to the site of Kamehameha's birth. It's a striking and empty spot, fitting for one whose name means "the lonely one." According to tradition, he was taken from this spot to Mo'okini Heiau for birth rituals at the temple dedicated to the god of war, again a fitting place for the baby who would grow up to be the warrior king who forged a united kingdom. Kamehameha, born about 1758, died in 1819 in Kailua-Kona. His burial site remains unknown.

Commissioned in 1878, the King Kamehameha statue in North Kohala was cast in Paris.

Kohala Coast

Fishponds

Ancient Hawaiians used brackish ponds along the ocean for aquaculture, or fish farming. Their methods were sophisticated, and they developed two types of ponds. Closed ponds were inland, without direct access to the ocean. For open ponds, the Hawaiians built rock seawalls that served as a low-tide barrier to escape for the unsuspecting fish that entered at high tide. Water circulated from the ocean through sluice gates keeping full-size edible catch from leaving. The Bishop Museum lists more than 350 fishponds circling the Big Island along a linked series of fishermen's trails and roads from the Hawaiian Kingdom. Although there are fishponds throughout Polynesia, this is where they evolved into feats of engineering.

The ponds, already the preserve of ruling chiefs, came under the control of Kamehameha

Words, Words, Words

You'll encounter new words as you explore sacred and ancient sites on the Big Island. Here's a brief glossary.

a'a—rough lava

ahu—a stone mound serving as an altar or shrine

ahupu'a—basic unit of ancient Hawaiian land distribution that ran from the high mountain uplands to the sea. It allowed access to the wide variety of materials and creatures needed for survival.

ala—waterworn stones used in heiau construction

ali'i—the ruling class, consisting of chiefs and nobles believed to have divine origins

'anu'u—wooden framework obelisk serving as oracle tower

'aumakua—an ancestral protective gods or god

hale noa—family sleeping house

heiau—temple used for worship or sacrifice

kahuna—priests and master craftsmen. Kahuna pule were priests presiding over each religious cult.

ko'a—a pile of stones designed as a shrine to attract fish to the area

ku'ula—a large smooth stone set upright on a platform as a religious effigy, often a shrine to the god Ku'ula used to attract fish

lele—sacrificial altar or stand

loko—any type of pond or enclosed body of water

luakini—temple where rituals for the Ku, the god of war, were held

Makahiki ceremony—annual harvest festival

mana—spiritual or supernatural power possessed most fully by deities, and less so by the ali'i, often referred to in terms of the sacred power in the land

mo'i—elaborately carved statue placed in front of altar

ohana—extended family

pāhoehoe—smooth lava

pali—cliff

pao—a building technique using several tiers of lava slabs or columns laid across the space between outer and inner retaining walls

wa'iea—small house for ceremonies on luakini platform

Source: www.nps.gov

I when he united the islands between 1790 and 1810. During his stays in Kailua-Kona, the catch from fishponds now found on the grounds of several Kohala Coast resorts would be wrapped in wet leaves and whisked either by canoe or special runner along the King's Trail, the Ala Loa.

Kahapapa and Kuʻualiʻi Fishponds

Waikoloa Beach Marriott Resort
808-886-6789
69-275 Waikoloa Beach Dr., Waikoloa, HI 96738
Open: Daily during daylight hours
Fee: Free

As you walk through the resort to the beach at ʻAnaehoʻomalu Bay, you'll cross the fishponds. Kahapapa, the smaller pond, is to the north, and you can see how it's connected to the sea and to Kuʻualiʻi, the larger pond. Because you're above the water on a bridge, it's often easier to spot fish in the ponds here than it is elsewhere.

While you're here, you can also see **petroglyphs**. If you park at the shopping complex, it's a quick walk along a signposted path to the first of the etchings of humans, birds, and canoes. Others are dots and lines. Please stay on the path. Walking on the petroglyphs causes irreparable damage. For a more extensive array of petroglyphs, go to the **Puʻakō petroglyph area**.

Kalahuipuaʻa Fishponds and Historical Trail

Mauna Lani Resort
808-885-6622
www.maunalani.com
68-1400 Mauna Lani Dr., Kohala Coast, HI 96743
Open: Daily
Fee: Free

Bottom samples taken from these seven fishponds south of the hotel date their use as far back as 250 B.C., or well before Western contact.

The hotel maintains and stocks the pools, moving the schools of mullet and *awa* from pond to pond as the fish go through their growth cycles, and offers tours of the ponds as part of its history program. Call for tour times.

You can also undertake a self-guided tour that includes an ancient settlement with lava tubes once used for shelter and goes out to a beach cove with good swimming. It loops through the grounds for about 1.5 miles, but if the guided tour fits your schedule, it's a more informative option.

Kaloko Fishpond

Kaloko-Honokohau National Historic Park
808-326-9057
www.nps.gov
Queen Kaʻahumanu Hwy., gate between mile markers 96 and 97, opposite the yellow Kona Trade Center, Kailua-Kona, HI 96740
Open: Daily 8–5
Fee: Free

The first references to this vast pond are in 300-year-old chants describing a massive sea-wall that is probably much older. The seawall, which is 30–40 feet wide and more than 6 feet high, created a pond fives times larger than the norm. It's an awesome spread, a place to believe the legend that the *menehune,* or little people, built all the fishponds in one night, their usual feat. Otherwise, you'll be overwhelmed by the full-size human effort that went into creating the wall. It's carefully positioned and angled just so. You'll see a reef where waves break. Then the waves build again, and just as they're set to break again, they run into the wall, their power diffused. Brilliant.

There are plans to resume traditional aquaculture at the pond, a move supported by the state's Office of Hawaiian Affairs.

Although there are bathrooms at the site, there is no drinking water. It can be a brutally hot place, so avoid visiting at midday and be prepared with sunblock and liquids no matter what time you arrive.

PETROGLYPHS

Very little is known about the petroglyphs found throughout the Hawaiian Islands. Who carved them? Unknown. What are they for? Unknown. You'll see family groups—father, mother, and children—incised in smooth lava. There are canoes, birds, and, after contact, guns, anchors, and imported animals such as horses. The earliest ones are stick figures. They're almost always found on smooth lava or cliff faces, and often along ancient trails.

One thing is known. Damage to the petroglyphs caused by walking on them or rubbing them is irreparable. They've endured for centuries, and if you want an image as a souvenir, please take a photograph.

Kaʻupulehu Petroglyphs

Kona Village Resort
808-325-5555, 800-367-5290
www.konavillage.com
Queen Kaʻahumanu Hwy., Kohala Coast, Hawaii 96740
Fee: Free. There are petroglyphs (and fishponds) on the resort grounds that are fully accessible via a boardwalk designed to protect the images. You must make an appointment to see them on your own, or to join a guided tour, so your name can be left at the guarded gate.

The Kaʻupulehu petroglyph field displays more than 400 of the best and most unusual images. There are human figures with paddles and fishing lines. Some figures are dancing; others appear to be walking. Once you start discerning the incisions, you'll spot fish, turtles, sailing canoes, chiefs in headdresses, a burial scene, and kites, which are extremely rare. Look carefully, and you will see the date 1820 and some carvings that include Western writing.

Puʻakō Petroglyph Archeological District

At the Holoholokai Beach Park, on the north side of the Fairmont Orchid Hotel in the Mauna Lani Resort
808-885-6622, 800-367-2323
www.maunalani.com
68-1400 Mauna Lani Dr., Kohala Coast, HI 96743

Open: Daily during daylight, but avoid midday
Fee: Free. The Muana Lani Hotel has a brochure and a map that you can obtain in the lobby, and they offer tours. Call for times.

Containing more than 3,000 images, this petroglyph preserve is one of the largest and oldest concentrations in Hawai'i and definitely worth a visit. There are two segments, the first paved with a special area just for making rubbings.

The second segment is a rough-ish trail through thickets of *kiawe* that opens into a barren flat lava viewing area. Most of the petroglyphs you'll see here seem to be facing Mauna Kea, but needless to say, the answer to "why" is unknown.

The district is larger than what is accessible, but in an effort to preserve the images, paths to many of the petroglyphs have been blocked. Please don't go into these areas.

Pu'ukoholā Heiau National Historic Site
808-882-7218
www.nps.gov/puhe
Kawaihae Harbor
62-3601 Kawaihae Rd., off HI 270, 0.25 mile north of the HI 19 intersection
Open: Daily 7:30–4
Fee: Free. Guided tours can be arranged for groups of 10 or more for $2 per person.
Facilities: Information center, restrooms, and a paved trail past the main *heiau*

Don't miss the Pu'ukoholā Heiau (Temple on the Hill of the Whales) built by Kamehameha I between 1790 and 1791 to fulfill a prophecy that if he built a temple and dedicated it to the god of war, he would unify the islands. The 86-acre site includes the homestead of Kamehameha's trusted advisor John Young and, in the bay, the submerged Hale o Kapuni Heiau, which is dedicated to the shark god.

All that remains of the *heiau* are the stone foundation and platforms. You'll see large circular rock formations that are the remnants of farming in the area prior to the *heiau*'s construction. There are stone walls built to keep domesticated animals out of the area, and some enclosures that served ancient Hawaiians as shelters and the modern U.S. military for observation and machine-gun nests during World War II.

When you're in the site, it's difficult to fully appreciate the size of the main *heiau*, so either coming or going, head down to the Kawaihae Harbor. Look for a track on the flat land beside the bay. It's opposite the *heiau*, and this long view provides the perspective needed to comprehend its size.

Kona Coast
A drive south along the coast from downtown Kailua-Kona passes many sacred sites and some beautiful scenery.

Ahu'ena Heiau
808-329-2911, 866-228-900
www.konabeachhotel.com
Off Ali'i Dr. on the grounds of the King Kamehameha Hotel, Kailua-Kona

On the National Register of Historic Places, this reconstructed *heiau* was Kamehameha's temple to Lono, the god of prosperity. His council met at the *heiau* for rituals and prayers, which was also the site of human sacrifices. The white structure in the rear is an oracle tower, and you'll see a nearby platform usually marked by offerings. The hotel is filled with artifacts related to Kamehameha, which you can view without being registered. Call the hotel for information about guided tours of the *heiau*, which is closed. Kulana Huli Honua, a local group dedicated to the preservation of the *heiau* as well as conducting tours, has had an uneasy relationship with the hotel at times. You may have to be satisfied with looking at the *heiau* from afar.

Kealakekua Bay State Historical Park
At the end of Nāpō'opo'o Rd. off HI 11, near mile marker 111, Captain Cook
Fee: Free
Facilities: Boat launch, restrooms, water, and food available

This is a stop that has it all—history, snorkeling (see chapter 7, Recreation), and terrific scenery. The **Hikiau Heiau** was the site of human sacrifices before Captain James Cook arrived in November 1778 during the harvest festival, and some Hawaiians saw him as Lono, the god of prosperity, but things went terribly wrong after he left in February. A storm damaged his ship, and he returned to the beautiful bay, not an event scripted in the Lono legend that boosted his first arrival. The welcome wasn't so warm the second time around—there were confrontations, thefts, and bad feeling all around. Tensions escalated, and a wounded Cook died in shallow water. The great seafarer couldn't swim. The white plinth across the bay from the beach park marks the site of his death. The memorial is occasionally vandalized. Unless you hike down to see it, the best view is by boat or from tiny, rocky Manini Beach, a short walk south of the boat launch.

Ku'emanu Heiau
Off Ali'i Dr. by Kahalu'u Beach Park near St. Peter's Catholic Church

You'll spot a rock platform, the remains of the *heiau* used to appeal for good surfing waves, to the right of the church (the Little Blue Church) as you face it.

Kuamo'o Battlefield and Lekeleke Burial Grounds
At southern end of Ali'i Dr., a 10- to 20-minute drive from downtown Kailua-Kona

More than 300 warriors died here in 1819 in a battle that saw the monarchists defeat the traditionalists with the aid of muskets obtained from foreigners. It is seen as one of the events marking the end of the old way of life. The terraced burial grounds are atop lava cliffs with surf roiling below. Many visitors leave offerings at the base of the historic marker.

South Kona

Pu'uhonua O Honaunau National Historical Park
808-328-2288, 808-328-2326
www.nps.gov/puho
Off HI 11 between mile markers 103 and 104; at the Honaunau Post Office, turn *makai*, or toward the ocean, onto HI 160. Go 3.5 miles, then turn left at the low, lava-rock sign at the park entrance.
Open: The park is open daily 7 AM–8 PM; the visitor center is open 8–5
Fee: $5 per vehicle per day

A structure at Puʻuhonua O Hōnaunau reveals ancient Hawaiian building techniques.

Facilities: Information center, restrooms, drinking water, sand-tire wheelchairs (they require the assistance of another person to push and guide the chair), gift shop, grills, and picnic tables (no umbrellas allowed). Fishing is permitted.

Allow yourself plenty of time to experience Pu'uhonua O Honaunau. It is one of the places you must visit on a trip to the Big Island, no matter how short your stay. Visit early in the morning or late in the day to avoid a very hot midday experience. The best time is the hour or so before sunset.

Please remember that this is a sacred place and treat it, along with other visitors, with respect. Take yourself and your cell phone to the visitor center or the parking lot. I've heard at full volume the details of a deal to buy several family-owned mortuaries and discussions of which dress to wear to an upcoming formal wedding. So much for imagining a terrified but determined ancient Hawaiian swimming to a place of refuge, one thoughtfully restored to enhance the spirit of peace and forgiveness.

Start at the visitor center to orient yourself and to find out if there are any cultural demonstrations scheduled for the park while you're there. Then embark on an excellent self-guided tour. In ancient Hawai'i, if you violated the *kapu* system by eating forbidden food or going onto land reserved for royalty, the penalty was usually death. If you could reach the nearest place of refuge and perform certain rituals before the priest, you would be spared. This park is the best example of a *pu'uhonua*, a sacred area, where murderers, defeated warriors, or anyone who had incurred the ruler's wrath could gain sanctuary and pardon.

A tall, thick lava wall built in the 1500s separates the areas that are royal grounds from the sanctuary. The royal grounds dotted with graceful coconut palms include fishponds, an area for games, and ancient trails that were laid down to take advantage of sunsets. Look

Ancient Hawaiians built impressive structures by hand using lava rocks.

Waters below the cliffs at South Point hold the promise of a good catch.

for the carved wooden images, *ki'i*. They set off the reconstructed thatched Hale o Keawe, which houses the bones of chiefs, remains believed to add to the area's natural power.

Try to budget time for a fairly easy 2-mile loop hike that most people skip. You'll need sturdy shoes for the route past smaller *heiau* and a course for *holua* sledding, a popular but dangerous sport for the *ali'i*. The track was made by building a rock foundation, then covering it with soil and grass. The long sleds were narrow and tapered, with crossbars to support the player in a lugelike position. It was fast, dangerous, and won by the person who traveled farthest, because the track is too narrow for racing. If you've seen sleds elsewhere—there are some at the Bishop Museum in Honolulu and Hulihe'e Palace in Kailua-Kona—it's interesting. If you're just looking for a way to burn kid energy, however, there's a snorkeling and swimming beach adjacent to the historical park.

Ka'u District

Ka Lae (South Point)

Off HI 11, turn *makai*, or toward the ocean, near mile marker 70 onto South Point Rd. Continue 12 miles, bear left at the fork, and keep going until you reach land's end.
Fee: Free
Facilities: None

Rugged, windswept, beautiful, yet desolate in the extreme even on a sunny day, this is where the first Polynesians are believed to have landed around A.D. 300. Artifacts found in the area suggest the area wasn't settled until later, nearer A.D. 750.

Hawai'i Volcanoes National Park

808-985-6000
www.nps.gov/havo
Off HI 11, 30 miles or 45 minutes southwest of Hilo; two to three hours or 96 miles southeast of Kailua-Kona
Fee: $5 per person on foot, bicycle, or motorcyle, or $10 per vehicle; pass valid for seven days
Open: The **park** is open 24 hours a day every day. The **Kīlauea Visitor Center**, just inside the park entrance, is open daily 7:45 AM–5 PM. The **Jaggar Museum** is open daily 8:30–5. The **Volcano Art Center** is open daily 9–5.

Facilities: Information center, restrooms throughout the park, food concessions in Volcano House hotel, art gallery, gift shop, accessible trails, roads. There are wheelchairs available on a first-come, first-served basis at the Kīlauea Visitor Center, Jaggar Museum, and at the ranger station at the end of Chain of Craters Rd.
Caution: Have a full as possible tank of fuel going into the park. It's big, 377 square miles. People with respiratory or heart problems and pregnant women should ask the park ranger at the entry gate if they should avoid some areas that day. It can get chilly here—it's 4,000

There are two kinds of lava: The first is pāhoehoe, which looks smooth or swirled. It comes from a fast flow, and is pronounced pa-HOY-hoy. The other kind, a'a, pronounced AH-ah, comes from a slow flow. It is crumpled, bumpy, and looks like a road crew has just finished drilling for the day.

The Crater Rim Road travels around the caldera that contains the crater Halema'uma'u.

feet above sea level—so bring a jacket. The park includes active volcanoes, which means areas can close without warning for eruptions, sulfur dioxide levels elevated to being dangerous for everyone, and earthquakes. For updates, check local media, ask at your accommodations, or best of all, call the park or go to www.nps.gov/havo/closed_areas.htm.

This is the place every Big Island visitor must visit even if it is the only place they experience. A UNESCO World Heritage Site, it is where you may be able to see and can almost always smell the Earth's creation process. If you only have a few hours, you can get a sense of the place. If you want to spend several days exploring the park, there are more than 150 miles of well-marked trails for casual hiking and routes that will take you away from it all for as long as you want to stay.

The big deal is **seeing lava**, but because you're dealing with Madame Pele, the goddess of volcanoes and her moods, it's not always possible to see lava without taking a private aerial tour (see chapter 7, Recreation). When Kīlauea oozes or spews lava, the park controls access for safety depending on the location. The danger is walking on hardened but hollow lava, not being consumed by its fiery forward onslaught. The usual viewing site has been the Pu'u O'o Vent, but there are no guarantees. Kīlauea has been active since January 3, 1983, and has consumed homes, churches, and more than 15,000 acres in its path while expanding the Big Island by over 500 acres as the lava has flowed into the sea.

Lush ferns line many of the roads in Hawai'i Volcanoes National Park.

PLANNING

The best way to prepare is to spend time on the park's Web site before leaving home. That way you won't be sitting on a beach the day there's a special event. The programs and the rangers who conduct them are top-notch.

While you can visit the park in one whirlwind day, it is more enjoyable to do it from a base in the village of Volcano, Hilo, or anywhere along that route. There are campgrounds in the park and a hotel (see chapter 3, Lodging, and chapter 6, Restaurants, for options).

If you have only a few hours in the park, hit the Crater Rim Drive, an 11-mile route that circles Kīlauea's summit. You'll pass through rain forests and desert and cross the caldera floor. There are lots of well-posted scenic stops and quick strolls to see steam vents; rift zones; the **Halema'uma'u Crater**, home to Pele; the **Devastation Trail**; the **Pu'u Pua'i Overlook**; the **Thurston Lava**

Please Don't . . .

Pick flowers or take samples of any other flora.

Feed the *nene*, the wild geese you'll see in the park.

Pile stones in an approximation of a sacred Hawaiian cairn, or *ahu*.

Leave offerings at the edge of the Kīlauea Caldera or toss them over the edge.

Cross into areas closed by park rangers for public safety.

Take stones home. It's illegal to remove even a pebble from a national park, so that should keep you in line if the belief about incurring bad luck and Pele's wrath by taking her lava doesn't.

Tubes; and the **Kīlauea Iki Overlook**. Each of the sights can be absorbed quickly but warrant longer stops. You can spend the better part of a day poking along the drive and its offshoots.

If you have more time, explore the park's coastal areas via the 40-mile round-trip on the **Chain of Craters Road**, which ends where lava closed it in 2003. There is no food, water, or fuel on this route.

Kīlauea Visitors Center
808-985-6000
Crater Rim Dr., just inside the park entrance

The first stop for any visit. The park offers a free brochure to visitors, and there is a more extensive guide for sale at the Kīlauea Visitors Center. There's a bookshop selling maps and special guides for hikers, birders, or amateur geologists, and there are special presentations that prepare you for what you'll see.

This is where to find information on the daily **ranger-led walks** across a variety of disciplines—vulcanology, botany, history—making it worth adjusting your plans to sally forth to see lava tubes or traverse a crater with them.

The schedule is posted each morning in the visitor center at 9. The first one, "How it All Began," with a talk on volcanology, usually gathers at 9:30 outside the Kīlauea Visitors Center and is repeated at 3:30. Other daily hikes—they're all easy—include the "Summit Walk" at 10:30 and 1:30. It is wheelchair accessible with less than half a mile of walking on a paved path and covers biology, geology, and the Hawaiian culture of Kīlauea.

There are special "After Dark in the Park" programs several Tuesday each month. Scheduled events are posted at the visitor center and online.

Volcano Art Center
808-967-7565, 808-967-8222
www.volcanoartcenter.org
Open: Daily 9–5
Next to visitor center

This historic building houses an art gallery and serves as a cultural center for the communities neighboring the part. See chapter 4, Culture, for more information on the center's gallery and activities.

Scientists at the Hawaiian Volcano Observatory monitor eruptions.

Volcano House
808-967-7321
Across from the visitor center off Crater Rim Dr.

There are terrific views of the Kīlauea and Halemaʻumaʻu craters from the dining room that caters to tour groups and the area outside it that extends past the snack bar to the hotel itself.

Steam Vents
As you drive along Crater Rim Dr., look for a marked turnoff. There may or may not be clouds of steam near the road, but carry on to the trail to the crater rim for a view that just doesn't quit, and bigger, better steam action.

Sulphur Banks
You'll find stinky volcanic gases wafting out of the ground just across the road from the steam vents. There's a wheelchair-accessible boardwalk and paved path that takes you through the banks so you can be enveloped in the stench of rotten eggs due to the carbon dioxide, sulfur dioxide, and hydrogen sulfide in the gas. The crystals are the result of sulfur gases. The reddish brown patches are clay formed when the sulfur gases form sulfuric acid, which breaks down the lava. If you have heart or respiratory problems, are pregnant, or have young children in tow, skip this.

Thomas Jaggar Museum

808-967-7643
Crater Rim Dr., about 3 miles west of the visitor center
Open: Daily 8:30–5
Fee: Free
Facilities: Restrooms, water, gift shop

Don't bypass these geologic displays showing the history of Kīlauea volcano. There's a working seismograph relating to the adjacent Hawaiian Volcano Observatory that lets you track all the burps and bubbles below Earth's surface. Unusual amounts of activity may presage a volcanic eruption. The hour-long film *Born of Fire, Born of the Sea* shows throughout the day, starting at 9. Some people walk in, watch for a bit, and drift out; others absorb it all. It's well done, but unless it's a cold, wet day, spend the time outside. The gift shop features a wealth of Pele and volcano material—books, posters, DVDs—and, of course, there are jaw-dropping views just outside.

Halemaʻumaʻu Overlook

A 10-minute walk from the Jaggar Museum

When you stare into Halemaʻumaʻu, you're looking down into home of Pele, the goddess of Hawaiian volcanoes. The crater, about 3,000 feet across, was a boiling lake of molten lava for most of the 19th century, a huge plus in building the nascent tourist trade. Visitors then used words like *indescribable*, and while it's a quieter scene now, the crater is twice the size it was in 1924. Such is the give-and-take of having a front-row seat for the volcano show. Scan the scene for a bit player: a large long-tailed white bird known locally as *Koaʻe*, or crater bird. It feeds at sea but nests in the crater wall.

The overlook is a sacred site for Hawaiians, so you may see offerings or people engaged in private rituals. Please treat the area with respect.

Keanakokoʻi Overlook

Off Crater Rim Dr.

On a clear day, this is a perfect spot to see Mauna Loa's 13,377-foot summit and Mauna Kea's 13,796-foot crown bejeweled with glittering astronomical observatories. The name means "cave of the adzes" because it was where Hawaiians came to find hard rocks to make tools.

Devastation Trail

Off Crater Rim Dr., about a mile past Keanakokoʻi Overlook

A half-mile-long wheelchair- and stroller-accessible trail through the cinders of Kīlauea Iki's 1959 eruption, which spat pulsating streams of lava as far as 1,900 feet into the air. The eruption, which scientists had correctly predicted, but at a different location, wiped out every living thing, as you can see along the trail, which is marked in parts by the shells of trees stripped bare. Notice little green signs that the forest is reclaiming its area.

Thurston Lava Tube

Off Crater Rim Dr.

The first thing you'll probably notice is that this stop is in a shady, cool area, bliss if you've taken a few walks in the hot sun. The entrance to the tube, discovered in 1913 by Lorrin

At Laupāhoehoe, the crashing waves can be mesmerizing as well as dramatic

Thurston, a local newspaper publisher, is in a fern forest filled with vociferous birds. The first part of the cavelike tube is illuminated, and the easiest way to see what it might be like to set off on a voyage to the center of the earth. If you've got a flashlight, you can go about half a mile along a subterranean route formed when an outer layer of lava cooled as hot stuff continued to run through the center.

Chain of Craters Road
Off Crater Rim Dr.

Turn off and keep going until the road ends. Turn around and drive back up the 4,000 feet you just descended. Dull and boring? No way. It got its name for a reason, so the scenery is primal, and the views are an ever-changing panorama of the ocean and clouds. As you proceed down to the sea, you'll better understand how lava flows through the area around mile marker 14 continuing past mile marker 15. There's a pull-off at the **Holei Pali Lookout**, which offers a sweeping view of old lava flows.

Be on the lookout for the Pu'u Loa Petroglyph Trail between mile markers 15 and 16. It's a doable 20-minute walk to access a large field of petroglyphs that you can view from a boardwalk.

The end of the road is often where you can see the lava meet the sea, sending clouds of steam up from the ocean. It is most dramatic at night, but there's enough drama in the steam to justify the park entrance fee and the drive down to sea level.

Hāmākua Coast

Waipi'o Valley
Waipi'o Rd. off HI 10. Go to the end of the road to the lookout.

Access: You cannot get to the valley floor on your own. The drive is extremely dangerous and potentially ruinous for a rented vehicle. There are half-day and longer horseback or wagon tours available (see chapter 7, Recreation), and the **Waipi'o Valley Shuttle**, 808-775-7121, offers two-hour tours every day but Sunday from 9 to 4. You need to make a reservation and then pick up your tickets at the **Waipi'o Valley Artworks** (808-775-0958, 800-492-4746; 48-5416 Kukuihale Rd.) in Kukuihale, where the tour begins and ends about 2 miles from the lookout. Tickets are $50 for adults, $25 for children 3–11. It is also possible to hike down to the valley on the road the tour van uses, but then you must hike up the car-killer grade the same day, as there's no official campground below.

Often thought of today as the ultimate E-ticket in an eco-theme park because of the adventure that is getting down to the valley floor, Waipi'o Valley was a special, sacred place to ancient Hawaiians. Chiefs met here to make important decisions. Kings, no matter where else on the island they maintained residences, had one here as well.

Embraced by 2,000-foot-high cliffs, the valley, a mile wide and more than 5 miles deep, was once home to thousands of people, and it is in this ancient surfing place where the infant Kamehameha was hidden in around 1758 to save him from a king who had heard the prophecy that the child would someday rule.

Within 150 years, non-Hawaiians were moving into the valley, drawn by the fertility of its soil and the grandeur of its cascading waterfalls—Hi'ilawe, more than 1,200 feet high, is the most famous. By 1946, when the tsunami struck, there were churches, schools, a post office, and even a hotel. After waves washed away almost everything, virtually everyone left, and it wasn't until the '60s that repopulation began. There are now about 100 or so people living in the valley.

NATURAL WONDERS

North Kohala

Pololū Valley Lookout
End of Akoni Pule, mile marker 29, Kapaʻau

Less well known than Waipiʻo Valley, the Pololū Valley was once inhabited by Hawaiians who cultivated wet taro patches. It was the source of smooth stones for many of the sacred structures and homes of ancient Hawaiʻi. The view from the lookout is worth the drive. The trail into the valley was destabilized by the October 2006 earthquake, closed, then reopened. The trail is steep and very slippery if wet.

Kohala Mountain Lookout
Kohala Mountain Rd.

Running between Waimea and Hāwī, this is one of the most scenic drives on an island where scenic drives define the daily commute. The road climbs and curves, each turn opening a vista more photoworthy, even when misty, than the last, before the scenery changes to that of a tree-lined rural road with the ocean visible beyond. This is the "old" road, and the views encompass the ocean and the coast, as well as three of the five Big Island mountains (Mauna Kea, Mauna Loa, and Hualālai), which were once active volcanoes, like Kīlauea on the other side of the island. A million shades of green cover the hillsides as you get closer to Hāwī. The road winds through tall ironwoods, emerald-covered cinder cones, and the undulating landscape of ranch lands. Often the Waimea mists roll in from the heights, bringing brilliant rainbows with them. Be sure to look for some of the highly decorative ranch entrances. There is no one designated lookout area, but you can find some of the best spots by looking for places where the shoulder of the road is worn from people pulling over.

Kaʻu (South Point)

Mark Twain's Monkeypod Tree
HI 11, near mile marker 64, Waiʻohinu

Mark Twain spent four months in Hawaiʻi in 1866. His dispatches for a California newspaper, collected as *Mark Twain's Letters from Hawaii* by the University of Hawaiʻi Press, are widely available throughout the Big Island, where he spent several weeks. He visited Kailua-Kona and Kealakekua Bay. He climbed Kīlauea during an eruption. He planted a monkeypod tree, which blew down in 1957, but enough survived that it flourished, and there is still an imposing tree on the site.

Kula Kai Caverns
808-929-7539
www.kulakaicaverns.com
Off HI 11, between mile markers 78 and 79, Ocean View

Open: Daily. All tours are by reservation only.
Fee: Prices for adults range from $15 to $195; there's a discount for children

These caverns are part of the 20-mile Kanohina labyrinth of braided lava tubes formed by Mauna Loa. Ancient Hawaiians used this network for water collection and as shelter from the wind, rain, or sun on trips from the mountains to sea level.

The tours range from a 30–45 minute walk on a lighted trail to a half-day experience for which the physical requirements range from being able to climb stairs to being very fit. The deal is simple: You show up equipped with long pants and sturdy shoes, and they'll supply the hard hat, lights, and knee pads.

I'm not a cave person—the Thurston Lava Tube gives me the willies—but I'm mentioning these caverns because I've been told by braver souls that even the brief, lighted tour is worthwhile as it provides insight into volcanoes and precontact life.

Puna District

Fill the tank, check the tires, put some bottled water in a cooler, and head off for some jungle exploring.

Lava Tree State Monument

Off the Pāhoa-Pohoiki Rd.—CR 132—2.7 miles southeast of Pahoa
Open: Daily during daylight
Facilities: Public toilets
Caution: Dense clouds of hungry mosquitoes

Part of the attraction to this park is the route in, under a canopy of interwoven tree branches far above you that create otherworldly lacelike shadows on the road. Do pull over and look up. I'll admit to climbing on the roof of my rental and lying back to get the full effect.

The park itself has an easy loop trail past "trees" created of lava in 1790 when an eruption from Kīlauea swallowed the jungle. The lava hardened around the trees, some tall, some not, which burned. The ferns, vines, and foliage crept back, but recently, the invasive, nonnative coqui frogs upset the park's ecosystem.

The Red Road

CR 137 (between CR 130 and CR 132)

Originally paved with cinders from the 1960 Kapoho lava flow, only the shoulders of this narrow county blacktopped road are red. It skims the eastern shores of the Big Island, through the Puna. If you don't understand the district's attraction, you may after experiencing the elemental contrasts this route between Kalapana to Kapoho offers: lava fields and low-slung hala trees so thick it's like driving through a tunnel. The road heaves up and down, a symptom of volcanic activity in the far and recent past. You'll see turnoffs marked with KEEP OUT signs, but the vibe isn't hostile so much as private. In some places the road floods. In others, it's so close to the shore that you're expecting spray to hit the windshield. Look *makai,* or toward the sea, and you'll occasionally see a picnic table in a small pull-out. While the entire route is worthwhile, the stretch between mile markers 14 and 17 is transcendent because you're so near translucent blue-green waves crashing on rocky black lava.

If you want to experience the Big Island at its most primordially lush, and have a four-wheel drive with high clearance as well as the skills needed for the possibility of navigating deep mud or large puddles, drive the Red Rd. from Kalapana to Isaac Hale Beach Park. Then keep going straight, to Kapoho, through the intersection of CR 137 (which you're on, but may not have seen identified on signs) and CR 132. This takes you off pavement and onto the road past Honolulu Landing, along a hidden coastal area of dense, almost unnervingly still jungle punctuated by quick views of the ocean. The KEEP OUT signs mean business, although anybody you see is likely to wave and smile. The roadside vegetation is thick. Look for orchids and ferns growing out of tree trunks. The road goes through an area of ancient burial grounds marked by white and red *KAPU—NO TRESPASSING* signs. Paving resumes after about 10 miles. Take a left on Paradise Dr., and you've jacked back into the world of today. Go straight to CR 130. Take a right at the intersection, and you're quickly back to the Kea'au intersection with HI 11 marked by the shopping center. Pinch yourself. It's a quick transition.

Hilo and Around

Rainbow Falls
Off Wainuenue Ave. heading west of town, just past Kamana Dr. The route is well marked.

Try to get here in the morning when there's a better chance of seeing rainbows, if the sun and the mist align, as water falls into the Wailuku River gorge. There's a parking lot with a nearby viewing area, and if there's been a heavy rain, you'll hear the waters roar down in a one-two drop that ends in a large pool.

Pe'epe'e Falls and Boiling Pots
Off Waianuenue Ave., about 3 miles north of downtown or 1.5 miles past Rainbow Falls. When the road splits, go right and follow the signs.

Four streams tumble down a series of falls into circular pools, making for very turbulent water in this part of the Wailuku River, particularly after a heavy rain.

Hāmākua Coast

Hāmākua Coast Drive
HI 19, the Belt Road

This 45-mile full-day drive features one breathtaking vista after another as you cross deep gullies on high bridges and curve through pastureland, jungle, and old plantation towns. It goes from **Hilo to the Waipi'o Lookout**, and while the route may appear direct on a map, take the time to slip off onto side roads, particularly **Old Māmalahoa Highway**, which roughly parallels the main road between mile markers 43 and 52. Most of them are narrow two-lane paved roads, what the main routes circling the island used to be like. There are enough of them that you can do the drive in both directions, taking detours to the ocean (*makai*) or to the mountains (*mauka*). You'll notice a dark red, yellow, and white sign with the image of a traditional Hawaiian warrior at sites of interest.

To enjoy exploring, you'll need more than the map that comes with your rental vehicle. The University of Hawai'i Press *Map of Hawai'i: The Big Island* is good to have at all times, but for secondary side roads get copies of *The Ready Mapbook of East Hawaii* and *The Ready Mapbook of West Hawaii*. Both are published by Odyssey Press.

How spectacular is the drive? Consider this: there's a scenic drive off the scenic route, the well-marked **Onomea Scenic Drive,** which is actually a segment of Old Māmalahoa Highway. It lives up to its name with a photo-ready view at each turn. Indeed, *onomea* means "the best place" in Hawaiian. Once the site of a Hawaiian fishing village, it became one of the first harbors for sailing ships in the 18th century. Stop, pull over, and get out. You'll hear birds, waves, and wind. Let yourself be surrounded by the jungle smells of dampness, evidence of which you can see on rocks and on stone bridges textured with mosses in innumerable shades of green.

Akaka Falls
Akaka Falls State Park
On CR 220, off HI 19 between mile markers 13 and 14. The route is well marked.

Many of the Big Island's choice waterfalls require some effort and sturdy shoes. Not this one. From the parking lot, a loop trail guides you through dense vegetation including ginger, orchids, and a bamboo grove, past the Kahuna Falls to the Akaka Falls, which plummets more than 400 feet. If there's been a heavy rain, it is something to see. If not, there's a steady cascade that's lovely if you catch it before the tour buses arrive.

Saddle Road
Road conditions: 808-935-6268
Between HI 11 in Hilo and CR 190 Waimea. From Waimea, turn off CR 190 near mile marker 7. From Hilo, take Waianuenue Ave., which is CR 200 west from town.

Before you head out on this narrow 55-mile road, be certain you have a full tank of gas and you know what your personal auto insurance covers, particularly for towing, unless you have rented a vehicle from a company that allows you take their property on this drive. The road is being straightened and evened out, section by section, but where that's yet to happen, it's windy and hilly and roughly paved. The plus is that you go through a landscape that in many places is gorgeous in a spooky out-of-this-world way at elevations of 6,000–7,000 feet above sea level. It's nicest early in the morning when the clouds are still low.

The road runs between the two largest volcanoes on the island, Mauna Loa and Mauna Kea. It's called the Saddle Road because it rolls through the valley between these two peaks. (You get a good view of the "saddle" from the Kohala Mountain Road.) The road was built by the military, and you may share the road with convoys or hear exercises from the Pohakuloa Military Training Area. It's also a shortcut for island residents who want to trim time and miles off the trip between Hilo and Waimea and beyond.

If you start from the Waimea end, the first portion of the drive takes you through rolling ranchland dotted with gated communities of spreads where small herds of sheep are moved from holding to holding to keep down the grass.

The turnoff for **Mauna Kea State Park** is at mile marker 35. It's quiet place on weekdays, with a few picnic tables. It's a pleasant break, a place to stretch your legs and look for hawks.

The road to the **Mauna Kea observatories** is near mile marker 28 (see chapter 4, Culture, for more information). This is also the marker for the **Hakalau Forest Refuge** (see chapter 7, Recreation, for more information). From here to Hilo, the road is noticeably better, a source of grumbling by residents of the other side of the island. The wider, smoother surface means faster traffic, so let people pass. The terrain changes, too. The scrubby growth of ferns and 'ōhi'a becomes markedly larger and greener as you approach Hilo.

Stone cookies from the Mt. View Bakery are a local favorite.

6

RESTAURANTS AND FOOD PURVEYORS

Breakin' da Mouth

Kau kau, pronounced "cow cow," means "food" or "meal" in Hawaiian pidgin. Or it could be "to eat." Whichever, whatever, you'll be doing lots of it, tasting new things or experiencing familiar ingredients used in ways that may be new to you. And then there's Spam. Hold that thought . . . of a blue can with yellow lettering.

The Big Island offers hundreds of restaurants serving everything from American diner favorites to exquisite Hawaiian regional dishes melding pan-Pacific influences with local flavors and techniques. In addition, there's a small army of food purveyors from coffee shacks to roadside stands offering prepared dishes, baked goods, fruit drinks, and sweets. Any diner, from picky to omnivorously adventuresome, will find their hunger pangs quelled. But pay attention to the timing of those tummy rumbles. Many restaurants close by 9 PM, so call ahead if you're looking for a late bite. And always call ahead on a holiday or if you're making a special trip to dine at a certain place. Hours and closing days change, particularly in family-owned businesses.

We searched for a variety of places and price ranges. We looked for truly local dining experiences, which meant we avoided fast-food outlets and chains even though McDonald's has localized its menu with Portuguese sausage, Spam, and green tea. It is the food that counts, so some of the places we like best aren't the fanciest. Other places we enjoyed are as fancy as anything you'd find in New York or Chicago. Thus, there's a range of dining experiences, from drive-through sandwich shops to the restaurants of celebrity chefs.

Food in Hawai'i provides a taste of immigration patterns. Polynesians, Americans, and groups including Korean, Japanese, Chinese, Filipino, Vietnamese, Thai, Puerto Rican, and a host of others contribute to the cuisine. For some of the best local tastes, you've got to be a salivatin' sleuth, checking out bulletin boards at grocery stores or looking for community bulletin boards to find fund-raisers selling *huli-huli* chicken or *kālua* pig. You'll need to slow down to read handwritten signs, because there, just ahead over by the cane road junction, might be pork *lau-lau,* straight from somebody's home and sold in a roadside stand. Or maybe you just need to see what looks like a fairground food truck with new eyes. In Hilo, I've noticed a bright blue shipping container with the words *Hawaiian Food* on a banner. It appears in different locations, and it's worth braking, then backing up or going around the block, to eat there. I can't be more helpful than to say it's all good.

Elsewhere, check out the parking lots when you're looking for a meal: In Waimea, Church Row lot; in Honoka'a, the gas station; in Kealakekua, it's the Bankoh, or Bank of Hawai'i; in Hilo, look along the bay front, near the canoe launch.

Another local treat is the plate lunch, a sturdy relation of the blue plate special. It includes at least two scoops of rice, a scoop of macaroni or potato salad or one of each, and at least one protein item. Vegetables, well, maybe yes, maybe no. It could be simple—today's catch (local), a hamburger patty (American), or *char siu* pork (Chinese) or *teri* beef (Japanese) or *kal bi* short ribs (Korean)—or a full Hawaiian special including ahi *poke*, lomi salmon, *kālua* pork, two scoops of rice, macaroni salad, potato salad, and *haupia,* a coconut pudding–like sweet. Local reviews of plate lunches, which include those served at food trucks, have been known to include the total weight.

Just as local, there is *loco moco,* or white rice topped with a hamburger, an egg sunny-side up, and brown gravy. That's the basic heart stopper, but the variations and add-ons are a cardiologist's nightmare: bacon, ham, Portuguese sausage, and teriyaki options in beef, chicken, pork, fish, shrimp, turkey, mahimahi, or ahi, and, of course, Spam.

There's little dispute that *loco moco* originated in Hilo in the 1940s, or at least is the creation of Hilo residents, but there is some debate as to the specifics. Some blame the Inouye family, who owned the Lincoln Grill, which closed in the '60s. They used rice as the starch—you're surprised?—and topped it with hamburger and gravy. The egg, which may have been an afterthought, gilded the lily. Many reports suggest the dish was created as a fast alternative to the traditional Japanese bento. Others believe *loco moco* originated at Café 100, a local restaurant founded by Richard and Evelyn Miyashiro, now in its third location. They named their restaurant in honor of his military unit, the famed 100th Infantry Army Battalion, the most decorated American unit in World War II. Which brings us to the angle that the battalion's cooks, many from Hilo, invented the dish to provide a taste of home using available Army ingredients, and the dish entered the local dining scene as men returned home. As for the name, *loco* is either Spanish for "crazy" or pidgin for "local," and the *moco* means—well, it rhymes.

As you can see, and as you will taste, everyday Big Island food marries the tastes and sensibilities of many cuisines. By the late 1980s, this carried over into some of the island's finest restaurants. Alan Wong, who first attracted attention as chef of the Big Island's Mauna Lani Bay Hotel, has famously said: "While I was growing up in Hawai'i, my grandfather cooked Chinese and my mother cooked Japanese, but she mingled in flavors of Filipino, Chinese, Japanese, and Hawaiian dishes." Wong was among a group of chefs, including Sam Choy, Mark Ellman, Amy Ferguson Ota, Beverly Gannon, Jean-Marie Josselin, Peter Merriman, Gary Strehl, and Roy Yamaguchi, who pioneered what is now known as Hawaiian Regional Cuisine.

The ingredients are locally sourced, so you'll savor Puna goat cheese, Keāhole lobsters, bananas from Keau, and salads featuring greens grown on farms owned by the restaurants. There's a microbrewery in Hilo, and one in Kailua-Kona. Thus wheat ale comes infused with *liliko'i*; don't miss it if it's available. Familiar items, such as simply grilled fresh-caught fish, appear with *liliko'i* butter, or ribs come with a sauce redolent of the sweet-sour-salt interplay of crack seed, a preserved fruit snack with Chinese origins. Pot stickers arrive with chicken satay stuffing. Ginger and soy, rather than salt and pepper, punctuate this vocabulary. Lychee ice cream topped with sauce from locally grown chocolate and a cup of Kona coffee ends a meal. There are tablecloths, there's fine service, and yet, there's more than a hint of a family kitchen.

There are few family kitchens without a can of Spam. Here are the facts. Hormel created Spam in the late 1920s as a way to cope with the scraps and leavings of its canned-ham processing. The company called the new product Hormel Spiced Ham, a neither here nor there name. A concocted name, Spam, fit on the can more easily. And because it was canned, needing no refrigeration, Spam became part of U.S. military rations in World War II. It became a hit in Hawai'i, where canned foods had long had a place in unrefrigerated pantries.

Just how much Spam is consumed each year in Hawai'i? In 2004, 7 million tins was the accepted number. It appears instead of bacon at breakfasts; slices float in soups. Diced, it bolsters salads and casseroles. Honolulu author Ann Kondo Corum's 1987 *Hawai'i's Spam Cookbook* sold so well that she came out with a second volume, *Hawai'i's 2nd Spam Cookbook*, filled with new recipes from local Spam-cooking contests. Aside from seeing Spam as a breakfast menu item, you're most likely to encounter it in Spam *musubi*, a ubiquitous offering found almost everywhere groceries are sold. Think of it as Spam sushi, since it is a crisply cooked slice of the luncheon meat plopped atop a lump of sushi rice molded to the meat's dimension. A swath of wasabi between the two adds zip, and the whole thing is wrapped in seaweed, then sealed in plastic wrap. Time and again, I've had to persuade doubtful friends to try it. When they head home, guess who's packing Spam *musubi* for the flight?

And yes, you'll find Spam on the breakfast menu at some of the island's posh spots. Which brings me to how to parcel out your dining dollars. The Big Island has a well-deserved reputation for being expensive. However, if you follow our suggestions and nose about on your own, you'll eat well, even on a budget. Part of the trick is following local residents to their favorite haunts. Ask people such as your masseuse at a resort, or the local bookseller, where they like to go. Chances are you'll have a good meal and feel pleased with your sharp traveler's instincts.

Before you dig in to this banquet of listings, you might consider using the two restaurant indexes at the end of the book. One lists restaurants according to cuisine, the other by price. The restaurants listed are given a price code based on the average cost of a meal for one of an appetizer, entrée, dessert, tax, and tip. We did not include the cost of alcoholic beverages, with or without tropical umbrellas.

Dining Price Codes

Inexpensive	Up to $20
Moderate	$20–40
Expensive	$40–$85
Very Expensive	$85 or more

Credit Cards

AE: American Express
CB: Carte Blanche
D: Discover Card
DC: Diners Club
MC: MasterCard
V: Visa

Meals Served

B = breakfast, L= lunch, D = dinner, SB = Sat. brunch, SSB = Sun. brunch

FINE DINING

Kohala Coast Resorts

Some of the most luscious and inventive dishes on the planet are served in the Kohala resorts. Each has a sumptuously designed dining room with sophisticated, knowledgeable staff, an interesting wine list, and a menu created by well-known if not celebrity chefs. All that's asked of you is to arrive in casually elegant resort wear and enjoy. Each resort also has a less formal dining option that is slightly less expensive with a more relaxed dress code. Selecting the best among them is impossible, as is selecting a favorite. I've listed them by resort from south to north.

FOUR SEASONS AT HUALĀLAI

Beach Tree Bar and Grill
808-325-8000
www.fourseasons.com/hualalai
72-100 Ka'ūpūlehu Dr., Kailua-Kona, HI 96740
Price: Moderate–Very Expensive
Cuisine: American
Serving: L, D
Credit Cards: AE, D, DC, MC, V
Handicapped Access: Partial
Reservations: Suggested for Sat. dinner buffet

The perfect food in the perfect setting for the perfect price. The beach and poolside alfresco offerings include grilled fish sandwiches, imaginative salads, and pizzas. Even the simplest is beautifully presented. The Saturday night buffet, "Surf, Sand, and Stars," is an array that shames any surf 'n' turf preconceptions. Maybe it's the sushi. Or the soufflés. There is contemporary Hawaiian music nightly, with hula Wednesday through Saturday.

The Hualālai Grille by Alan Wong
808-325-8525
www.fourseasons.com/hualalai
72-100 Ka'ūpūlehu Dr., Kailua-Kona, HI 96740
Price: Moderate–Very Expensive
Cuisine: Hawaiian Regional
Serving: D
Credit Cards: AE, D, DC, MC, V
Handicapped Access: Partial

Reservations: Suggested for Sat. dinner buffet

Alan Wong, one of the chefs who originated Hawaiian Regional Cuisine, oversees a sophisticated open-air setting accented with koa and marble that overlooks the grounds and the golf course. The menu includes some of his signature dishes, such as ginger crusted onaga, which consists of local red snapper with miso vinaigrette, shiitake and enoki mushrooms, and corn, and a soup-and-sandwich combo that is a chilled red and yellow tomato soup served with a foie gras, *kālua* pig, and grilled cheese sandwich. Chocolate appears prominently among the desserts, and the coffee selections include some of Kona's finest estate-grown and roasted coffees. An added attraction is the exhibition kitchen that lets you watch the pros make it look easy.

Pahu i'a
808-325-8000
www.fourseasons.com/hualalai
72-100 Ka'ūpūlehu Dr., Kailua-Kona, HI 96740
Price: Expensive–Very Expensive
Cuisine: Hawaiian Regional
Serving: B, L
Credit Cards: AE, D, DC, MC, V
Handicapped Access: Partial
Reservations: Required for dinner

The aquarium, or the *pahu i'a*, is a nice touch, but the drop-dead ocean view takes your breath away. Request a table on the intimate Naupaka Terrace with Pacific views that subliminally suggest fish. Act on that with the seafood sampler, or opt for Big Island goat cheese panna cotta, Hāmākua mushrooms, and a macadamia nut pesto. Signature dishes, including lobster, Dungeness crab, and Kona kampachi, are harvested from the nearby Natural Energy Laboratory of Hawai'i Authority. Breakfast choices include *loco moco,* huevos rancheros, a Japanese "set" (the healthy option), or a buffet that is vast, elegant, and among the state's best.

Kona Village Hotel

Hale Samoa

www.konavillage.com
1 Kahuwai Bay Dr., Kohala Coast, HI 96740
Closed: Tues. and Wed.
Price: Expensive–Very Expensive
Cuisine: Hawaiian Regional
Serving: D
Credit Cards: AE, DC, MC, V
Handicapped Access: Partial
Reservations: Essential for nonguests so your name will be at the gate

Formal yet unpretentious and exquisite Hale Samoa is right on the beach and something of a secret because many people aren't aware they can dine here if they're not staying at Kona Village. The menu for the five-course prix-fixe dinner changes daily, and the preparations often carry hints of French, Italian, or Polynesian cuisines. Expect dishes such as abalone with a citrus beurre blanc. If you can, arrive for sunset over Kahuwai Bay, a romantic way to end the day.

Hilton Waikoloa Village

Donatoni's

Hilton Waikoloa Village
808-886-1234
www.donatonis.com/donatonis
www.hiltonwaikoloavillage.com
69-425 Waikoloa Beach Dr., Waikoloa, HI 96738
Price: Expensive
Cuisine: Italian
Serving: D
Credit Cards: AE, D, DC, MC, V
Handicapped Access: Partial
Reservations: Yes

Ahhhh, romance! Designed as an Italian villa, perhaps the only one extant with a lanai, Donatoni's is widely acclaimed as one of the state's most appealing and intimate restaurants. The food lives up to the setting, showcasing Hawaiian ingredients in northern Italian preparations. Dishes are beautifully presented. Servers aim to please. The cellar wins kudos from the *Wine Spectator* year after year. Go ahead, play footsie under the table, and don't rush off without dessert.

Imari

808-886-1234
www.hiltonwaikoloavillage.com
69-425 Waikoloa Beach Dr., Waikoloa, HI 96738
Price: Expensive
Cuisine: Japanese
Serving: D
Credit Cards: AE, D, DC, MC, V
Handicapped Access: Partial
Reservations: Yes

In a teahouse overlooking a pond, Imari sets the stage for a traditional Japanese dining experience, then the curtain opens on an updated version of the classics. Yes, there are teppenyaki, sukiyaki, and shabu-shabu dinners, but there's also sautéed fois gras and unagi on a rice cake drizzled with mirin balsamic glaze and truffle oil to give a delicious edge to the refined surroundings.

Kamuela Provision Company

808-886-1234
www.hiltonwaikoloavillage.com
69-425 Waikoloa Beach Dr., Waikoloa, HI 96738
Price: Expensive

Cuisine: American
Serving: D, SB
Credit Cards: AE, D, DC, MC, V
Handicapped Access: Partial
Reservations: Yes

Relaxed and refined, next door to the hotel's wine bar, this is a delightful way to end a day, sitting on the lanai under tiki torches. Because there are so many wines served by the glass, it's tempting to dine only from the appetizer menu just to keep playing with pairings: *kālua* clams with Chinese sausage, chicken sate over potato salad flavored with wasabi, shrimp poached in a lemongrass, and ginger broth. Yet the roasted chicken with guava barbeque sauce shouldn't be missed, and there's a fine assortment of surf 'n' turf options. For dessert, roast s'mores. Homemade graham crackers do make a difference. Be sure to ask for an ocean-view table outside and time your meal to include the sunset.

WAIKOLOA BEACH MARRIOTT RESORT

Hawai'i Calls

808-886-6789
www.marriott.com
69-275 Waikoloa Beach Dr., Waikoloa, HI 96738
Price: Moderate–Expensive
Cuisine: American
Serving: B, D
Credit Cards: AE, MC, V
Reservations: Recommended at dinner

The Hawai'i Calls offers an expansive breakfast buffet where the custom-made omelets are a popular choice. The continental breakfast is a generous, less expensive option. The dinner menu features American favorites touched by Pacific and Hawaiian flavors. Hawai'i Calls isn't in quite the same league as other resort restaurants on the Kohala Coast. However, much like the hotel it serves, it is a very good value and a dependable option, particularly the catch of the day at an outdoor

table, a meal made memorable by the staff's genuine aloha spirit.

KING'S SHOPS

Roy's Waikoloa Bar and Grill

808-886-4321
www.roysrestaurant.com
250 Waikoloa Beach Dr. Waikoloa, HI 96738
Price: Expensive–Very Expensive
Cuisine: Pacific Rim
Serving: D
Credit Cards: AE, D, DC, MC, V
Handicapped Access: Partial
Reservations: Yes

For terrific food in a lively setting, Roy's is tough to beat, even if it is in what is essentially a strip mall overlooking a lake and a golf course. It may not be the place to take your sweetie to gaze deeply into those beloved eyes. This crowded place bustles, and all that action makes noise, lots of it. As is true of Roy Yamaguchi's other outposts, there are always some of his signature dishes on a menu that changes with the season. If you want to understand why *Gourmet* described Yamaguchi as "the father of modern East-West cooking," order the seafood tasting platter, which includes his hibachi-grilled salmon, blackened ahi, and misoyaki butterfish. There's always other fish on the daily menu, and Szechuan baby back ribs, another classic, will please carnivores.

Merriman's Market Café

808-886-1700
250 Waikoloa Beach Dr. Waikoloa, HI 96738
Price: Moderate–Expensive
Cuisine: Mediterranean
Serving: L, D
Credit Cards: AE, MC, V
Handicapped Access: Partial
Reservations: Suggested at dinner

This is Peter Merriman's break from Hawaiian Regional Cuisine. A casual place with indoor and outdoor dining, it is an affordable alternative to his Waimea base, and as such has become popular with local residents as well as visitors. It can get crowded, but if there is a wait, it is worth it. There's sausage made in-house, an array of pastas and delectable salads at both meals, with sandwiches at lunch and pizza and light entrées such as lamb kebabs or grilled fish at dinner. The wine list is extensive for a bistrolike restaurant, and the children's menu includes a very popular variation on spaghetti and meatballs.

THE FAIRMONT ORCHID RESORT

Brown's Beach Houses

808-887-7368
www.fairmont.com
1 North Kaniku Dr., Kohala Coast, HI 96743
Price: Moderate–Very Expensive
Cuisine: Hawaiian Regional
Serving: L, D
Credit Cards: AE, DC, MC, V
Handicapped Access: Partial
Reservations:

Go early to get a table near the path by the water as the sun goes down and watch the torches being lighted among the palm trees. The Hawaiian dreams-come-true setting doesn't change, but the splurge-worthy food seems to get better year after year, or so repeat diners tell me, friends who get dreamy-eyed talking about miso-marinated fish and crisp wontons. I can't disagree with the superlatives they use. Even the local musicians who entertain nightly are among the island's best. If you're budgeteering, go for lunch and try the lobster fried rice; it will ruin you for fried rice anywhere else ever again.

The Grill

808-885-2000
www.fairmont.com
1 North Kaniku Dr., Kohala Coast, HI 96743
Price: Expensive–Very Expensive
Cuisine: Hawaiian Regional
Serving: D
Credit Cards: AE, DC, MC, V
Handicapped Access: Partial
Reservations: Yes

Unless you prefer the terrace, the Grill exudes a clubby yet not stiffly formal atmosphere thanks to the abundance of koa in the decor. This is a good opportunity to discover what Hawaiian Regional Cuisine, so often stereotyped as fish-oriented, means for meat, specifically a rack of lamb. If you must have seafood, you can add a grilled half Keāhole lobster to your order. The wine list is extensive, as is the dessert menu.

MAUNA LANI RESORT

Canoe House

808-885-6622
www.maunalani.com
68-1400 Mauna Lani Dr., Kohala Coast, HI 96743
Price: Expensive–Very Expensive
Cuisine: Hawaiian Regional
Serving: D
Credit Cards: AE, D, DC, MC, V
Handicapped Access: Partial
Reservations: Yes

At one point the Canoe House, with its koa canoe suspended from the ceiling and soulful sunset views, was *the* restaurant on the Kohala Coast. Then chef Alan Wong, one of the originators of Hawaiian Regional Cuisine, left in 1995, and the word was that the food, while good, wasn't as blazingly amazing as it had been. That said, if you weren't aware of the past, you'd find much to enjoy about the present. There's been enough of a comeback that it won the 'Ilima Award in 2005 as best Big Island restaurant largely on the strength of its seafood dishes. So live for today. Arrange to have sunset cocktails on the terrace. Order fish, maybe in a risotto, and a great bottle from the extensive wine list. Enjoy your meal.

Glossary of Grinds (*grindz*, pidgen for "food" or "to eat")

Adobo (a-dough-bo; Filipino)—It's a dish! No, it's a cooking technique! What do you care? It's good. Expect meat that has been marinated, then stewed in a mixture of garlic and vinegar.

'Ahi (AH-hee; Hawaiian) and **Aki** (AH-kee; Hawaiian)—These are the two types of tuna most often found in sashimi. Rich, fatty, flavorful fish that works well in many preparations.

Bento (ben-toh; Japanese)—In Japan, this was traditionally a movable meal served in a lacquer box. Today, in Japan and Hawai'i, it usually means a prepackaged takeout meal.

Char siu (char-shyoo; Chinese)—Barbecued pork.

Chili pepper water—Made with scalding Hawaiian chilis, water, and vinegar, it is a condiment you'll find in many restaurants. You may hear this called *wai nīoi* (vai nee yoi).

Crack seed—Dried, salted fruit such as lemon, ginger, or tamarind seeds or seafood that is the local version of a Chinese snack. It takes a bit of getting used to, but once you do, it becomes an essential Hawaiian taste.

Haupia (how-pee-ah; Hawaiian)—A firm pudding of coconut cream.

Izakaya (ee-zah-kah-yah; Japanese)—Beer nibbles.

Kalbi (kahl-bee; Korean)—Korean barbecued short ribs, made with soy sauce, sesame oil, garlic, and other flavorings.

Kālua (kah-loo-ah; Hawaiian)—A traditional preparation. Food is wrapped in leaves and steamed over hot rocks in an earthen pit.

Kalo (KAH-low; Hawaiian)—Taro, the base for poi, which is taro steamed, then mashed with a little water to achieve the proper texture. The leaves can be boiled and eaten, and the tuber can be sliced thin and prepared as a chip.

Kiawe (ke-ah-veh; Hawaiian)—Wood of the *algaroba* tree that is often used for grilling.

Ko cho jang (koh choh jahng; Korean)—Red chili paste.

Lau-lau (lauw-lauw; Hawaiian)—Foods wrapped in leaves and steamed or baked. Usually you find pork or fish wrapped in taro leaves, but other combinations are often available.

Li hing mui (lee hing moo-ee; Chinese)—A mixture of Chinese five-spice, sugar, and salt. Once used to preserve fruit, it's now used widely in cooking.

Liliko'i (LEE-LEE-koh-ee; Hawaiian)—Passion fruit.

Lomi salmon (loh-me salmon; Hawaiian)—Boneless salt salmon that is pounded into thin strips to tenderize it. It is often served in a salad or as a relish with onions, tomatoes, green onions, and Hawaiian salt. Yes, *lomi* means massage.

Lū'au (loo-ow; Hawaiian)—A feast or taro leaves.

Mahimahi (mah-hee-mah-hee; Hawaiian)—Dolphin fish, which is not a porpoise or the mammalian dolphins people swim with. It has a light, moist flesh that adapts well to many preparations.

Malasada (mah-lah-sah-dah; Portuguese)—A doughnut without a hole, deep-fried and rolled in sugar.

Manapua (mah-nah-poo-ah; Hawaiian)—Chinese-style steamed buns often containing barbecued pork. The name, according to some, is derived from the Hawaiian words *mea 'ono pua'a*, meaning "delicious pork thing," which sums it up nicely.

Man doo (mahn doo; Korean)—Pasta dumplings, generally filled with cabbage and meat.

Mochi (moh-chee; Japanese)—A steamed cake made with glutinous rice flour. It is often filled with sweet red beans in paste form. The cake may be flavored.

Moi (moy; Hawaiian)—Pacific threadfin, a delicately flavored, light-fleshed fish. Originally cultivated in ancient fishponds and reserved for royalty, it is now farmed and available to all.

Musubi (moo-sue-bee; Japanese)—A slice of fried Spam atop sushi rice usually shaped to fit the meat's dimensions, then wrapped with a strip of toasted seaweed. In Japan, it would be a ball of shaped, perhaps flavored, rice.

Namul (nah-mool; Korean)—Seasoned vegetable dishes.

Nishime (nee-shee-meh; Japanese)—A vegetable stew.

ʻŌhelo berries (O-hello; Hawaiian)—Considered sacred to Pele, the volcano goddess, these are related to cranberries, grow in the higher altitudes of Volcano National Park, and make delicious jams and pies.

Onaga (oh-nah-gah; Japanese)—Ruby snapper; moist, mild-flavored.

Ono (oh-no; Hawaiian)—Wahoo fish; firm-fleshed.

ʻŌpakapaka (oh-pah-kah-pah-kah; Hawaiian)—Pink or crimson snapper.

Pāo doce (pown dosh; Portuguese)—A rich, sweet bread. It makes terrific French toast and often comes flavored with guava or taro.

Pasteles (pah-TELL-ay; Puerto Rican)—A tamale-like dish of mashed green banana and spiced pork. Look for it at roadside stands.

Phō (fuh; Vietnamese)—Noodle soup of clear beef broth with transparent slices of raw meat or meatballs. It is served with fresh bean sprouts, basil, and sauces that you add in to suit.

Pipikaula (pee-pee-kow-lah; Hawaiian)—Salted beef that is sun dried. It is often broiled and sliced thin.

Pohole (po-ho-le; Hawaiian)—Shoots of a fern that grows in the Waipiʻo Valley, they evoke asparagus in taste and are often served in a simple salad.

Poke (poh-kay; Hawaiian)—An appetizer or a snack that's usually bite-size pieces of seasoned raw, fresh fish mixed with seaweed. *Poke* means cubed or chopped.

Portuguese sausage (Portuguese)—A garlicky pork sausage similar to pepperoni or chorizo.

Puaʻa (poo-ah-ah; Hawaiian)—Pig or pork.

Pul goki (pull go-kee; Korean)—Korean-style barbecued beef, marinated in soy sauce and sesame oil. You sometimes see it on a menu spelled *bul go gi*.

Pūpū (poo-poo; Hawaiian)—Appetizers, snacks. Heavy *pūpūs* allow you to make a meal of finger food.

Saimin (sigh-min; Japanese)—The local version of Japanese ramen or Chinese lo mein is made with Japanese fish stock and wheat noodles. It's 24/7 comfort food often topped with cooked eggs, green onions, barbecued pork, or Spam.

Shave ice—Not quite snow in a paper cone. The syrup flavors are different than the lemon, lime, and cherry available on the mainland, and the mound of shaved ice, which is grittier than the ice on a snow cone, often hides a serving of ice cream or adzuki beans.

Tsukemono (tsoo-keh-moh-no; Japanese)—Pickled vegetables usually served as side dishes to eat alone or as garnish.

Udon (oo-doan; Japanese)—A white, thick noodle often served in soup or stir fried. You'll also see udon offered cold with dipping sauce.

MAUNA KEA RESORT AREA

Batik
Mauna Kea Beach Hotel
808-882-7222
www.maunakeabeachhotel.com
62-100 Mauna Kea Beach Dr., Kamuela, HI
96743

Like the hotel, Batik has been closed for
renovations since the 2006 earthquake.
There is every reason to believe it will
reopen with food as good as, if not better
than, before.

HAPUNA BEACH PRINCE HOTEL

Coast Grille & Oyster Bar
808-880-1111
www.hapunabeachhotel.com
62-100 Kauna'oa Dr., Kohala Coast, HI
96743
Price: Expensive
Cuisine: Seafood
Serving: D
Credit Cards: AE, D, MC, V
Handicapped Access: Partial
Reservations: Yes

The seafood selection here ranges far beyond Hawaiian waters, but the *poke* reminds
you where you are, as if you could forget.
After all, the split-level, open-air dining
room has views so encompassing you're
almost forced to stare. If you like oysters,
you're in for an excellent experience—the
variety is extensive. The tempura soft-
shelled crab is a winning appetizer. For
those eager for an alternative to fish, the
lamb chops are grilled perfectly.

Hakone Steakhouse Sushi Bar
808-880-1111
www.hapunabeachhotel.com
62-100 Kauna'oa Dr., Kohala Coast, HI
96743
Price: Expensive
Cuisine: Steak, sushi
Serving: D

Credit Cards: AE, D, MC, V
Handicapped Access: Partial
Reservations:

The treat here is the Japanese buffet on Fri.
and Sat. night. If you can, plan for it even
though it may not be as traditional as the
offerings on other evenings. However,
be sure to stray from the buffet and order
the vegetable tempura if it is available à la
carte, and do ask for assistance in selecting
sake. The selection is extensive, and the
differences are not as subtle as you might
expect.

RESTAURANTS

Beyond the Gold Coast

KAILUA-KONA

Aki's Café
808-329-0090
75-5699 Ali'i Dr., Kailua-Kona, HI 96740
Closed: Major holidays
Price: Inexpensive
Cuisine: American and Japanese
Serving: B, L, D
Credit Cards: AE, MC, V
Handicapped Access: Partial
Reservations: No

Although Aki's is open all day, breakfast is
the crowd-pleaser. Get here at 8 when the
doors open, or even a bit before. The breakfast menu is extensive. The Japanese dishes
are popular at lunch and dinner. I like the
ramen. Remember: It's OK to slurp.

Ba-Le
Kona Coast Shopping Center
808-327-1212
74-5588 Palani Rd., Kailua-Kona, HI 96740
Closed: Christmas, New Year's Day
Price: Inexpensive
Cuisine: Vietnamese
Serving: L, D
Credit Cards: MC, V

Handicapped Access: Partial
Reservations: No

This is the only Big Island outpost of a small Hawaiian chain that made its reputation with Vietnamese sandwiches. All the food's good, but the Vietnamese sandwiches are exceptional and make a filling, but not heavy, meal.

Big Island Grill

808-326-1153
75-5702 Kuakini Hwy., Kailua-Kona, HI 96740
Closed: Sun.
Price: Moderate–Expensive
Cuisine: American and Hawaiian
Serving: B, L, D
Credit Cards: MC, V
Handicapped Access: Partial
Reservations: Not taken

The line can be long when you're hungry, the service can sometimes be slow, but the huge portions of local comfort foods suggest the slogan on the menus, "Well Worth the Wait," is no lie. "Biggie's" is a local family institution filled with loyal fans who know a deal when they taste it. The chicken katsu is popular, and this is a good place to try a side of Spam with your breakfast favorites.

Fujimamas

808-327-2125
75-5719 Ali'i Dr., Kailua-Kona, HI 96740
Price: Moderate–Expensive
Cuisine: East-West fusion
Serving: L, D, SSB
Credit Cards: MC, V
Handicapped Access: Partial
Reservations: Dinner

I came to Fujimamas by way of the original in Tokyo, which is excellent. Nothing's been lost in translation. It won the 2007 Hale Aina Award for best new Big Island restaurant. The bar serves sakes, shochus, and inventive cocktails suited to a palate adult enough to drink them. Standout dishes include the crispy scallion and sesame noodle cake, the wok-tossed (local) lamb, Parker Ranch angus steak with miso mashed potatoes, corn-crusted *opakapaka,* and the Chinese noodles in a truffle-oil stir fry. The decor's fun, but sit outside because you can. The service is relaxed in an efficient way and friendly.

Huggo's

808-329-1493
www.huggos.com
75-5828 Kahakai Rd., off Ali'i Dr., Kailua Kona, III 96740
Price: Inexpensive–Expensive
Cuisine: Pacific Rim seafood
Serving: B, L (weekdays), D (nightly)
Credit Cards: AE, D, DC, MC, V
Handicapped Access: Partial
Reservations: Suggested

Huggo's windows open over the rocks at the edge of the Pacific. Sunsets are something—the thatched-roof outpost next door, Huggo's on the Rocks, is a hot spot for tropical drinks and light meals. Once night falls, you can often see manta rays seeking out the bright lights of town. What started in 1969 as a dependable place for fresh fish and steak has morphed into a serious kitchen—don't let the postcard setting dissuade you—serving dishes featuring local ingredients. Seafood is the star. Try the Kailua Bay Cioppino as either an appetizer or an entrée. The mahimahi and ono give it an island twist. The chocolate and ice cream desserts can be overwhelming; a slightly lighter option is the ginger crème brûlée. Don't miss the transformation of a bar into a morning destination for espresso drinks and breakfast. Java on the Rocks opens at 6:30 AM, and wave contemplation with caffeine is a must.

Jackie Ray's Ohana Grill
In the Pottery Terrace Building
808-327-0209
www.jackierays.com
75-5995 Kaukini Hwy., Kailua-Kona, HI
96740
Price: Moderate–Expensive
Cuisine: Eclectic
Serving: L, D
Credit Cards: MC, V
Handicapped Access: Partial
Reservations: For dinner

What to say about Jackie Ray's? You've got to
love a place where the menu for fancy cocktails is "Da Fou Fou Drinks." It's packed with
local families, kids happily tucking into teri
chicken, pizza, or pork chops from the *keiki*
menu. Adults face a bewildering array of
choices, beef Stroganoff to grilled fish tacos
or seared 'ahi *poke* (and that's just at lunch).
At dinner, the *pūpūs,* or appetizers, are
fit for sharing, and the short ribs with
ko-chu-jang chili sauce could be an entrée
if you're not hungry. Try the curry-crusted
'ahi. There's a takeout menu and entertainment with dancing on the weekends.

Jameson's by the Sea
At Magic Sands Beach
808-329-3195
77-6452 Ali'i Dr., Kailua-Kona, HI 96740
Price: Moderate–Expensive
Cuisine: Continental
Serving: L (weekdays), D
Credit Cards: AE, DC, MC, V
Handicapped Access: Partial
Reservations: Yes

If you manage to reserve a table outside on
the lanai, it's the setting more than the food
that makes Jameson's a draw, particularly if
you're staying in the Keauhou neighborhood. It's a fine place for a sunset cocktail,
again if you're outside. If you dine, fresh
fish is the way to go.

Kenichi Pacific
808-322-6400
Keauhou Shopping Center, #D125
78-6831 Ali'i Dr., Kailua-Kona, HI 96740
Closed: Mon.
Price: Moderate–Expensive
Cuisine: Asian fusion and sushi
Serving: L, D
Credit Cards: AE, D, DC, MC, V
Handicapped Access: Yes
Reservations: Dinner

Terrific food, good service, and tasteful
decor hidden—or so it seems—in a shopping center. Go figure. You can make a meal
from appetizers like lobster spring rolls,
focus on the sushi bar, or splash out with a
full dinner. If you like duck, don't miss the
confit; the duck is cured with Chinese five-
spice. Leave room for the molten cake. It
really is as good as people say.

Killer Tacos
808-329-3335
74-5483 Kaiwi St. # 145, Kailua-Kona, HI
96740
Closed: Sun.
Price: Inexpensive
Cuisine: Surfer Mexican
Serving: L, D
Credit Cards: No
Handicapped Access: Partial
Reservations: No

Where there are surfers, there are tacos
(and burritos and beer). These, by the Old
Kona Airport State Park off HI 19, are worth
seeking out if you want a quick, casual
meal. Everything's very fresh and the *kālua*
pig crispy tacos will remind you that you're
not in Baja.

Kona Inn Restaurant
Kona Inn Shopping Village
808-329-4455
75-5744 Ali'i Dr., Kailua-Kona, HI 96740
Price: Inexpensive–Moderate
Cuisine: American and Hawaiian

Serving: L, D
Credit Cards: AE, MC, V
Handicapped Access: Partial
Reservations: No

Stop by for a sunset umbrella drink and appetizers, but consider dinner elsewhere unless something appeals from the daily specials. This is a touristy spot with lots of history and comfortable chairs. It's right on the waterfront, which may be why you should stick with the fish dishes, even though the menu, with children's selections, offers everything from Caesar salads to ribs.

Kona Natural Foods
Crossroads Shopping Center
808-329-2296
75-1027 Henry St., Kailua-Kona, III 96740
Price: Inexpensive
Cuisine: Healthy
Handicapped Access: Yes
Reservations: No

Open from 8:30 AM to 9 PM every day but Sunday, when it closes two hours earlier, this is where to grab a sprout-laden sandwich, an organic salad, or a fresh-fruit smoothie at the takeout counter of a well stocked supermarket. The produce section features greens grown in the South Kona area, and there are some prepared main entrées available.

O's Bistro
Crossroads Shopping Center
808-327-6555
www.osbistro.com
75-1027 Henry St., Kailua-Kona, HI 96740
Price: Moderate—Expensive
Cuisine: Hawaiian Regional
Serving: B, L, D, SSB
Credit Cards: AE, D, DC, MC, V
Handicapped Access: Partial
Reservations: Suggested

Chef Amy Ferguson-Ota melds Hawaiian Regional Cuisine with hints of the Southwest and Italy to create her healthy and flavor-filled dishes. The "Kona Style" no-tuna noodle casserole on the vegetarian menu and the version with wok-seared spiced 'ahi are nothing like my mother ever made—maybe it's the fresh shiitake cream instead of Campbell's cream of mushroom soup. Breakfast starts at 10 AM, and the offerings include breakfast tacos and French toast with pecans. Don't be put off by the location near Wal-Mart. Ferguson-Ota, a native Texan who trained at Le Cordon Bleu, appeared on the late Julia Child's PBS series *Lessons with Master Chefs*.

Ocean View Inn
808-329-9998
75-5683 Ali'i Dr., Kailua-Kona, HI 96740
Closed: Mon.
Price: Inexpensive—Moderate
Cuisine: Chinese-Hawaiian, American

The Natural Energy Laboratory of Hawai'i Authority was founded in 1974 at Keāhole Point as a research center for ocean thermal energy conversion. The surrounding technology park is now a center for aquaculture, and it's changing the way some of the Big Island's best restaurants find their fish.

The attraction at NELHA has always been the extraordinarily pure, bacteria-free water pumped up from 2,000 feet below sea level. Although it arrives at 43 degrees Fahrenheit, entrepreneurs can warm it to temperatures best suited for the cultivation of seafood such as lobster, flounder, crab, shrimp, oysters, and even abalone.

Aside from the availability of extraordinarily fresh fish to stimulate chefs' creativity, this high-tech take on the Big Island's ancient fishponds reduces the potential for overfishing and expands the notion of sustainability.

Serving: B, L, D
Credit Cards: No
Handicapped Access: Partial
Reservations: No

This is a local institution across from the Kailua Pier. It's a casual place with an extensive menu of Chinese selections. The Hawaiian food's a sure bet, and while you won't be the only island visitor in the place, you'll be well outnumbered by the regulars.

SOUTH OF KAILUA-KONA

Aloha Angel Café
808-322-3383
www.alohatheatre.com
79-7384 Māmalahoa Hwy., Kainaliu, HI 96750
Closed: No dinner Tues. and Wed.
Price: Inexpensive–Expensive
Cuisine: American eclectic
Serving: B, L, D
Credit Cards: MC, V
Handicapped Access: Partial
Reservations: Dinner

For years, I'd driven by the Aloha Angel Café. I'm over the angel thing, it's in a theater, and somehow, I decided it would be too granola-crunchy. How I discerned all this in passing what started as a silent-movie house is a mystery. What a fool I was. It's a treat. Breakfast and lunch are casual, served on a lanai with sweeping views that steps down a thickly planted hillside. The daytime offerings lean just a bit to the Southwest with burritos, but local dishes like *loco moco,* a tofu scramble, and grilled fresh fish hold the center. The baked goods—and this includes the French toast—are notable. Dinner is in a small dining room, an inviting space. The yellow curry is good no matter which option—chicken, seafood, or tofu—you choose. Save room for sweets.

The Coffee Shack
808-328-9555
www.coffeeshack.com
83-5799 Māmalahoa Hwy., Captain Cook, HI 96704
Price: Inexpensive
Cuisine: American
Serving: B, L
Credit Cards: MC, V
Handicapped Access: Partial
Reservations: No

Eat. Here. Now. You can see the trees where your coffee grew. There are fruit pies available at breakfast and serious sandwiches on an assortment of wonderful homemade breads at lunch. The salads and soups are exquisitely fresh. The pizzas are good, but if you have one of those for lunch, how can you justify Kona lime pie or *liliko'i* cheesecake with a cup of their estate-grown coffee for dessert? The panoramic view of Kealakekua Bay from the lanai is just icing on the (carrot) cake. And when the memories start to fade, call and sharpen them by ordering fresh roasted beans by the pound. You saw the trees. You're practically family.

Holuakoa Café
808-322-2233
76-5901 Māmalahoa Hwy., Hōlualoa, HI 96725
Closed: Mon.
Price: Inexpensive–Moderate
Serving: B, L, D (Wed. through Sat.)
Credit Cards: MC, V
Handicapped Access: Partial
Reservations: No

What was once a little café is growing into a full restaurant. They just started serving dinner in February 2008, so I've yet to try it, but if lunch is any indication, food will be fresh, simple, and homemade. The soups are usually winners, as are the specials.

Keei Café

808-322-9992
Māmalohoa Hwy. 11, Kalakekua, HI 96704
Closed: Sun., Mon.
Price: Moderate
Cuisine: Eclectic
Serving: L, D
Credit Cards: No
Handicapped Access: Partial
Reservations: A must for dinner

Less than 30 minutes from Kailua-Kona,
the Keei Café is one of those places that had
great food and went through some growing
pains as word got out. The ingredients are
local and fresh. The day's catch receives
inventive treatment and is reliably good.
Service can sometimes be shaky, but bear
with them. The lemongrass curry is popular, and the setting is attractive with South
Kona views. Try the mango cobbler, or
actually any of the sweets that strike you.
They're good.

Manago Hotel

808-323-2642
www.managohotel.com
82 6155 Māmalahoa Hwy., Captain Cook,
HI 96704
Closed: Mon.
Price: Inexpensive–Moderate
Cuisine: Japanese
Serving: B, L, D
Credit Cards: D, MC, V
Handicapped Access: Partial
Reservations: Recommended for dinner

This local institution is beloved for its
pork chops and other inexpensive, simple, and tasty meals. The atmosphere is
nostalgic, the service friendly, and the
crowd convivial. The pork chops are
served at lunch and dinner, so there's
really no excuse to miss them.

Nasturtium Café

808-322-5083
79-7491 Māmalahoa Hwy., Kealakekua,
HI 96750
Closed: Sun., Mon.
Price: Inexpensive–Moderate
Cuisine: Healthy eclectic
Serving: L
Credit Cards: MC, V
Handicapped Access: Yes
Reservations: No

Round and round the globe we go, and still
it's the Nasturtium menu. All of it is healthy,
tasty, and presented with thought. The
problem: decisions. Roasted red pepper
soup or gingered carrot? There's traditional
salad nicoise, or you can replace that tuna
with ostrich. A tempeh Reuben or a goat-
cheese wrap? A Mexican quesadilla or
Indonesian gado-gado? BYOB, toss a coin,
and be sure to save room for dessert. You
can also order "nourishment," as the menu
calls it, to go. What a clinical word for such
good food.

Anpan from the Standard Bakery come two to a bag.

Standard Bakery

808-322-3688

79-7394 Māmalahoa Hwy., Kealakekua, HI 96750

Closed: After noon

Price: Inexpensive

Cuisine: Bakery

Serving: B

Credit Cards: No

Handicapped Access: Partial

Reservations: No

If you're making an early-morning drive from Kailua-Kona to Puʻuhonua O Hōnaunau National Historical Park, you can grab a bento here to eat there, or a quick cup of 100 percent Kona coffee to have with a warm malasada or with their anpan, a Japanese-style pastry filled with sweet red bean paste. A little bit old fashioned, the anpan come two per bag. They're not very sweet, which is how they should be, but they're filling and they keep, so you can have your malasada and an anpan, too.

Teshima's

808-322-9140

79-7251 Māmalahoa Hwy., Kainaliu, HI 96750

Closed: Call on holidays

Price: Inexpensive

Cuisine: Japanese

Serving: B, L, D

Credit Cards: No

Handicapped Access: Partial

Reservations: No

This is as local as it gets, from the Japanese breakfasts of fish, rice, and miso to complete sukiyaki dinners. Opened in 1929 as a general store and transformed into a restaurant in the early 1940s, it's a reminder of the days before resorts, private jets, and big name chefs. The sashimi is fresh, the shrimp tempura light, the pickles crispy and fine. The No. 3 teishoku dinner gives you tasty bites of all these many nice things.

KAʻU (SOUTH POINT) AREA

Hana Hou Restaurant

808-929-9717

95-1148 Nāʻālehu Spur Rd., Nāʻālehu, HI 96772

Off HI 11 (turn south at the intersection with Ace Hardware and Island Market)

Closed: Call

Price: Inexpensive–Moderate

Cuisine: Local-style American

Serving: B, L, D

Credit Cards: No

Handicapped Access: Partial

Reservations: Recommended for dinner

On my last visit, I felt as if I'd entered the first line of a joke: Three cops and a priest are eating at two tables in a restaurant . . . Claiming to be the southernmost eatery in the United States, a distinction once trumpeted by nearby Shaka's, the folks at Hana Hou believe in making sure that you will not go away hungry. Maybe their goal is that you will never be hungry ever again. The portions are large, and there's an enthusiasm for whipped-cream toppings at breakfast, so ask if you don't want to be surprised. Some of the plate lunches are served by weight: 8 ounces or 1 pound. The fresh fish options are usually good—try "whatever takes the bait" panko style.

Pāhala Town Café

808-928-8200

96-3163 Pikake St., Pāhala, HI 96777

Corner of Kamani and Pikake Sts.

Off HI 11 at mile marker 52

Closed: Call

Price: Inexpensive

Cuisine: Local-style American

A very simple café with friendly staff, this is a good place to try dishes like saimin while checking the bulletin board for local events. The Little Smokies breakfast includes eight Vienna sausages. The tasty, generous bentos—usually there's a teriyaki option and fresh fish option—are good to go. Daily specials often include a stew. If the malasadas are fresh, they're worth the calories. Skip the ones with fillings.

Punaluʻu Bake Shop

808-929-7343
www.bakeshophawaii.com
HI 11, Nāʻālehu, HI 96772
Closed: Christmas, New Year's Day
Price: Inexpensive
Cuisine: Bakery and light meals
Serving: B, L
Credit Cards: MC, V
Handicapped Access: Yes
Reservations: No

The southernmost bakery in the United States is known for its sweet bread (and, frankly, a constant stream of tourists). There are three varieties—traditional, taro, and guava—and there are sample trays out all the time. The traditional is faintly yellow, the taro's vaguely purple, and the guava's quite pink. The long, square loaves slice up nicely for toast, but I usually use it for French toast, adding fresh-grated orange zest and a bit of guava or mango juice to the egg batter, just as I do with all sweet bread. The shape makes this bread easier to work with than dome-topped round loaves found elsewhere. There's a hospitable garden for stretching your legs if you're taking a break from driving. Stick with baked goods and Kaʻu coffee.

Shaka Restaurant

808-929-7404
HI 11, Nāʻālehu, HI 96772
Closed: Call
Price: Inexpensive–Moderate
Cuisine: Local-style American
Serving: B, L, D
Credit Cards: MC, V
Handicapped Access: Partial
Reservations: No

It's hard to miss Shaka's, a low-slung blue building with a big parking lot out front. The lot fills up because Shaka's is dependable and the portions substantial. Plate lunches draw local residents. If you order a burrito, be sure you're up to the challenge.

NEAR HAWAIʻI VOLCANOES NATIONAL PARK

Kiawe Kitchen

808-967-7711
19-4005 Haunani Rd.
Volcano, HI 96785
At the intersection of Old Volcano and Haunani Rds.
Closed: Wed.
Price: Moderate
Cuisine: Italian
Serving: L, D
Credit Cards: MC, V
Handicapped Access: Partial
Reservations: Dinner

For a nice low-key meal, the Kiawe Kitchen hits the spot. For lunch, try a perfect, if pricey, individual pizza from the wood-fired oven—the simple margarita perhaps—and a salad of local greens in an airy room that has walls painted lava red. The sandwiches are large enough to share. The Caesar salad came with slivers of toast rather than croutons, a nice change. The specials change daily and are often a good choice, particularly the soups. At dinner, the pasta dishes can be comforting, and the lamb is popular. Service can be a bit scattered if there's a rush. Pacific Rim regions are well represented on the wine list, along with Big Island microbrews. Watch your step—the fern tracery on the walkway is a nice touch to the exterior.

Kīlauea Lodge

808-967-7366
www.kilauealodge.com
Old Volcano Rd., Volcano, HI 96785
Closed: Call for holiday hours
Price: Expensive

Cuisine: European
Serving: B, D
Credit Cards: AE, MC, V
Handicapped Access: Partial
Reservations: Dinner

Kīlauea Lodge may come as a surprise to anyone who expects Hawai'i to be all about blue drinks and grilled fish. This is a dining room that feels like a stone hunting lodge dropped in from Europe or the Rockies. It's casual but dressy enough for a fine-dining experience, with koa tables, polished wood floors, and friendly servers, many of whom have worked here for years. The fireplace is tall and wide, throwing out welcome heat in this often chilly village. A single malt or a chewy red wine won't go amiss as you burrow into the sofa with your drink. The menu features solid meaty fare: lamb Provençal, excellent free-range venison, a Parker Ranch steak, a German sausage plate that, with the *hasenpfeffer* (braised rabbit), reveal the kitchen's German roots. Fish—there's some surf but overall much more turf—and always a vegetarian dish. Breakfasts, which are part of the room fare if you stay at the lodge, are substantial. The choices are limited but hearty, and it's fine to linger while planning the day. Of all the dining options in Volcano, this is the nicest, and well worth the drive from Hilo if you're staying there.

Lava Rock Café

808-967-8526
19-3972 Old Volcano Hwy., Volcano, HI 96785
Closed: Call on holidays
Price: Inexpensive–Moderate
Cuisine: American eclectic
Serving: B, L, D
Credit Cards: MC, V
Handicapped Access: Partial
Reservations: Suggested at dinner

This is a good place for meals with kids. The prices are right, the service sympathetic, and the food's simple enough for picky eaters, yet tasty enough for adults. (Try the chili.) The atmosphere isn't much, but the servings are generous, particularly the plate lunch, and the menu ranges far: it includes Chinese and Mexican dishes as well as the usual local favorites like teriyaki chicken. The desserts are multifork experiences best shared.

Thai Thai Restaurant

808-967-7969
19-4084 Old Volcano Rd., Volcano, HI 96785
Closed: Call on holidays
Price: Inexpensive–Moderate
Cuisine: Thai
Serving: D
Credit Cards: AE, D, MC, V
Handicapped Access: Partial
Reservations: No

As far as I can tell, the reason it's called Thai Thai is because the food is spiced without regard for non-Thais. It's real Thai food relying on fresh local herbs to make your mouth tingle. Consider yourself warned. You'll find all your favorites— pad Thai, larb—on the menu, and they're expertly prepared. The curries are uniformly good; try them with the catch of the day. Don't miss the green papaya salad. It has heat and it's crunchy fresh, a winning combination.

Volcano Golf and Country Club

808-967-8228
Pii Mauna Dr., Hawai'i Volcanoes National Park, HI 96718
Off HI 11, about 2 miles west of the park entrance at mile marker 30
Closed: Call on holidays
Price: Inexpensive–Moderate
Cuisine: American
Serving: B, L
Credit Cards: AE, DC, MC, V
Handicapped Access: Partial
Reservations: No

Volcano can be chilly, and a hearty breakfast or hot lunch here can be a smart move. I particularly like it for a late breakfast when the greens are still damp and the clouds hang low, because the windows are so big. The service is good, and because there's rarely a crowd, you can sit without feeling pressured. The menu offers reliable standards, many with punny names like "Birdie on the First Hole," which is a breakfast of two eggs, side of meat, toast, rice, or potatoes. Nonetheless, there are enough local dishes like the beef stew or saimin that you know you're not at a golf course at home. This a good choice if you're traveling with children.

Volcano House
Hawai'i Volcanoes National Park, HI 96718
808-967-7321
Closed: Call on holidays
Price: Inexpensive—Moderate
Cuisine: American
Serving: B, L, D
Credit Cards: MC, V
Handicapped Access: Yes
Reservations: Suggested for dinner

Volcano House operates the only restaurant in the park. The best option at the Ka Ohelo Dining Room and the snack bar is the view. The breakfast buffet is ample but uninspired.

Volcano True Value Hardware
808-967-7969
Old Volcano Rd., Volcano Village, HI 96785
Closed: Call for hours
Price: Inexpensive
Cuisine: Hot dogs to go
Serving: L
Credit Cards: MC, V
Handicapped Access: Partial
Reservations: No

These folks serve up a substantial all-beef hot dog with a large soda and a bag of chips. No more, no less. Pick up fruit at a roadside stand and carry on.

IN AND AROUND THE PUNA DISTRICT

Black Rock Café
808-965-1177
15-2872 Government Rd., Pāhoa, HI 96778
Closed: Call
Price: Inexpensive—Moderate
Cuisine: American, Hawaiian
Serving: B, L, D
Credit Cards: MC, V
Handicapped Access: Partial
Reservations: No

A casual place that's part bar, part dining room, Black Rock serves a mean hamburger and a good grilled catch-of-the-day sandwich. The salads are generous, as are most portions, and local families fill big tables to keep things lively.

Luquin's Restauant
808-965-9990
www.luquinsmexicanrestaurant.biz
15-2942 Pāhoa Village Rd., Pāhoa, HI 96778
Closed: Call
Price: Inexpensive—Moderate
Cuisine: Mexican
Serving: L, D
Credit Cards: MC, V
Handicapped Access: Partial
Reservations: No

Luqin's draws a crowd for dinner. Expect a line on weekends. Portions are big, and the food is good, if a bit bland at times, but a *liliko'i* or mango margarita can make up for that. Vegetarians do well with the tofu enchiladas.

Ning's Thai Cuisine
808-965-7611
15-2955 Pāhoa Rd., Pāhoa, HI 96778
Closed: Call
Price: Inexpensive—Moderate
Cuisine: Thai
Serving: L, D
Credit Cards: No

Handicapped Access: Partial
Reservations: No

A small rustic place with a fully deserved local following that is almost worshipful, Ning's uses local organic ingredients and gets the spicing right. It's one of those places where each dish is better than the last. The vegetarian options are delicious. They do takeout; indeed, table service can be delayed because of the volume. The tofu spring rolls carry particularly well.

Pāhoa Natural Foods
808-965-8322
15-2903 Government Rd., Pāhoa, HI 96778
Closed: Call
Price: Inexpensive–Moderate
Serving: B, L, D
Credit Cards: MC, V
Handicapped Access: Yes
Reservations: No

A funky grocery with a hot food bar, ready-made sandwiches, and wraps. It's a good option if you're self-catering in the area. There's a coffee scene in the morning, with folks catching up on town talk, and the bulletin board's filled with announcements of local events.

GREATER HILO

Abundant Life Natural Foods and Café
808-935-7411
292 Kamehameha Ave., Hilo, HI 96720
Closed: Call for holiday hours
Price: Inexpensive
Cuisine: Healthy light meals
Serving: B, L
Credit Cards: MC, V
Handicapped Access: Partial
Reservations: No

This natural foods grocery store in downtown Hilo offers creative salads, nourishing sandwiches, and other options when you want a healthy meal while shopping along the bay front in downtown Hilo.

Café 100
808-935-8683
969 Kīlauea Ave., Hilo HI 96720
Closed: Call for holiday hours
Price: Inexpensive
Cuisine: Local style (plate lunches, *loco moco*)
Serving: B, L, D
Credit Cards: No
Handicapped Access: Yes
Reservations: No

The purported home of the *loco moco* now serves more than a dozen variations on this island staple, consisting of a hamburger patty and egg on white rice topped with gravy. There's also a brisk trade in plate lunches—the macaroni salad is particularly good—both to go and to eat at picnic tables on the shady, wraparound lanai with a striking view of the parking lot, which is never empty. If you like iced tea, be sure to ask for half unsweetened regular tea and half *liliko'i* tea, a local concoction worth trying.

Café Pesto
808-969-6640
www.cafepesto.com
308 Kamehameha Ave., Hilo, HI 96720
In the S. Hata Building
Closed: Mon.
Price: Inexpensive–Expensive
Cuisine: Italian, local style
Serving: L, D
Credit Cards: AE, MC, V
Handicapped Access: Partial
Reservations: Recommended at dinner

Pizzas, calzones, big salads of local organic greens, fresh fish, and pasta highlight the menu at this dependable local favorite. Every so often I stray from the pizza menu, but I always return. It's a lively scene, there's a full bar, and the service is friendly.

Cronies
808-935-5158
11 Waiānuenue Ave., Hilo, HI 96720
Closed: Sun.

Price: Inexpensive–Moderate
Cuisine: Pub food
Serving: L, D
Credit Cards: MC, V
Handicapped Access: Partial
Reservations: No

At this sports bar gone local, try the fish 'n' chips made with mahimahi, or have a burger or a grilled catch-of-the-day sandwich. The service is fast and friendly, which makes up for the no-frills atmosphere.

Harrington's
808-961-4966
135 Kalaniana'ole Ave., Hilo, HI 96720
Closed: Call for holiday hours
Price: Moderate
Cuisine: Fish, steaks
Serving: L, D
Credit Cards: MC, V
Handicapped Access: Partial
Reservations: Suggested at dinner

With the white fairy lights along the edge of the roof and an open-air dining room that lets you watch the koi below in Reed's Bay, this is a pretty place for a meal that can fall short of expectations. But if you stick with the fresh catch of the day in a simple preparation, you should have a fine evening. Service is willing but sometimes slow.

Hilo Bay Café
808-935-4939
www.hilobaycafe.com
315 Maka'ala St., Hilo, HI 96720
Near Waiākea Center
Closed: Call for holiday hours
Price: Moderate–Expensive
Cuisine: Hawaiian Regional
Serving: L (daily except Sun.), D
Credit Cards: AE, D, DC, MC, V
Handicapped Access: Yes
Reservations: Recommended for dinner

Honolulu Advertiser readers selected this chic restaurant in a big-box shopping mall

as one of the state's best in 2004, and the place isn't resting on its laurels. Don't miss it. To counter expansive views of a parking lot from the bar area, the interior forces you to look inward at details like clouds of orchids, blown-glass light fixtures, and the striking presentations emerging from the kitchen. The menu changes frequently. It is inventive, making good use of local, fresh products, and varied—steak to tofu. The bar gets its island on with creations like lychee mojitos. Try to get a table in the boothlike area in back and hunker down over a chicken potpie.

Ken's House of Pancakes
808-935-8711
1730 Kamehameha Ave., Hilo, HI 96720
Closed: One day a year for the staff Christmas holiday party: Call
Price: Inexpensive–Moderate
Cuisine: American, local-style
Serving: B, L, D, SB, SSB
Credit Cards: AE, D, DC, MC, V
Handicapped Access: Partial
Reservations: No

The only lull at Ken's occurs between 2 and 3 AM, but even then, it's hardly slow. In 2008, *USA Today* selected this family-friendly institution as one of the 10 best breakfast joints in the country. It's like your favorite diner during college; smart, friendly service, comfy booths, bountiful servings, and a never-ending menu—oxtail stew and burgers and taco salad and eggs any way you want them whenever you want them. There can be a short wait at peak times, and it's the kind of local spot where an anonymous patron picked up the tab for a dozen or so U.S. Army reservists one Sat. morning when I was there. If you hear a gong and the staff yelling "sumo," that means somebody's ordered a super-duper-size dish, a brave move considering the norm. And yes, the pancakes are good, but to start my day, I have a bowl of the delicious saimin, *keiki*-size. (Sumo-size is so big it comes with inflatable pool toys.)

Miyo's

Waiākea Villas
808-935-2273
400 Hualani St., Hilo, HI 96720
Closed: Sun.
Price: Inexpensive–Moderate
Cuisine: Japanese
Serving: L, D
Credit Cards: MC, V
Handicapped Access: Partial

A gem. From the miso to the pickles, Miyo's food is uniformly delicious. It's healthy, home-style Japanese cooked without MSG and served in an open room in the trees by Wailoa Pond. At night it can be tricky to find, so plot your route before you leave. The tempura is practically greaseless, the daily specials won't lead you astray, and if you can't decide—it is hard—give in to one of the combination dinners. Miyo's is BYOB, and bringing your favorite among the many locally available Japanese beers is the best choice.

Naung Mai

808-934-7540
86 Kīlauea Ave., Hilo, HI 96720
Behind the Garden Exchange
Closed: Sun.
Price: Inexpensive
Cuisine: Thai
Serving: L, D
Credit Cards: MC, V
Handicapped Access: Partial
Reservations: No

It might not look like much from the outside, but seek it out, because one taste of the cucumber salad reveals why this is a popular local spot. Add the tofu spring rolls, and a curry . . . what a meal. The curries—red, green, yellow, and Mussaman—contain seafood, vegetarian, chicken, or meat and are served with white, jasmine, sticky, or brown rice. The options seem endless, but there's one constant—your meal will be very satisfying no matter what you choose.

Nihon Restaurant & Cultural Center

808-969-1133
123 Lihiwai St., Hilo, HI 96720
Closed: Sun.
Price: Moderate–Expensive
Cuisine: Japanese
Serving: L, D
Credit Cards: AE, D, DC, MC, V
Handicapped Access: Partial
Reservations: Recommended at dinner

For a memorable meal in Hilo, book a bay-view table at the Nihon Restaurant and arrive in time to watch night fall. It's a lovely experience, one that is matched by the food, particularly the sushi. The teriyaki steak is a good choice if you want an alternative to fish. The servers wear kimono and the decor is Japanese, which, with the art, explains the cultural element in the name. Given the paucity of dining options in the Banyan Dr. hotels, the Nihon Restaurant is an excellent choice if you don't want to drive into town, and worth a drive if you're staying elsewhere if only because you can combine the trip with a stroll through the lovely Liliʻuokalani Gardens. Lunch is a good deal.

Nori's Saimin and Snacks

808-935-9133
688 Kinoʻole St., Hilo, HI 96720
Near Hilo Lanes Bowling Alley
Closed: No dinner Mon., no lunch Fri. and Sat.; call for holiday hours
Price: Inexpensive
Cuisine: Japanese noodles
Serving: L, D
Credit Cards: AE, D, MC, V
Handicapped Access: Partial
Reservations: No

Tucked in the back of a low-rise commercial complex, Nori's offers real food for real people, a formula that earned it the 'Ilima Award for Best Big Island Restaurant in 2007. Diners at Nori's don't care about Formica-topped tables, low ceilings, and florescent lighting, because the saimin—in a delicious broth—is that scrumptious even if you don't slurp. It's just one of more than a dozen noodle soups available, along with plate lunches and dinners that feature ribs, 'ahi, and daily specials. Try the Hilo-style saimin with won-ton. Or the chicken or beef sticks if you want nibbles. The sushi is fresh and creative. There's a steady takeout traffic that includes orders of cookies and pies. Open until midnight Tuesday through Saturday.

Ocean Sushi Deli
808-961-6625
239 Keawe St., Hilo, HI 96720
Closed: Sun.
Price: Moderate
Cuisine: Japanese
Serving: L, D
Credit Cards: MC, V
Handicapped Access: Partial
Reservations: No

There's not much atmosphere, but the price is right. That's what made this a local notable, but service can be so erratic that it can spoil the meal. Which is too bad, because when the creativity flows here, the special rolls offer insight into how something very traditional bends to accommodate a new place and new ways. The result—ahi *poke* in a roll. There's a brisk to-go business, so if you only want traditional sushi, do it. The uni is often outstanding.

Puka Puka Kitchen
808-933-2121
270 Kamehameha Ave., Hilo, HI 96720
Closed: Call for hours
Price: Inexpensive
Cuisine: Japanese
Serving: L, D
Credit Cards: No

Handicapped Access: Partial
Reservations: No

Don't be surprised if you see a fast-moving line outside this little restaurant during lunch hours as local people pop in to grab a bento to take away. The unagi goes quickly, as does the 'ahi, but don't worry if they're gone—the other options are all good. If there is a wait for a table, it'll be short. The lamb curry is delicious, make sure to have the garlic-fried rice, and the chicken katsu is a fine example of Japanese home-style cooking.

Royal Siam Thai Restaurant
808-961-6100
70 Mamo St., Hilo, HI 96729
Closed: Dinner Mon., lunch Sun.
Price: Inexpensive   Moderate
Cuisine: Thai
Serving: L, D
Credit Cards: AE, D, DC, MC, V
Handicapped Access: Partial
Reservations: No

A simple place serving Thai food in all its complex glory. Trust whatever appeals from the daily specials and order off the menu with impunity. The curries are uniformly good, and the garlic chicken in coconut milk is delicious.

Seaside Restaurant and Aquafarm
808-935-8825
www.seasiderestaurant.com
1790 Kalaniana'ole Ave., Hilo, HI 96720
Closed: Mon.
Price: Moderate—Expensive
Cuisine: Fish
Serving: D
Credit Cards: AE, D, MC, V
Handicapped Access: Partial
Reservations: Dinner

The Nakagawa family does one thing superbly: fish. They raise seven kinds, including aholehole, in 30 acres of ponds they first cultivated in 1921. If you want fish fresh from the pond, say so when you make your reservation, and it will be plucked from the water moments before you arrive. Sautéed, steamed, or fried: those are the preparations. Simple, but sophisticated. If it is available, order the aholehole in advance. This is a local favorite and has been for generations. Don't be put off by the location past the light-industrial jumble surrounding the airport.

What's Shakin'
808-964-3080
27-999 Old Māmalahoa Hwy., Pepe'ekeo, HI 96783
On the Hāmākua Coast 4-mile scenic drive outside Hilo
Closed: Call for holiday hours
Price: Inexpensive
Cuisine: Healthy sandwiches, smoothies
Serving: Late B, L
Credit Cards: MC, V
Handicapped Access: Partial
Reservations: No

It's hard work, navigating the twists and turns of the scenic drive outside Hilo, stopping to take pictures of Onomea Bay, maybe even visiting the Hawai'i Tropical Botanical Garden. Reward yourself with a stop at this yellow plantation-style health food deli with superfresh options from snacks to serious sandwiches and salads. The smoothies alone are worth the stop.

HĀMĀKUA COAST

Cafe Il Mondo
808-775-7711
45-3626 Māmane St., Honoka'a, HI 96727
Closed: Mon.
Price: Inexpensive–Moderate
Cuisine: Pizza, salads, espresso
Serving: L, D
Credit Cards: No
Handicapped Access: Partial
Reservations: Suggested at dinner

Although hand-crafted pizzas are the primary food group at this tempting café, there's plenty on the adult and children's menus that doesn't involve a stone oven. The daily soup is usually a good choice, particularly with one of the salads of organic greens grown nearby. There's local art on the walls, a vintage koa bar, and something about the place that makes you want to linger a little bit.

Māmane Street Bakery
808-775-9478
45-3625 Māmane St., Honoka'a, HI 96727
Closed: Weekends
Price: Inexpensive
Cuisine: Bakery with espresso drinks
Serving: B
Credit Cards: MC, V
Handicapped Access: Partial
Reservations: No

Get here early or forget it. The retail outlet of this well-known bakery opens at 6 AM and closes around noon. Although there are sandwiches and other choices, do the right thing and caffeinate with the pastries or Portuguese sweet bread. If you want a snack for later or are cooking dinner at a rental, grab the focaccia. It's good, but it's hard to resist. In a bag. In the backseat. It smells so . . . tasty.

Simply Natural
808-775-0119
35-3625 Māmane St., Honoka'a, HI 96727
Closed: Christmas, New Year's Day
Price: Inexpensive
Cuisine: Healthy
Serving: B, L
Credit Cards: No
Handicapped Access: Partial
Reservations: No

An unpretentious place that uses local organic products for hearty sandwiches, salads, and smoothies. Breakfast offerings are fairly standard, but the banana pancakes are made with taro.

Tex Drive-In
808-775-0598
HI 19, Honoka'a, HI 96727
Closed: Call
Price: Inexpensive
Cuisine: Local style
Serving: B, L, D
Credit Cards: D, DC, MC, V
Handicapped Access: Partial
Reservations: No

The attraction at this time-honored road-side stop is the malasadas, a Portuguese doughnut missing the hole. When they're fresh, they're exceptional—light, sweet, a bit doughy in the center, as they should be. I prefer mine plain, but there are many fillings, including guava and other tropical options. The plate lunches are filling, and there are usually Filipino dishes available. There's food to go, but part of the fun here is hanging out, particularly in the early mornings when those yummy warm malasadas fly out the door.

NORTH KOHALA AND WAIMEA (KAMUELA) AREA

Bamboo
808-889-5555
Akoni Pule Hwy. at HI 270, Hāwī, HI 96719
Closed: Mon.
Price: Moderate–Expensive
Cuisine: Asian fusion
Serving: L, D, SB
Credit Cards: MC, V
Handicapped Access: Partial
Reservations: Dinner

About 30 minutes north of the Kohala Coast resorts, Bamboo exudes the kind of funky charm a hotel would be hard-pressed to replicate. The restored building remains old style, the welcome is warm, and drinks are generous. (The *liliko'i* margaritas are pretty and potent.) And the food fits right in. Don't try to decide among the *pūpūs;* you want the Big Bamboozle with two of everything, including the house specialty,

chicken sate pot stickers. Somebody took a sensible approach to the menu because many of the entrées can be ordered as half portions, which makes baby back ribs with pineapple sauce doable rather than daunting. Grilled fish on spicy somen noodles is also good. The local-style entrées aren't afterthoughts, and there's a children's menu. John Keawe, the well-known slack-key guitarist, provides the entertainment several times a month. Check his calendar at www.johnkeawe.com and try to catch one of his shows.

Café Pesto
808-882-1071
www.cafepesto.com
Kawaihae Harbor, HI 270, Kawaihae, HI 96743
Kawaihae Shopping Center (across from the harbor)
Closed: Call for holiday hours
Price: Inexpensive–Expensive
Cuisine: Eclectic
Serving: L, D
Credit Cards: AE, D, MC, V
Handicapped Access: Partial
Reservations: Helpful at dinner

Always busy, always popular, Café Pesto bumps up standards like calzones, pizzas, and pasta. Spinach salad is served with seared *poke* or marinated fresh fish, and you can get Japanese eggplant as a pizza topping. The portions are fit for sharing, and there's a children's menu. It's not unusual to see kids asleep at the table during a family gathering, and it's the kind of place where the servers take it all in stride.

Daniel Thiebaut
808-887-2200
www.danielthiebaut.com
65-1259 Kawaihae Rd., Waimea, HI 96796
Closed: Call for holiday hours
Price: Expensive
Cuisine: French-Asian

Serving: D, SB
Credit Cards: AE, D, MC, V
Handicapped Access: Yes
Reservations: Recommended

French-trained Thiebaut, who once cooked down the hill at the Mauna Kea Beach Resort, uses Big Island products to create a cuisine that fuses French and Asian influences. From Hunan-style rack of lamb to sautéed macadamia-nut chicken breast, this is inventive food in congenial surroundings, a series of small rooms in what was once the Chock In store. Vegetarians get treated well; for example, a crispy avocado spring roll, and, just like everyone else, a daily special.

Huli Sue's BBQ and Grill

808-885-6288
64-957 Māmalahoa Hwy., Waimea, HI
96743
Closed: Call for holiday hours
Price: Inexpensive–Moderate
Cuisine: BBQ
Serving: L, D (to-go orders available)
Credit Cards: MC, V
Handicapped Access: Yes
Reservations: No

Don't miss this cowboy roadhouse serving comfort food with style and good cheer to families or solo diners. Everything's fresh—you can walk up the road to fields where the salads grow—and organic when possible. Chicken soup (for the *paniolo* soul) is rich in noodles and shiitake mushrooms. Don't miss the *poke* with corn nuts. Treat yourself to the onion rings. The BBQ meats come with one of four sauces: Southwestern, Caribbean citrus, chili

Huli Sue's menu features locally grown, caught, raised or produced product.

water–pineapple–sugarcane, and my favorite, crack seed. It makes BBQ sublime. Crack seed brisket with sides of grilled pineapple and corn pudding . . . oh my, my. So very good to the last morsel; I've never been able to contemplate dessert. The coconut layer cake looks real fine in passing, though.

Kohala Coffee Mill

808-889-5577
Akoni Pule Hwy., Hāwī, HI 96719
Closed: Call for holiday hours
Price: Inexpensive–Moderate
Cuisine: Coffee, light meals, Tropical Dreams ice cream
Serving: B, L
Credit Cards: MC, V
Handicapped Access: Partial
Reservations: No

In Hāwī, this is the morning gathering point that keeps hopping most of the day. Bagels and other baked goods suit morning coffee; the salads, burgers, soups, and stews appear a bit later. The ice cream is a Big Island–made treat. It's a good place to hear about local events and to hang out, imagining that you live nearby.

Kohala Rainbow Café

808-889-0099
54-3897 Akoni Pule Hwy., North Kohala, HI, 96755 (opposite King Kamehameha statue, Kapa'au)
Closed: Weekends
Price: Inexpensive
Cuisine: Wraps, bagels, ice cream, espresso drinks
Serving: L
Credit Cards: MC, V
Handicapped Access: Partial
Reservations: No

It's healthy, low-key, light-filled, and airy, and just about the last dining option before you go off a cliff into Pololū Valley several miles down the road. The ingredients are very fresh and mostly local. The wraps, the café specialty, are tasty and imaginative: *kālua* pig is the protein element in the Kamehameha. You order at the counter, sit down, and lunch arrives. If you don't want a meal, there are other lighter options, served cheerfully.

Merriman's

808-885-6822
www.merrimanshawaii.com
Opelo Plaza, Waimea, HI 96743
Off HI 19
Closed: Call for holiday hours
Price: Expensive
Cuisine: Hawaiian Regional
Serving: L, D
Credit Cards: AE, MC, V
Handicapped Access: Yes
Reservations: Recommended

Waimea is a little like north Berkeley's gourmet ghetto in that great food is part of the landscape. Year after year authoritative voices such as *Gourmet* magazine and the *Wine Spectator* sing the praises of Peter Merriman's original restaurant. The menu and the specials reflect what's available from local farmers. If you can't decide, order the famous platters for a selection of appetizers and signature dishes like wok char 'ahi. Lunch doesn't offer that luxury, so arrive with a similarly curious eater to trade and taste offerings like the *kālua* pig and sweet onion quesadilla, Chinese short ribs, and whatever is on offer as sandwich of the day.

Nanbu Courtyard

808-889-5546
54-3885 Akoni Pule Hwy., Kapa'au, HI 96755
At the Nanbu Hotel
Closed: Call for holiday hours
Price: Inexpensive
Cuisine: Coffee and light meals
Serving: B, L
Credit Cards: MC, V

Handicapped Access: Partial
Reservations: No

The Nanbu Building is on the National Register of Historic Places, and the courtyard is tucked away behind several retail outlets facing the street. The food is simple but good, and this is a quiet alternative to other cafés in town.

Sushi Rocks
808-889-5900
55-3435 Akoni Pule Hwy., Hāwī, HI 96719
Closed: Wed.
Price: Moderate
Cuisine: Sushi
Serving: D
Credit Cards: AE, DC, MC, V
Handicapped Access: Partial
Reservations: Suggested

The traditional concept of sushi is a starting place. Listen to your server, ask questions, and be brave. You'll be rewarded with an adventure in sushi. There is a changing array of cooked fish dishes, noodles and salads, and a full bar that does to generous standard cocktails what the sushi bar does to rice, fish, and seaweed. It's a fun room, and everything's beautifully presented; hang on for a tasty ride.

Tako Taco Taqueria
808-887-1717
64-1066 Māmalahoa Hwy., Waimea, HI 96743
Closed: Call for holiday hours
Price: Inexpensive
Cuisine: (Healthy) Mexican
Serving: L, D
Credit Cards: MC, V

Busy, busy, busy at lunch with to-go orders flying out the door, this simple place provides fast food far removed from a chain environment. The fresh fish burritos or tacos are good bets, although carnivores and vegetarians will find options. Do what everyone does and get takeout for the beach or elsewhere.

FOOD PURVEYORS

Bakeries

HILO

O'Keefe and Sons Bakery and Garden Café
Owners: Jim and Clarita O'Keefe
808-934-9334
374 Kino'ole St., Hilo, HI 96720
Closed: Sun.

Jim and Clarita O'Keefe oversee a growing empire of outlets for their tasty products. There's the bakery on Kino'ole St.—two blocks from the farmers' market—with a welcoming outdoor area for taste testing. Ono Kona Coffee at 835 Kīlauea Ave. is a red-roofed drive-through for a quick, powerful caffeine fix with grab'm sandwiches and baked goods. (If you park and go inside, Ono Kona coffee beans are available in vacuum-packed half- and full-pound bags.) They also operate the café at the 'Imiloa Astronomy Center in the University of Hawai'i–Hilo Science and Technology Park off Komohana St. It's all good.

Two Ladies Kitchen
Owners: Nora Uchida and Tomi Tokeshi
808-961-4766
246 Kīlauea Ave., Hilo, HI 96720
Closed: Sun., Mon., and Tues.

Two Ladies Kitchen always runs out of mochi, a traditional Japanese confection made from pounded rice. Nora Uchida and Tomi Tokeshi think that's the right way to do business, because it means the mochi is fresh each day. Stop by their happy small shop and try any of the 6 to 20 varieties of shaped and colored mochi they make. What's available changes with the season. The big draw is the strawberry mochi, a fresh fruit covered with a skin of mochi.

The ladies may arrive before dawn, but the screen door doesn't open until 11 AM, when the ladies are often greeted with a line.

MOUNTAIN VIEW

Mt. View Bakery
Owner: Larry Sueda
808-968-6353
18-1319 Old Volcano Rd., Mountain View, HI 96771
Closed: Sun.

Stone cookies sounds like the title for an illustrated children's book, but they are well-loved sweets best purchased from the source on Old Volcano Rd. in Mountain View. Dentally dangerous unless dunked in milk, coffee, or hot chocolate (I've never tried them in tea, but feel free), consider them the Big Island version of biscotti, because they're hard rather than chewy, and dense. Make sure to try the chocolate chip and remember: dunk'm.

Breweries

HILO

Mehana Brewing Company
Owner: Calvin Shindo
808-934-8211
275 E. Kāwili St., Hilo, HI 96720
Closed: Sun.

Mehana Brewing Company is a microbrewery owned by the Shindo family. There's a no-frills tasting room plopped inside a vast corrugated metal building. All the beers are on tap. They sell T-shirts emblazoned with the striking labels. Be sure to try the Humpback Blue Beer and the Mauna Kea Pale Ale.

KAILUA-KONA

Kona Brewing Co.
808-334-2739
www.konabrewing.com
75-5629 Kuakini Hwy., at Palani Rd., Kailua-Kona, HI 96740

This is the Big Island's first microbrewery. Start off with a sampler, four 6-oz. glasses of beers, ales, and porters. The selection changes by the season. The food is pub basics, and sitting outside on the vast lanai under tiki lamps is congenial. You're surrounded by corrugated tin buildings, so it isn't as romantic as it sounds. The pizzas are good, and while most have an island name—Pele's Own, the Kohala—most of the toppings are familiar. You can order a pizza in advance and pick it up to cook at your rental. There's beer to go as well, but the selection is not as extensive as what's on tap. Brewery tours Monday through Friday at 10:30 AM and 3 PM.

Cafés & Roasters

Aloha Outpost (808-965-8333) in the Pāhoa Marketplace features Puna coffee and rotates the house brew daily, but it always has a T1 line open for in-house gaming that includes "Return to Castle Wolfenstein" and "Halo 2."

Bears' Café
808 935 0708
106 Keawe St., Hilo, HI 96720
Closed: Call for holiday hours

The coffee is strong and the waffles light, a scenario that changes only slightly at lunch, when menus adjusts to offer generous sandwiches and salads. Service can be slow, but the flip side is that you can take your time people-watching (and being watched) in a spot filled with bears that children may find fun.

Bong Brothers and Sistah
808-328-9289
84-5227 Māmalahoa Hwy., Hōnaunau, HI 96726

A coffee stand in a coffee mill, where nearby farmers bring their beans for roast-

Coffee Culture

Coffee is the Big Island's wine, an exceptional product grown under specific circumstances for fanatical consumers. Hawai'i is the only state in the United States where coffee is grown commercially.

The trees arrived in Hawai'i from Brazil aboard the British warship H.M.S. *Blonde*. Chief Boki, then governor of O'ahu, had acquired them on his way back to the islands from London. The coffee was planted in Mānoa Valley on O'ahu. Rev. Samuel Ruggles, who established a mission station in Hilo, took coffee trees to Captain Cook in 1828. It was ideal coffee country with a subtropical climate, sun blessed in the morning, cloud dappled in the afternoon on the slopes of Hualālai and Mauna Loa. The soil, rich from their past eruptions, encouraged development of large plantations, but the coffee crash of 1899 found owners leasing their land to smallholders, most of them Japanese farmers who had completed the indentured servitude entered to make the voyage east. From Hōlualoa above Kailua Bay, these family farmers spread coffee into Kealakekua and Hōnaunau, towns connected by scenic roads today.

By the 1930s there were more than 1,000 farms in Kona alone. Today there are about 700 coffee growers statewide, 600 of them on the Big Island. They're spread out along a 2-mile-wide corridor that runs 25 miles from 2,500 to 500 feet above sea level. Kona coffee is one of the top gourmet coffees in the world due to its aroma, mellowness, and full-bodied flavor. About 150 of the farms control their own production, marketing their coffees as estate-grown identifiable brews. This has created a boutique coffee industry akin to California's vineyards, with self-drive tour maps available at the Kona Historical Society and from www.konacoffeefest.com.

In the same way that awareness of California wine has spread from the Napa and Sonoma regions to include Santa Barbara, Monterey, and the San Pasqual Valley near San Diego, there is a growing interest in coffee grown in the Ka'u, Hāmākua, and Puna districts.

Commercial coffee production in Ka'u started after the sugar plantation closed in 1996. Roughly 90 percent of the coffees produced in Ka'u are farmed on approximately 330 acres in Moa'ula at an elevation of 2,000 to 2,500 feet. Another area that grows Ka'u coffee is Wood Valley. Ka'u coffee has a floral bouquet, distinctive aroma, and very smooth taste. Indeed, in 2007, two Ka'u coffees placed in the top 10 out of 104 entries from around the world at the Specialty Coffee Association of America's Roasters Guild Cupping Pavilion Competition.

Coffee's history in the Puna area is similar. Over 6,000 acres of coffee growing in the area were plowed under when the Puna Sugar Plantation was established in 1891. Today there's about 125 acres of coffee under cultivation. Most of the farms are located in Hawaiian Acres, between 1,000 and 2,500 feet elevation. They produce a very full-body, heavy coffee with nutty overtones.

After a missionary brought coffee plants to families along the Hāmākua Coast, small coffee farms sprang up in the coastal villages in the mid-19th century. Growers introduced Guatemalan coffee cultivars in the late 19th century, and commercial cultivation centered in the Kuka'iau, Honoka'a, Pa'auilo, and Poha-kea areas. By the 1950s, most of the coffee fields had reverted to pastures. Today there are about 150 acres of coffee, most between 350 to 2,000 feet elevation. Hāmākua coffee is rich with a chocolaty-smooth finish.

Tours and tastings are available at many Kona coffee farms. It is more difficult to find coffee from the other areas. Look in farmers' markets and local markets like the Pāhala Town Café. While cafés and espresso stands serving 100 percent Big Island coffee are easy to find, it may not be available where you're staying. Consider traveling with a hot pot, filters, and a cone, then buying a fresh roasted half-pound bag and having it ground so you have a personal ready-to-brew stash in your room.

ing. Of course there are Bong T-shirts, but the more unusual souvenir is one of the coffee bags with the family's logo.

Café Il Mondo
808-775-771
45-3626 Māmane St., Honoka'a, HI 96727

An espresso bar that takes the Italian theme a step further and serves pizza and baked goods. There's indoor and outdoor seating and often entertainment in the evening.

Coffees 'n' Epicurea
808-328-0322
83-5315 Māmalahoa Hwy., Captain Cook, HI 96726
At mile marker 106

Perfectly roasted coffee and light, flaky pastry make this a tasty option.

Hilo Coffee Mill
Owners: Katherine Patton and Jeanette Baysa
808-968-1333, 866-982-5551
17-995 Volcano Rd., Mountain View, HI 96760
Between mile markers 12 and 13

The Hilo Coffee Mill is a reliable place to taste Ka'u and Puna coffees if you have had trouble finding them. The owners work with many small growers in those two districts, helping them process, roast, and market their beans as part of the renaissance of East Hawai'i coffee. The mill carries the air of a boutique wine shop. There are tastings and knowledgeable staff to answer questions. It's also a good stop for finding out about local events, and because of its midway location between Hilo and Hawai'i Volcanoes National Park, it's worth taking a break in their café.

There are many coffee samples to sip on a tour of Greenwell Farms.

Hōluakoa Café
808-322-2233
76-5901 Māmalahoa Hwy., Hōlualoa, HI
96725-9717

Hōluakoa opens at 6:30 for an early morning fresh roasted cup, roasted and ground
on-site from beans grown from one of the
local farms. Fueled up, you can embark on
the coffee tour south along picturesque HI
180, which is also known as Māmalahoa
Highway.

Island Lava Java
808-327-2161
75-5799 Ali'i Dr., Ali'i Sunset Plaza,
Kailua-Kona, HI 96740

Across the street from the water, this is a
wireless hot spot where you can relax and
watch the passing scene as you check your
e-mail or enjoy a light meal. Sunsets are
marvelous.

Java on the Rocks
808-329-1493
75-5828 Kahakai Rd., off Ali'i Dr., Kailua-
Kona, HI 96740

This is not to be missed, as you can watch
waves crash with your first cup of caffeine
at what was the bar, Huggo's on the Rocks,
the night before.

Kohala Coffee Mill
808-889-5577
Akoni Pule Hwy., Hāwī, HI 96719

In Hāwī, this is the all-day gathering place,
so grab a seat where you find it, and linger.

This fresh-picked produce from Fujifarms is bound for Fujimama's restaurant.

At Kona Joe's, coffee grows on trellises like those winemakers use for grapes.

Kope Kope
808-933-1221
1261 Kīlauea Ave., Hilo, HI 96720
Hilo Shopping Center

A source for Kaʻu, Puna, and Hāmākua Coast beans; there's often live music at lunch as well as on Thursday, Friday, and Saturday nights.

Ono Kona Coffee
835 Kīlauea Ave., Hilo, HI 96720

This red-roofed drive-through provides a quick, powerful caffeine fix, a lifesaver on your way to or from the airport because you can pick up fresh roasted Hāmākua Coast beans here as well.

Starbucks
808-887-6409
67-1185 Māmalahoa Hwy. # D108, Waimea, HI 96743

It's the constant fire in the fireplace that makes this link in the ubiquitous chain cozier than the norm.

Waimea Coffee Co.
808-885-8915, 866-885-1104
63-1279 Kawaihea Rd. #114, Waimea, HI 96743

Tucked into Parker Square, Waimea Coffee is an agreeable place to sit with a cup of coffee inside as the screen door slaps open and closed. Or go sit outside on the lawn, under the trees. They serve estate-grown coffees from Kona, Hāmākua, and Puna, as well as from Molokaʻi, Kauʻi, and Maui.

Coffee Farms

KEALAKEKUA

Greenwell Farms

Owners: Tom and Jennifer Greenwell
808-323-2276
www.greenwellfarms.com
81-6581 Māmalahoa Hwy., Kealakekua, HI
Closed: Sun.

Founded by Henry Nicholas Greenwall and his wife, Elizabeth Caroline, the farm's coffee was first recognized at the 1873 World's Fair in Vienna, Austria. Today the couple's descendants run the 150-acre spread behind the original farmhouse, which now houses the Kona Historical Society. The low-key tour allows lots of time for questions and photographs. It was here, as I climbed up a small incline, then walked among the trees feeling the heat as the sun climbed in the sky, and saw how the machinery operated, that I realized how much work goes into my morning cup. (I also learned that the darkest roast doesn't make the strongest coffee.)

Kona Joe

Owners: Joe and Deepa Alban
808-322-2100
www.konajoe.com
79-7346 Māmalahoa Hwy., Kealakekua, HI
Between mile markers 113 and 114
Closed: Sun.

Others may talk about Kona coffee as if it is wine, but Joe Alban grows it like grapes—trained to grow along the wires of trellises with advice from his brother, John, a graduate of the viticulture and oenology department at University of California–Davis. Joe believes this patented technique allows the Arabica coffee to develop with a more uniform exposure to sunlight than it would get on a tree. It puts ripe cherries (the ripened fruit of a coffee bush is called cherry) within easy reach of pickers, and the resulting brew wins prizes as well as recognition from the governor. Which is all very nice, but what you'll remember is the view from the espresso bar.

HOLUALOA

Hōlualoa Kona Coffee Company

Owner: Desmond Twigg-Smith
808-322-9937
www.konalea.com
77-6261 Māmalahoa Hwy., Hōlualoa HI 96725
Open: 7:30-4 weekdays

The estate tour, recognized in the book *Watch it Made in the USA: A Visitor's Guide to the Best Factory Tours and Company Museums* covers what goes into one of the world's finest coffees from the tree to the cup. In addition to the estate's coffee orchards, guests can view the thriving mill and roasting operation that handles coffee for more than 100 nearby farms. It's a good way to get a sense of what's going on behind the farm signs you see along the up-country coffee corridor.

HONOKA'A

Long Ears Coffee

Owners: Netta and Wendell Branco
808-775-0385
www.longearscoffee.com
Honoka'a, HI 96727

Contact the Brancos directly to set up a farm tour for a minimum of two people. (Her mother, Wailani, is recognized as a Hawaiian Living Treasure for her quilts.) The Brancos enjoy talking story, and theirs is a good one. They began coffee farming almost accidentally because wild coffee plants left from the late 19th century grew on their land, the 3B Half Horse Ranch, a mule-breeding operation in Āhualoa. They picked the red coffee cherry (the ripened fruit of a coffee bush is called cherry), and after discovering little interest in the stuff, roasted it for themselves. Gradually, they found others picking the wild coffee, bought their cherry, and now they're coffee farmers; coffee processors, using an old drum roaster; and coffee sellers. The mule "factory" continues, and that's the late Ozark Red, a Catalonian jackass, on the label.

Chips

HILO

Atebara Chips
Owners: Nimr Tamini and Clyde Oshiro
808-969-9600
717 Manono St., Hilo, HI 96720

When World War II rationing threatened the Hilo potato chip business Raymond Atebara started in 1936, he turned to locally grown taro. When the 1946 tsunami destroyed his factory, he moved Atebara Chips to Manono St., where they're still made today, along with sweet potato, potato, and shrimp chips. Now made by Nimr and Clyde as part of their business, Hawaii Island Gourmet Products, Atebara chips cost more than others, but they're worth it. The gift shop, which is closed on Sunday, will ship chips to your home by the case.

Farmers' Markets

Farmers' markets offer the best introduction to local foods. Fresh-caught fish, locally grown produce, farm-made specialties, Japanese radishes, eggplants, cucumbers, Hawaiian chili peppers, Thai basil, and Portuguese sweet bread, sausage, and malasadas, which are doughnuts without the holes. All are reasons to stay in a place with a kitchen, or at least a refrigerator, and to carry a cooler in your car.

The biggest is the Hilo Farmers' Market, and like the other markets, it operates on a limited schedule. The Hilo market is open just two days a week, Wed. and Sat. Hopping by 7, it's almost empty by early afternoon. Launched in 1988 with just a few produce sellers, it now sprawls over parts of two downtown blocks centered at the corner of Mamo St. and

Fresh cut orchids are abundant and inexpensive at Big Island farmers' markets.

Kamehameha Ave., across from Mo'oheau Park. There's plenty of on-street parking despite the crowd swarming to see what about 200 vendors, including real estate agents, have on offer. They sell everything from exotic fruits, such as lychees and infrequently, mangosteens, to jewelry, island-made clothing, and traditional Hawaiian crafts. It's is a terrific place to find special local vendors like the Rainbow Falls Connection (try the 'ōhi'a lehua honey and *liliko'i* curd), coffee from smaller growers like Hawai'i Rainforest Coffee, dressings and sauces from Broke the Mouth (their papaya lime dressing is a treat), ready-made meals like green papaya salad, and tiny bananas that taste like strawberries or vanilla. And it is astonishing how inexpensive the cut flowers can be here. I end up with big bouquets in my room wherever I'm staying.

However, there's also a significant amount of Pacific Island kitsch, the brightly colored silk or synthetic wraps featuring smiling, leaping dolphins, hibiscus and birds of paradise, silver beaded this and that, shell jewelry, and cheap luggage in island-print fabric. It's the same merchandise available in Penang and Phuket, so if you're looking for something local, be sure you're not buying something that's locally imported rather than locally made.

Despite Hilo's big-deal reputation, there are other farmers' markets throughout the island. My favorite is the smaller one in Waimea, held in a field each Sat. It's relaxed, uncrowded, and very local, from the array of goods to the vibe.

Here's a listing of some Big Island farmers' markets. The hours and days may change, so check local newspaper listings or ask people where you're staying. Although some vendors may take credit cards, play it safe and bring cash, particularly small bills for making change. Don't eat ahead of time. There are plenty of samples and chances to have a walkabout feast.

HILO

Hilo Farmers' Market
www.hilofarmersmarket.com
Open: Wed. and Sat. 7–3
Kamehameha Ave. and Mamo St., Hilo, HI 96720

HĀMĀKUA COAST

Honoka'a Farmers' Market
Open: Sat. 7:30–2
Old Botelho Bldg., Honoka'a, HI 96727

Laupāhoehoe Market
Open: Sat. from 8:00 AM–noon
9652 Kaumali'i Hwy., Laupāhoehoe, HI 96764

KOHALA

Hawaiian Homestead Farmers Market
Open: Sat. 7–noon
Kuhio Hale Building, 64-759 Kahilu Rd., Waimea, HI

The Hawaiian Homesteaders Assn. Farmers Market offers organic produce, flowers, baked goods, potted plants, and crafts that are usually nicer and less expensive that what's on sale at resort boutiques. Among the goods on offer are the fragrant lavender products from nearby Honopua Farm. I've sent the scented laundry spray to friends who've swooned over it. (The trick is to send a lot home in a USPS flat-rate box rather than haul it with you.) Be on the lookout for delicious cheeses from Dick and Heather Threlfall's Hawai'i Island Goat Dairy and Carol Pegg, a.k.a. The Fudge Lady, whose "sometimes nutty, sometimes not" selections aren't too sweet. My favorite is the dark chocolate fudge with ginger. Matthias Seelis can help you select and ship plants from his stand, Wonderful Orchids.

Many craftspeople work on their wares in their booths at the Hilo Farmers Market.

WAIMEA

I Ka Pono Farmers' Market
Open: Sat. 7:30–noon
Parker School, at I Ka Pono Community
Garden, Waimea

HĀWĪ

Under the Banyans Farmers' Market
Open: Sat. 7:30–1

KONA

Ali'i Garden Market Place
Ali'i Dr., 2 miles south of Kailua Pier, Kona
Open: Wed.through Sun. 9–5

Kona Farmers' Market
Open: Sat. and Sun. 8–2:30
Old Industrial Park, Kaiwi Square

KAILUA-KONA

Kailua Village Farmer's Market
Open: Thurs., Fri., Sat., and Sun.
Across from Hale Hālāwai, Kailua-Kona

SOUTH KONA

Kealakekua Flea Market
Open: Tues., Thurs., and Sat. 8–3
Haleki'i St.

Kona Pacific Farmers' Co-op
Open: Fri. 8–4
82-5810 Nāpō'opo'o Rd., Captain Cook, HI

South Kona Fruit Stand
Open: Mon. through Sat. 9–6
84-4770 Māmalahoa Hwy., Captain Cook,
HI

KA'U (SOUTH POINT)

Nā'ālehu Farmers Market
Open: Wed. 10–2; Sat. 8–noon

PUNA AREA

PĀHOA

Akebono Farmers' Market
Open: Sun. 8–1
Akebono Theatre, HI 130

Caretakers of Our Land Farmers' Market
Open: Sat. 7:30–noon
Sacred Heart Church

Maku'u Farmers' Market
Open: Thurs., Sat., and Sun. 6–3
HI 130

Offerings at the twice-weekly Hilo Farmers Market include locally-grown produce.

This roadside stand operates on the honor system for fruits, vegetables and flowers.

MOUNTAIN VIEW

Island Fruits
At mile marker 12 on HI 11.
Open: Mon. through Fri. 10–5:30;
Sat. 9–4

Kea'au Village Farmers' Market
Open: Daily 7–5

VOLCANO

Volcano Village Farmers Market
Open: Sun. 8:30–11 AM
Cooper Center, Volcano

Lots of local produce, flowers, prepared
foods, baked goods, and an occasional
clothing swap.

Grocery Stores

THE SHOPS AT MAUNA LANI

Foodland Farms
808-887-6101
68-1330 Mauna Lani Drive, #200., Kohala
Coast, HI 96743

HILO

KTA
808-959-9111
50 E. Pū'ainakō St., Hilo, HI 96720

KTA
808 935-3751
321 Keawe St., Hilo, HI 96720

Sack 'n' Save
808-935-3113
250 Kino'ole St., Hilo, HI 96720

Safeway
808-959-3502
111. E. Pū'ainakō St., Hilo, HI 96720

WAIKOLOA HIGHLANDS CENTER

KTA
808-883-1088
68-3916 Paniolo Ave., Waikoloa, HI 96738

WAIMEA

KTA
808-885-8866
65-1158 Māmalahoa Hwy., Waimea, HI
96743

Waimea Foodland
808-885-2022
Parker Ranch Center, Waimea, HI 96743

KONA COAST SHOPPING CENTER

KTA
808-329-1677
74-5594 Palani Rd., Kailua-Kona, HI 96740

Sack 'n' Save
808-326-2729.
75-5595 Palani Rd., Kailua-Kona, HI 96740

CROSSWINDS SHOPPING CENTER

Safeway
808-329-2207
75-1027 Henry St., Kailua-Kona, HI 96740

KEAUHOU SHOPPING CENTER

KTA
808-322-2311
78-6831 Ali'i Dr., Keauhou, HI 96739

KEA'AU SHOPPING CENTER

Sure Save Supermarket
16-128 Orchidland Dr.
Kea'au HI 96749
808-966-9009

HĀWĪ

K. Takata Store
808-889-5261
54-3627 Akoni Pule Hwy., Hāwī, HI 96719

Natural Food Stores
Abundant Life Natural Foods: 808-935-7411; 292 Kamehameha Ave. Hilo, HI 96720
Island Naturals: 808-965-8322; 15-1403 Nanawale Homestead, Pāhoa, HI 96778

Island Naturals: 808-935-5533; 3030 Maka'ala St., Prince Kuhio Plaza; Hilo, HI 96720
Kona Natural Foods: 808-329-2296; 75-1000 Henry Street Kailua-Kona, HI 96740
Puna Fresh Foods: 808-966-9316; Kea'au Shopping Center; Kea'au, HI

Sweets

HILO

Big Island Candies
Owner: Allan Ikawa
808-935-8890
585 Hinano St., Hilo, HI 96720

Big Island Candies has a sales area out of Madison Ave. by way of Omotesando, a glass-walled production like the one *I Love Lucy,* and treats that are out of this world. Get to 585 Hinano St. in Hilo early in the day—before the tour groups—and nibble samples rich in local ingredients as you try to decide which of the exquisitely presented treats you'll take home. The shortbread cookies are justly famous. Try the Bien Vivente sesame and almond cookies and the golden macadamia nut brownies. As for the chocolates, betcha can't eat just one (box). They're worthy of worship.

Itsu's Fishing Supplies
808-935-8082
810 Pi'ilani St., Hilo, HI 96720

This family-owned business has been serving what many consider to be the best shave ice in Hilo—where it is called "ice shave"—for decades. It's the texture. Not too grainy, not too soft. Try it with adzuki beans if they're available.

KAILUA-KONA

Kailua Candy Company
Owners: Cathy Smoot Barrett and Robin Barrett

808-329-2522
www.kailua-candy.com
73-5612 Kauhola St., Kailua-Kona, HI
96740
Between Home Depot and Costco

The Barretts are known for carrying on a long tradition of hand-dipped chocolates (her parents, Jack and Ginny, started the business) like guava-rum truffles and Kona coffee swirls, but the macadamia nut brittle needs a shout-out, as do the ginger macadamia nut clusters enrobed in white chocolate.

Scandinavian Shave Ice
808-331-1626
75-5699 Ali'i Dr., Kailua-Kona, HI 96740

More like fluffy flavored snow than a crunchy snow cone, shave ice is a local treat. You can get as many as three flavors of syrup, so go for it and walk around with something that looks like a football fan's wig. The flavors range from vanilla to *li hing mui*. If you want a substantial treat, have a scoop of yogurt or ice cream hidden in the middle.

Tropical Dreamin'
Would you plan a trip around ice cream? On the Big Island, you should at least add it to your "To Taste" list, because this is the land of coffee and fruits like white pineapple, poha berries, 'ohelo berries, dragon fruit, lychee, mango, passion fruit, guava, and apple banana. John and Nancy Edney start with those flavors and end up with Tropical Dreams, a superpremium ice cream, meaning it is made with cream containing 18 percent butterfat and is "low overrun" (the amount of air mixed in during the freezing process). The ice cream is rich and dense. They also make Hilo Homemade ice cream, a premium ice cream made with 16 percent butterfat with a little higher overrun. And they make gelato as well as yogurt. Chances are you'll see some of their products in the island's best restaurants because they make custom flavors for many chefs. Be on the alert for scoop shops, but the **Kohala Coffee Mill** (808-889-5577; Akoni Puli Hwy., Hāwī, HI 96719), **Daylight Donuts** (808-324-1833; 78-6831 Ali'i Dr., Suite C122, Kailua-Kona, HI 96740), and **Hilo Homemade** (41 Waiānuenue Ave., Hilo, HI 96720), are sure bets.

Wineries
Volcano

Volcano Winery
Owners: Scott and Liz Ratcliff
808-967-7479
www.volcanowinery.com
35 Pi'i Mauna Dr., Volcano, HI 96785

Using a white grape that is a cross between muscat and Grenache gris, the winery creates wines blended with local fruits for a unique island taste. They use macadamia nut honey in their signature honey wine. They ship quarter, half, and full cases.

Wine and Liquor Stores

Most grocery stores and Long's Drugs sell beer, wine, and liquor. These independent shops have knowledgeable staff and often have tastings.

Kadota's Liquor: 808-935-1802; 194 Hualalai St., Hilo, HI 96720
Kamuela Liquor: 808-885-4674; 64-1010 Māmalahoa Hwy., Waimea, HI 96743
Kona Wine Market: 808-329-9400; 75-5626 Kuakini Hwy., Kailua-Kona, HI 96740

A monument to the mystical Kauila
at Punalu'u Beach Park where
turtles swim and bask.

7

RECREATION

Fun in the Sun

With beaches, forests, jungles, lush valleys, pasturelands, rolling hills, and mountains, the Big Island offers a spectacular year-round backdrop for outdoor activities. Not surprisingly, water sports—swimming, snorkeling, scuba diving, fishing, boating, and more—are available for every level of skill, at every price. Golfing, horseback riding, and even skiing are all accessible. Hikes range from easy loops on flat ground to challenging adventures in demanding terrain. For birders, it's a cornucopia of species, many of them endangered and found nowhere else. That's just as true for gardeners; the resources are rich and varied.

Whatever you do, wear sunscreen and drink plenty of water.

BICYCLING

For the avid cyclist or the happy-go-lucky pedal pusher, the Big Island offers a variety of rides, from smooth beachside roads to rugged off-road rides. From road bike to mountain bikes, rentals are available by the hour or by the day or longer. However, you might be better off bringing your own and renting something different for a specific route, say a road bike for tackling the Kona Coast highway. You can also rent racks for your rental vehicle, a combo that lets you design your own drive 'n' pedal tour of the Big Island.

Most roads are flat or have gradual grades, with notable exceptions, such as the roads from Kawaihae to Waimea, Waimea to Hāwī, and Kailua-Kona to Hōlualoa, as well as the road up Mauna Kea. While main roads are well paved, secondary roads and back roads are often rough and narrow. A popular ride is Mana Road. It starts in Waimea and goes around Mauna Kea to the Saddle Road, more than 40 miles, much of it on packed dirt.

The Ironman Triathlon is the major cycling event. It's a 2.4-mile ocean swim near the Kailua pier, followed by a 112-mile bike race through ancient lava fields and lush forests from Kailua to Hāwī, then back, and a 26.2-mile run along the bike race route. Competitors, as many as 1,800 of them, have 17 hours to finish. The event is usually scheduled in October. If you're thinking of entering, be aware that most entrants log between 18 to 24 hours a week in training, including 7 miles of swimming, 225 miles of biking, and 48 miles of running. For more information, see www.ironman.com.

Detailed descriptions of more than two dozen of the island's best rides are available from **Peoples Advocacy for Trails Hawai'i** (808-936-4635; www.pathhawaii.org). The roster includes every area of the island, and routes for all skill levels, meaning that a family can split up—some driving and some biking—to see the same sights. The **Big Island Mountain Bike Association** (808-961-4452; www.homepages.interpac.net/mtbike) provides similarly detailed route descriptions for those who prefer to go off road. Another useful resource for cyclists is the second edition of *Mountain Biking the Hawaiian Islands* by John Alford (Ohana Publishing, Honolulu).

Bike Rentals, Repairs, and Sales

HILO

Da Kine Bike Shop (808-961-4452; www.bicyclehawaii.com), 2 Furneaux Lane, Hilo
Hilo Bike Hub (808-961-4452; www.hilobikehub.com), 318 E. Kawili St., Hilo
Mid-Pacific Wheels (808-935-6211; www.midpacificwheels.com), 1133 Manono St., #C, Hilo

KAILUA-KONA

Dave's Bike & Triathlon Shop (808-329-4522; www.bigislandweb.com/daves), 75-5669 Ali'i Dr., Kailua-Kona
HP Bikeworks (808-326-2453; www.hpbikeworks.com), Hale Hana Centre, 74-5583 Luhia St., Kailua-Kona
Hawaiian Pedals (808-329-2294; www.hpbikeworks.com), Kona Inn Shopping Village, 75-5744 Ali'i Dr., Kailua-Kona

WAIMEA

Mauna Kea Mountain Bikes (808-883-0130, 888-682-8687), P.O. Box 44672, Waimea, HI 96743

Bicycling Tours

Another option is to sign on for an organized cycling tour with a guide, a support vehicle, repair services, and hotel accommodations. There are Big Island cycling tours from budget to luxurious customized outings, often with other activities such as snorkeling, sailing, or sightseeing.

Orchid Isle Bicycling (808-327-0087; www.orchidislebicycling.com), P.O. Box 3486, Kailua-Kona, HI 96745, a local company owned by Oliver and Julia Kiel, offers daily bike tours as well as four-, five-, and six-day packages. If one of their packages doesn't work for you, they can custom-design cycling tours for as few as four people. Prices start at $1,895. Day tours are four to six hours long, and prices start at $100. Again, custom tours are available.

Other tour guides include the following:

Backroads (800-462-2848; www.backroads.com)
Bicycle Adventures (800-443-6060; www.bicycleadventures.com)
Womantours (800-247-1444; www.womantours.com)

Breathless in the Vog

If on some days you find it difficult to breathe or your eyes water and your throat's sore, blame erupting Kīlauea. The volcano emits noxious sulfur dioxide gas and other pollutants that react with oxygen and atmospheric moisture to produce volcanic smog. Other complaints associated with vog, as it is known, include a general lack of energy, flulike symptoms, and an increased susceptibility to respiratory ailments. When the trade winds are blowing, the vog moves southwest—it's been detected 1,000 miles away on Johnston Island—and west from the volcano to the Kona Coast, where it's trapped by sea breezes. Vog also reduces visibility, so use your headlights during the day.

BIRDING

That you see as many birds throughout the Big Island as you do is remarkable when you consider that experts believe fewer than two dozen original species remain of the more than 70 that occupied the Hawaiian islands before humans arrived. Since then, it's been grim. Hawaiians may have wiped out as many as 40 species before European explorers arrived in the 1770s. Today, Hawaiian birds account for almost half of all the endangered species in the United States.

You'll often see yellow caution signs depicting *nene*, which resemble Canada geese. The state bird, the *nene* is an endangered species gaining in numbers. Look for them on the slopes of Mauna Kea, Mauna Loa, and Hualālai, and in Hawai'i Volcanoes National Park, where you should be sure to take the Kipuka Puaulu Bird Preserve 1-mile loop trail.

The best season to see forest birds is late winter and springtime, and seabirds are best spotted in February and March, when they breed, through early fall. The best place to see forest birds is the **Hakalau Forest National Wildlife Refuge**, open to the public for birdwatching, pig hunting, hiking, and photography on weekends and holidays. You'll need a four-wheel-drive vehicle, and entry is off the Saddle Rd. However, before entering you must obtain a permit from the refuge management office in Hilo (808-443-2300), which also oversees the **Kona Forest National Wildlife Reserve**.

Hawaii Forest and Trail (808-331-8505, 800-464-1993; www.hawaii-forest.com) offers two daylong birding tours. The Rainforest and Dryforest Birding Adventure regularly takes birders into dryland forest on the west side of Mauna Kea and through misty forest on the northeastern slope of Mauna Loa. Birders may find *iiwi, apapane, amakihi,* and *omao* in the rain forest along the Pu'u 'ō'ō Trail and Hawai'i *amakihi* in the dry Mauna Kea Forest Preserve. The Hakalau Forest Wildlife Refuge tour takes birders a few times a year to an area not open to the general public. Look for the endangered *akepa, akiapolaau,* and Hawai'i creeper.

Victor Emanuel Nature Tours (800-328-8368; www.ventbird.com) includes the Big Island as part of their multiday statewide birding itineraries.

Other useful resources include:

The **Hawai'i Audubon Society** (www.hawaiiaudubon.com) publishes *Hawai'i's Birds,* a guide filled with color photos. They also sponsor hikes and bird-watching expeditions. The invaluable Web site provides detailed directions to areas where you are most likely to see marine, wetland, forest, and open-country birds.

A Pocket Guide to Hawai'i's Birds, by H. Douglas Pratt (Mutual Publishing) has many color photos and lists birding hot spots.

CAMPING

The Big Island offers many opportunities to get up close and personal with nature in campgrounds in national, state, and county parks.

Permits are required for camping at county parks, and reservations may be made up to a year in advance. Fees ranging from $6 for adults to $1 for children under 12 are assessed by the day. All reservations are made by campground and can be made using a credit card online at: www.ehawaii.gov/Hawaii_County/camping/exe/campre.cgi. County parks with camping facilities, which usually include grills, bathroom, and pavilions, are **Isaac Hale** in Puna, **Kolekole** and **Laupāhoehoe** on the Hāmākua coast, **Kapaʻa** and **Mahukona** in North Kohala, **Spencer** in South Kohala, **Hoʻokena** and **Miloliʻi** in South Kona, and **Punaluʻu** and **Whittington** in Kaʻu. The surrounding parks can be very busy on weekends and holidays. The campsites are often booked well in advance. Descriptions of available facilities—most are quite basic—pictures, and updates on closures, maintenance, and construction are available at: www.hawaii-county.com/parks.

State parks also require permits for camping and cabin use. Camping is allowed at **Kālōpa and McKenzie State Recreation Areas** on the Hāmākua Coast and in the Puna respectively and the **Manukā State Wayside** in the Kaʻu. There are cabins at Kālōpa and Hāpuna Beach SRAs. There's also a state site off the Saddle Rd., **Mauna Kea SRA**. Camping fees are $5 per campsite per night. Lodging fees range from $20 to $55 per night per person for a group cabin. All the cabins are very rustic. Check availability at www.hawaiistateparks .org/camping, then download a permit application. Reservations are not confirmed until payment by check or money order is received. Credit cards are not accepted.

Hawaiʻi Volcanoes National Park has drive-in campgrounds. The main campground is **Nāmakani Paio**, located off HI 11, and **Kulanaokuaiki**, located off Hilina Pali Rd.,which has two wheelchair-accessible sites, but no water. They are both free after payment of the park entry fee. Camping is available on a first-come, first-served basis. There are cabins at Nāmakani Paio, which can be booked through the Volcano House (808-967-7321; www .volcanohouse.com). Backcountry camping is by permit only, and you must register at the Kīlauea Visitor Center. There is an 8-bunk cabin at **Puʻu Uʻlaʻula** at 10,035 feet and a 12-bunk cabin at **Mokuʻaweoweo** at 13,250 feet. Both are available on a sharing, first-come, first-served basis. For details see: www.hawaii.volcanoes.national-park.com/camping.htm.

DOLPHINS

An encounter with a dolphin is a dream-of-a-lifetime experience, and one the dolphins seem to enjoy, too. However, to get the party started, you must reserve two months in advance at the **Dolphin Quest** program. Sign up for a group session or book an encounter that is just you and up to six of your guests. (If you didn't make a reservation, call. Somebody's cancellation can be your opportunity, but don't count on this.) There's also a five-hour-long program that has you shadow the trainers as they work with the dolphins. Although the program operates at the Hilton Waikoloa Village, you don't have to be a hotel guest to participate. The dolphins are about a 30-minute walk from the parking lot, and you will be charged for parking. No children younger than five. Prices start at $195, and special needs can be accommodated.

Dolphin Quest (808-886-2875; www.dolphinquest.org), Hilton Waikoloa Village, 425 Waikoloa Beach Dr., Waikoloa

FISHING

Wherever there's an opportunity to fish on the Big Island, somebody's there. At South Point, at the ocean side edge of tidal pools, off rocky promontories at beach parks and pullovers, on Coconut Island, or at where the mouth of the Wailuku River flows into Hilo Bay, people are fishing.

The big deal, however, is the big fish. Kona hosts the **International Billfish Tournament** each August, but fish are plentiful year-round. If you're not sure of how well you'll handle the water, go out in the calmer mornings. Because boats, captains, and crews come and go, it's easier to arrange an outing by using a charter company. Prices vary widely. If you do catch a record-breaking big one, it will be appear on the "Big Fish List," a weekly feature in the sports section of *West Hawaii Today* that includes species, weight, angler, skipper, boat, and date. Have the clipping framed.

Charter Services Hawaii (808-334-1881, 800-567-2650; www.konazone.com), Kailua-Kona, HI 96745

Honokōhau Marine Charters (808-329-5735, 888-566-2487; www.charterdesk.com), Honokōhau Harbor, north of Kailua-Kona

GARDENS

Hawai'i's biodiversity is nothing short of astonishing. Trying to make sense of what you see can be difficult, and a visit to one of the island's signed gardens helps.

Amy B. H. Greenwell Ethnobotanical Garden
808-323-3318
www.bishopmuseum.org
82-6188 Mamalohoa Hwy. at mile marker 110, Captain Cook, HI 96704

Part of the Bishop Museum, this fascinating garden focuses on the traditional Hawaiian uses of plants and land, and on conservation. It includes a 5-acre remnant of the prehistoric agricultural Kona field system of the *ahupua'a* of Kealakekua. The garden layout illustrates the four vegetation zones in the Kona region: coastal, dry forest, agricultural, and upland forest. Of the 200 species in the collection, 28 are endangered. Like everything the Bishop oversees, this is well presented, well signed, and well worth a visit. The suggested donation is $4. Guided tours are available on Wednesday and Friday at 1 PM; there is a $5 charge for these tours. Free, guided tours are available at 10 AM on the second Saturday of the month. Closed weekends, holidays.

Senior Discounts

Many attractions offer discounts for AARP members or anyone who is over a certain age. Be sure to ask, because these rates are not always published, and carry your membership card as well as proof of age. Don't forget to ask at hotels, rental car agencies, and elsewhere. The savings can add up. Ask about discounts for children under a certain age, too.

Hawai'i Tropical Botanical Gardens

808-964-5233
www.htbg.com
27-717 Old Māmalohoa Hwy., Papa'ikou, HI 96781

This 40-acre nonprofit collection of tropical plants from around the world is worth the price of admission. In addition to the plant and bird collections, trails in the garden lead to waterfalls, streams, and views of Onomea Bay. It's a beautiful lesson in botany for even a hard-core urbanite. Tours are self-guided, and it takes about an hour and a half to walk the loop trail that's just over a mile long. $15 for adults, $5 for children 6–16. Closed: Thanksgiving, Christmas, and New Year's Day. Open 9–5 daily (last admission at 4 PM).

Lili'uokalani Gardens

808-961-8311
Banyan Dr., Hilo, HI 96720

This public park is bordered by the rocky shoreline of the Waiākea Peninsula facing Hilo Bay and a nine-hole golf course on the other. The Japanese-style Lili'uokalani Gardens, named for the Hawaiian monarch Queen Lili'uokalani, surrounds a pond with charming footbridges and gazebos, weeping willow trees, azaleas, bamboo, and well-maintained lawns. What the park lacks in informative signage—there is none—it makes up for with atmosphere. It is very popular with local residents who use it for walking and jogging and hanging out. The gardens are just across from Coconut Island, a little island with a tiny beach, picnic tables, and pavilions. Hawaiians considered it a place of healing. (Be sure to look for the palms with markers showing the height of various tsunami.) Banyan Dr. is a pleasant walk shaded by more than four dozen banyan trees planted by celebrities, including Cecil B. DeMille in 1933. Over the years Amelia Earhart, Franklin D. Roosevelt, Louis Armstrong, and Richard Nixon were among those who planted saplings.

Manukā State Wayside Park

Māmalahoa Hwy., north of mile marker 81, near Miloli'i in the Ka'u District

This arboretum planted in the mid-19th century includes many species of native plants in a park that leads into the trails in the South Kona Forest Reserve. The park has picnic tables, but there is no drinking water.

Pua Mau Botanical Gardens

808-882-088
www.puamau.com
10 Ala Kahua, off HI 270 at mile marker 6 near Kohala Estates, Kawaihae, HI 96743

This 45-acre low-rainfall garden focuses on the use of perpetually blooming woody plants in an arid Hawaiian environment. It features a maze with over 200 varieties of hibiscus, an aviary with exotic birds, a collection of original sculptures, and spectacular views. The nonprofit gardens are dedicated to the preservation and propagation of plant life indigenous to the Big Island's arid climate. There is a self-guided tour with booklet with plant names and descriptions. Admission is $10 for adults; $8 for those over 64 and students with an ID. Open 9–4 daily.

Lush plantings mark a path at Hawai'i Tropical Botanical Gardens in Papa'ikou.

University of Hawai'i at Hilo Botanical Gardens
808-974-6200
200 W. Kāwili St., Hilo, HI 96720

The University of Hawai'i at Hilo Botanical Gardens includes a large collection of cycads, many of which can be seen in cone year-round. There's also an array of palms from around the world, including a near complete collection of endemic *loulu* palms. The gardens are open daily to the public for self-guided tours.

World Botanical Garden
808-963-5427
www.wbgi.com
At HI 19, turn at mile marker 16, Honomū, HI 96728

On 275 acres of what were once sugarcane fields, the garden contains thousands of plant species. The major feature, however, is Umauma Falls, a three-tiered, 300-foot waterfall. Admission is $13 for adults, $6 for teens aged 13–17, and $3 for children aged 5–12. Open 9–5:30 daily.

GOLF

The hazards of golfing on the Big Island are legion: smooth *pāhoehoe* lava, rough *a'a* lava, nearby humpback whales, ocean spray, rock slides, and some of the most challenging courses the world's top designers could configure. That's just on the fabled Kohala Coast, where reservations are a must. Elsewhere on the island, play on the southernmost course in the United States, on the honor system along the Hāmākua Coast, or more than 4,000 feet above sea level.

KOHALA COAST

Francis H. I'i Brown North Course
808-885-6655
www.maunalani.com
Mauna Lani Resort, Kohala Coast, HI 96743

Smooth *pāhoehoe* lava and *kiawe* groves make for challenging golf on course designed by Homer Flint and Raymond Cain as the lead architects. Carts, lessons, club rental. 18 holes, par 72, 6,913 yards. Fees: $145–210.

Francis H. I'i Brown South Course
808-885-6677
www.maunalani.com
Mauna Lani Resort Kohala Coast, HI 96743

The rough is thick and lined with both *pāhoehoe* and *a'a* lava. Avoid both if you can. Homer Flint and Raymond Cain led the design team for the course, which affords views of hump-back whales in the winter. 18 holes, par 72, 6,983 yards. Fees: $145–210.

Hāpuna Golf Course
808-880-3000, 866-774-6236
www.hapunabeachprincehotel.com
62-100 Kauna'oa Dr., Kamuela, HI 96743

Touted as environmentally sensitive by the USGA, which called it "the course of the future" in 1997, this links-style golf course is tucked into the land's natural contours. Designed by Arnold Palmer and Ed Seay, it rises from sea level to about 700 feet. Driving range, club rental, lessons, pull carts. 18 holes, par 72, 6,875 yards. Fees: $105–165.

Hualālai Golf Course
808-325-8480
www.fourseasons.com/hualalai
100 Ka'upūlehū Dr., Kailua-Kona, HI 96745

The Jack Nicklaus–designed course begins in an area of lush greenery, flows across a lava field, and ends at the Pacific shore. Restricted to resort guests and club members. 18 holes, par 72, 7,100 yards. Fees: $250.

Mauna Kea Golf Course
808-882-5400, 866-774-6236
www.maunakeabeachhotel.com
Mauna Kea Beach Hotel, 62-100 Kauna'oa Dr., Kohala Coast, HI 96743

Offering dramatic elevation changes, Mauna Kea Golf Course has beautiful panoramic views from nearly every hole. Designed by Robert Trent Jones Sr., it is undergoing a comprehensive upgrade and is expected to reopen December 2008.

Waikoloa Resort Golf—Beach Course
808-886-6060
www.waikoloagolf.com
1020 Keana Pl., Waikoloa, HI 96738

Robert Trent Jones Jr. designed this course that wends through lava flows along 'Anaeho'omalu Bay. Expect to see other Hawaiian islands year-round, and whales in season. 18 holes, par 70, 6,566 yards. Fee: $130–195.

Waikoloa Resort Golf—King's Course
808-886-7888
www.waikoloagolf.com
600 Waikoloa Beach Dr., Waikoloa, HI 96738

A Tom Weiskopf and Jay Morrish–designed Scottish links-style course, consisting of a double green, drivable par 4s, and large pot bunkers. 18 holes, par 72, 7,074 yards. Fee: $130–195.

Waikoloa Village Golf Club
808-883-9621
6801792 Melia St., Waikoloa, HI 96738

A Robert Trent Jones Jr.–designed course in the Mauna Kea foothills that overlooks the Kohala Coast. It is a favorite among local residents. 18 holes, par 72, 6,791 yards. Fee: $25–80.

KAILUA-KONA

Kona Country Club

808-322-2595

www.konagolf.com

78-7000 Ali'i Dr., Kailua-Kona, HI 96740

The Ali'i Mountain Course, designed by William Bell, Robin Nelson, and Rodney Wright, is rated four and a half stars by *Golf Digest*. It has a cool upland setting overlooking the ocean. Ancient Hawaiian rock slides run through its center. Carts, lessons, club rental. 18 holes, par 72, 6,634 yards. Fee: $97–150.

The Ocean Golf Course, designed by William Bell, is so close to the Pacific golfers are often refreshed with spray from breaking waves. The fairways are adjacent to the ocean, and most greens break toward the ocean. Carts, lessons, club rental. 18 holes, par 72, 6,748 yards. Fee: $60–165.

Makalei Hawaii Country Club

808-325-6625

72-3890 Hawai'i Belt Rd., Kailua-Kona, HI 96740

A public course designed by Richard P. Nugent with tree-lined fairways. 18 holes, par 72, 7,091 yards. Fee: $99.

VOLCANO

Volcano Golf and Country Club

808-967-7331

Pi'i Mauna Dr., off HI 11, Hawai'i Volcanoes National Park, HI 96718

A 1920s course with an updated design by Jack Snyder, this is a quiet course set on the slopes of Mauna Loa. At 4,280 feet elevation, the air is crisp, and some players insist that balls travel farther than you'd expect because the air's thinner than found at sea level. 18 holes, par 72, 6,547 yards. Fee: $65.

KA'U (SOUTH POINT) AREA

Sea Mountain Golf Course

808-928-6222

HI 11, Pāhala, HI 96777

A public course designed by Jack Snyder that is the southernmost in the United States. 18 holes, par 72, 6,416 yards Fee: $50. Credit Cards: MC, V.

HILO

Hilo Municipal Golf Course

808-959-7711

340 Ha'iha'i St., Hilo, HI 96720

A short but challenging course designed by Williard G. Wilkinson. 18 holes, par 71, 6,325 yards. Fee: $45. No credit cards.

Naniloa Country Club
808-935-3000
120 Banyan Dr., Hilo, HI 96720

A flat tree-lined course designed by Alexander Kahapea with a lake on the second and fifth holes. 9 holes, par 35, 2,875 yards. Fee: $45.

HĀMĀKUA COAST

Hāmākua Country Club
808-935-3000
HI 19, Honokaʻa, HI 96727

A semiprivate executive-length course designed by Frank Anderson in 1927. It is one of the oldest on the island. There are hills, but no carts. 9 holes, par 33, 2,490 yards. Fee: $20. No credit cards.

Waimea Country Club
808-885-8053
47-5220 Māmalahoa Hwy., Waimea, HI 96796

Scottish-style course with bent grass greens designed by John Sanford, who laid it out on up-country pastureland where ironwood trees, not waves and lava flows, are the challenge. It can be cooler than coastal courses, so bring a sweater or, better yet, a waterproof jacket. 18 holes, par 72, 661 yards. Fee: $45.

Hiking on the Big Island presents some specific challenges beyond the need to wear sunscreen and dark sunglasses, and to drink plenty of liquids. The heat and humidity can reduce your stamina, so don't expect to go as far and as fast as you might normally. Slopes are often extremely eroded and the vegetation poorly anchored, offering no help when you grab it for support. It gets dark fast in the tropics, so plan your outing accordingly. If you're not carrying bottled water, treat all drinking water, because much of the fresh water is contaminated with leptospirosis, a bacteria. Watch out for big centipedes. Their bite isn't serious, but it hurts.

Hawai'i suffers from the many nonnative invasive plants and animals that have been introduced over the years. To reduce the likelihood of spreading these from an area where you have been hiking to a place they've yet to infest, wash your boots or shoes at the end of hike before you trek anywhere else.

Many pleasant walks in Hawai'i Volcanoes National Park are on paved paths.

HELICOPTER TOURS

The best way to get the full impact of Kīlauea erupting or the wild verdant lushness of the Hāmākua Coast is to take a helicopter tour. It's a splurgeworthy experience. **Blue Hawaiian** (808-961-5600, 800-754-2583; www.bluehawaiian.com) is the operation of choice. More importantly, the Federal Aviation Administration has given the maintenance crew a Diamond Award every year from 1998 to 2007. The tour to take is the two-hour-long "Big Island Spectacular," which costs $440-495 per person depending on the helicopter used, or $380-427 if booked online. The tour departs from Waikoloa Heliport, which is close to the Kohala Coast resorts, every day but Christmas. The "Circle of Fire plus Waterfalls" tour leaves from Hilo Airport and takes 45 minutes. It costs $217.80 per person, $177.72 if booked online. Both tours fly over the steaming volcano and areas destroyed by recent flows. What makes the "Spectacular" just that is the additional tour of the Kohala Mountains. From the air, you can see traces of ancient Hawaiian settlements as well as valleys with a depth you can only sense by driving the scenic coastal route.

HIKING

The Big Island offers hikes ranging from those suitable for an enthusiastic preschooler to ones that will test superfit, experienced outdoor types who can live for a week on bark and water. Thus, if you're reasonably fit and can follow a trail, you'll find many outings that you can call hikes if you want bragging rights, but which are walks where you get an aerobic workout if you go faster than a stroll. (These are my speed. No great changes in elevation, no scrambling over loose rocks or jumping down "little" 6-foot drops.) This is true particularly in **Hawai'i Volcanoes National Park,** where you can also find some of the most taxing hikes.

The park is the best area for day hikes. The Web site is www.nps.gov/havo. Before setting out, always check current volcano eruption information at 808-985-6000. The visitor center, where you can obtain helpfully detailed maps, is open from 8 to 5 daily.

The 11-mile **Crater Rim Trail** passes through rain forest and desert as it circles the Kīlauea Caldera. It is a full daylong hike but not overly strenuous.

The **Earthquake Trail** and **Waldron Ledge** walk is an 0.8-mile stroll through native plants with views of the Kīlauea Caldera. It is wheelchair accessible.

The 4-mile round-trip **Kīlauea Iki Trail** is an easy hike that passes through native forest filled with ferns and a crater. Start at the Kīlauea Iki overlook rather than the visitor center and go counterclockwise. It's supposed to take about three hours, but there are spur trails to explore, views to ogle, and a bounty of plant life to look at—I brake for ferns. The tricky part of the trail comes when you drop down into the crater, but there are steps and railings to help you get to the lava field. The contrast between the fecund forest and the barren lava of the crater floor showcases the Big Island's multiple personalities.

Feeling ambitious? Then tackle the 7.5 miles from the Mauna Loa Strip Rd. to Red Hill, a large cinder cone close to the main vent of the 1984 eruption. You ascend from 6,662 feet to just over 10,000 feet.

A well-marked trail to the Pu'u-loa petroglyph field starts at mile marker 16 on Chain of Craters Rd. It's less than 2 miles round-trip. There's a pullout for parking.

Outside the park, the **Donkey Hike** down to Onomea Bay is strenuous, but the views are great. To find the trail, start at the Hilo end of the Onomea Bay Scenic Dr. It's a well-

In North Kohala, horses occupy fields with spectacular views.

marked turnoff from Māmalahoa Hwy. to Old Māmalahoa Hwy. Pass Hawai'i Tropical Botanical Garden; go past its parking lot. On the opposite side of the road, just beyond the end of the fencing, you will see a small sign and a rough trail descending down the right side of the road. Do not attempt this trail if it is raining or has been raining.

A very easy amble of less than a mile is at the Mauna Lani Resort, which has preserved many sites of historical and archeological interest. The path across a lava field is paved, and you'll see ancient fishponds that are still in use.

Other resources:

Hawai'i Trails: Walks, Strolls and Treks on the Big Island by Kathy Morey (Wilderness Press) sets out a variety of outings classified by difficulty. The maps and trail notes are helpful.

The venerable **Hawaiian Trail and Mountain Club** is based on O'ahu, but it has a wealth of information on Big Island hikes on its Web site, www.htmclub.org.

USGS Topographical maps are available from **Hilo's Basically Books** (808-961-0144, 800-903-6277; www.basicallybooks.com).

The **Sierra Club** has a chapter, the **Moku Loa Group**, on the Big Island (www.hi.sierra club.org).

The **Audubon Society** (www.hawaiiaudubon.com) sponsors bird-watching hikes.

Hawaiian Walkways (808-775-0372, 800-457-7759; www.hawaiianwalkways.com) and **Hawaii Forest and Trails** (808-331-8505, 800-464-1993; www.hawaii-forest.com) offer menus of guided hikes. Including gear and snacks, prices start at $95. Both operators offer customized hikes. Because I'm not a regular hiker, I appreciate a guide. I find I see more and have a richer experience if I'm not worrying about where I'm going in an area I don't know.

HORSEBACK RIDING

Cowboy culture colors the Big Island, where it is *paniolo* culture, after the Spanish and Mexican cowpokes brought in by Captain George Vancouver in the 1800s. He'd given cattle to King Kamehameha, and the beasts, running wild, were damaging forested areas until rounded up. It was tough work, and the cowhands were among the best anywhere. Eben Parker Low, who managed the Pu'u-hue Ranch in Kohala, decided to prove that, and in 1908, he sent Archie Ka'au'a, Jack Low, and Ikua Purdy to participate in Wyoming's Cheyenne Frontier Days, a kind of cattle ranchers' Olympics. Purdy won the steer roping championship and put Hawaiian *paniolo* on the map. The others took third and sixth place.

Riding continues to be a magnificent way to see the Big Island. All rides require advance reservations, and there are often age and weight restrictions. Most of the ranches will create custom rides for special celebrations, such as proposals or honeymoons. Yeee-haw!

Cowboys of Hawai'i (808-885-5006; www.cowboysofhawaii.com), Waimea. Rides cover some of the 175,000 acres of the Parker Ranch. They also offer wagon rides and ATV tours. Prices start at $79.

Dahana Ranch (808-885-0057, 888-399-0057; www.dahanaranch.com), Waimea, offers rides across a working ranch owned and operated by third-generation Hawaiian cowboy Harry Nakoa. Their round-up ride gives you a taste of working the herd. Prices start at $60 per person.

King's Trail Rides (808-323-2388; www.konacowboy.com), Kealakekua. Their 2-mile ride to Kealakekua Bay, and out to the Captain Cook monument on the north shore, is mostly downhill. Of course, there's snorkeling once you get there, and it's some of the best on the island. Prices start at $130.

Na'alapa Stables (Kakua Ranch 808-889-0022; Waipi'o Valley 808-775 0419; www.naalapastables.com), North Kohala. The open-range rides cross a 12,000-acre ranch in North Kohala or traverse Waipi'o Valley. Prices start at $68 per person.

Paniolo Adventures (808-889-5354; www.panioloadventures.com), North Kohala. These folks know their customer base and conduct a nothing-faster-than-a-walk "City Slicker" ride, which, like others on their menu, explores part of the 11,000-acre Ponoholo Ranch. Prices start at $69.

Waipi'o on Horseback (808-775-7291, 877-775-7291; www.waipio.homestead.com), Honoka'a, leads you along the valley floor to explore this historic area of farms, streams, and waterfalls. Vans take you into the valley, where you meet your mount. Prices start at $85.

Waipi'o Ridge Stables (808-775-1007, 877-757-1414; www.waipioridgestables.com), Honoka'a, rides out along the top edge of the valley. Their five- to six-hour ride includes swimming in a waterfall pond. Prices start at $85 per person.

HUNTING

On the Parker Ranch, there is **year-round game hunting** for Polynesian boar, Spanish goat, Vancouver bulls, and Axis deer, and an upland game bird season from October through February. Meat handling and caping is included with the hunts. Mounts can be arranged by request. All this can be expensive. A hunter education card is required to purchase a Hawai'i hunting license. A current license from any state may be used to purchase a Hawai'i preserve license. For more information, call 808-960-4148. For a rundown of state regulations, go to www.state.hi.us/dlnr/dcre/know.htm.

SKIING

Yes. You can. *Mauna Kea* means "White Mountain" in Hawaiian, and that's where the action is. There are 2-mile runs with 2,500 to 4,500 feet of vertical per run. That comes with panoramic views that often extend to Maui. Snowboarding and cross-country skiing are also available, conditions permitting. **Ski Guides Hawaii** (808-885-4188; www.skihawaii .com) offers tours for groups with a minimum of three people, with all equipment provided. Prices per person start at $250.

SPAS

More than being relaxed, you want to be reduced to a human noodle. No need to get tense finding a treatment. Some spas have offerings so extensive that the temptation is to check into the massage room rather than your room.

KOHALA COAST

Fairmont Orchid
808-885-2000, 800-441-1414
www.fairmont.com
Open: Daily
Reservations: Suggested

The Spa without Walls is just what it says: 10 private outdoor waterfall huts, five at the ocean's side, and three indoor treatment rooms. The signature Awa Earth & Fire treatment begins with traditional *lomi lomi* massage with warm coconut oil and ends with Hawaiian medicinal herbs compressed into the skin with a warm lava stone.

Four Seasons Resort Hualālai
808-325-8000, 800-332-3442
www.fourseasons.com
Open: Daily
Reservations: Suggested

The signature hot-rock massage employs hot and cold basalt stones to help restore balance. The stones are left outside at night to absorb the moon's energy.

Mauna Lani Resort
808-881-7922
www.maunalani.com
Open: Daily
Reservations: Yes

Indoors, outdoors, and in the sauna, it's all about Lava Love. The Lava Flow body treatment detoxifies. Products are made with lava. The sauna is lava. Gotta love the lava.

Waikoloa Beach Marriott Resort
808-886-8191
Open: Daily
Reservations: Yes

The resort's Mandara Spa offers the Elemis Aromastone massage, which uses warm stones and aromatherapy oils to reduce stress while increasing blood and lymph flow with the goal of balance.

KAILUA-KONA

Hawaii Healing Ohana
808-331-1050
www.hawaiihealingohana.com
Open: Tuesday–Saturday
75-5799 Aliʻi Dr., Kailua-Kona, HI 96740

Located in the Aliʻi Sunset Place behind Lava Java, this spa gets the local vote for best spa and kudos from *Forbes Traveler*. The available massage techniques include reiki, craniosacral, and *lomi lomi.* They custom-blend therapeutic aromatherapy massage oils to help heal what ails you.

HILO

Banyan Massage Hale
808-969-1044
71 Banyan Drive #115, Hilo, HI 96720
Open: Daily
Reservations: Yes

I have fallen asleep on the massage table here during the two-hour Relaxation Massage, which is described as an eclectic blend of massage styles including Swedish and *lomi lomi.* Formerly known as Tranquil Waters Massage, this unpretentious place, located in the Hilo Hawaiian Hotel, has therapists who can feel what needs to be fixed.

Most county beach parks have pavilions so you can get out of the sun.

Pay attention to signs in beach areas of the Big Island.

TENNIS

Most of the Kohala Coast resorts have tennis courts. Friends have praised the 10-court facility at the **Fairmont Orchid.** Call 808-885-2000 for reservations. In Kailua-Kona, the **Keauhou Beach Resort** has six courts. Call 808-322-3441. There are 20 county parks with more than 40 well-maintained free tennis courts, half of them lighted. Call the **Department of Parks & Recreation** (808-961-8311) for courts near you or print out the list available at: www.co.hawaii.hi.us/databook_98/Table%207/7.35.pdf before you leave home. It's from 1998, but tennis courts are unlikely to move.

WATER SPORTS

Beaches

You want white sandy beaches? Don't be dissuaded by the Big Island's reputation for lacking this attraction central to any Hawaiian holiday. You need to know where to look and, sometimes, be willing to walk a bit. Your efforts will be rewarded. Look for signs that say BEACH ACCESS or for well-worn paths leading in the right direction. Not all beaches have lifeguards. If you're in doubt about the water conditions, don't go in. All the Kohala Coast resorts have beaches, some of them man-made. If you're not a guest and want to sun on their sand, remind the guards that you have the right of public access. Virtually all beaches in Hawai'i are public.

To check daily safety conditions at many popular state and county beaches, go to www.hawaiibeachsafety.org, which is a cooperative effort by the Hawai'i Lifeguard Association and five other state and local government groups. You can sign up for daily e-mail, RSS feeds, cell phone, and SMS messaging on Big Island beach conditions.

KOHALA COAST AREA

'Anaeho'omalu Beach
Public access at the Waikoloa Beach Marriott Resort

Almost everybody calls this marvelously long, curved beach fringed with palm trees A-Bay. It's popular with locals as well as visitors, and because of its proximity to the Waikoloa resort area, it can be busier than others during the week. If you want to do more than just sit in the sun, there are trails with signs for a self-guided tour through ancient fishponds and ruins. On the north end of the beach there's a concession stand that rents boogie boards and snorkel and windsurfing equipment. While the beach has facilities, you can also eat at the hotel or buy food to go at the resort shops.

In Kalapana, the sea-soaked lava is good for sunning but not swimming.

Hāpuna Beach
Off HI 19 near mile marker 69

Hāpuna's white sands have earned it a reputation as one of Hawai'i's finest beaches and indeed, one of the top beaches in the United States. It may well be the beach of your dreams, half a mile or so long, with good swimming when there's no surf. There's a protected cove at the north end that's perfect for young children. Dive instructors also use it for classes. There's good snorkeling at the south end. The afternoons can get breezy, and jellyfish can be a problem. During the week, the beach can be fairly quiet, but on weekends and holidays, it's a scene. Facilities include restrooms, showers, camping, and cabins.

Kekaha Kai State Park
Off HI 19, north of Keāhole-Kona International Airport between mile markers 90 and 91. There should be a sign KEKAHA KAI STATE PARK at the mouth of an unpaved road.

At the end of the access road, you'll find pretty Mahai'ula Beach. With salt and pepper sand, it's the most used beach in the park, and the easiest to reach. There are restrooms, picnic tables, grills, and shade. A 30-minute hike north via a trail that passes several ponds and crosses a lava field brings you to white-sand dunes and Makalawena Beach.

Mahukona Beach Park
Off HI 270 turn toward the ocean, or *makai,* at mile marker 14 and follow the road to the water. When you're almost at the shore, take a right (you'll see the pavilion).

This is an abandoned Kohala Sugar Company harbor. There's no beach, but if it's calm, and you want to snorkel, you can descend into the clear water via a new-ish ladder on an old

The county beach parks in Hilo have protected waters that are good for families.

cement landing. You see lots of fish and abandoned industrial equipment. It can be tricky getting back up the ladder, so the usual rule applies: If you're in doubt, don't go in. It's a pleasant enough place for a picnic, or a break from driving along the coast highway, but not a destination unless you want to glimpse some remains of Big Sugar. Restrooms, showers, picnic tables, pavilions. No drinking water.

Mauna Kea Beach
Off HI 19 at the Mauna Kea sign

Of course the beach at one of the finest resorts would be as close to perfect as possible. Also known as Kauna'oa Beach, public access is controlled by limiting cars to 30 designated spots, so arrive early. Restroom, showers.

Old Kona Airport Beach
Off HI 19 at Makala Blvd.

A family beach complete with ballparks, shade pavilions, ample parking, restrooms, and showers. Rarely crowded during the week, there can be a small surge at sunset. In January 2008, the County of Hawai'i took ownership of the facility from the state, which has been criticized for inadequate maintenance almost since the park opened in 1976, six years after the airport closed. The county says it will increase staff and that maintenance will improve over time.

Spencer Beach Park
Off HI 270 between mile markers 2 and 3

Spencer Beach is south of Kawaihae Harbor, on the shore below Pu'ukoholā Heiau, built by Kamehameha I. This is a fine, fine family beach that's very popular with local residents and visitors. A long shallow reef directly offshore provides good protection from the winds and waves. Swimming and snorkeling are excellent. There are lots of shade trees and lifeguards, and the facilities include grills, picnic tables, and a camping area. Parking is fairly easy.

KAILUA-KONA

Kahalu'u Beach Park
Ali'i Dr. between Kailua-Kona and Keauhou

A premier beach for kids because it's safe and there's usually a lifeguard on duty. It's also a prime snorkeling spot because the sheltered bay harbors so many kinds of fish. To see them, go out about 30 or 40 yards. There's a good chance you'll see sea turtles. Food is available at concession stands and oftentimes from lunch trucks. There are also snorkel and other equipment rentals available nearby. Restrooms, showers.

Kamakahonu Beach
Kailua Pier, Kailua-Kona

The protected waters off the slivers of beach surrounding the pier make this a sweet little family beach with decent snorkeling. It is, however, in the heart of tourist town, which is good or bad, depending on your perspective.

Magic Sands Beach
Ali'i Dr. between Kailua-Kona and Keauhou

This white-sand beach is also known as White Sands Beach and Disappearing Sands Beach. Tidal shifts or strong surf can suck it away overnight, but it always returns, as will you. Located on Ali'i Drive just south of Kailua-Kona, often crowded, it's good for boogie boarding and is a popular sunset spot. Restrooms, showers, difficult parking, lifeguard.

South of Kailua-Kona

Papakōlea Beach
Off HI 11, follow South Point road 12 miles south. When you come to a fork, go left until you arrive at an unofficial "visitor center." You can park here free, but you may be asked to pay or for a donation by scammers. Your call.

The big attraction at this beach is the presence of olivine, which means the sand is green. Consider that word *olivine* . . . and rein in expectations of emerald or grass-green sand. The trail to the beach starts at the boat ramp near the parking, and it is hard to spot. Once you're on it, walk 3 miles, usually into the wind, until you reach the beach. There's a scramble with some manageable drops at the end to actually get down to the beach. It's not a good idea to swim here. There are no facilities, and no shade, so bring water for the hike in and out.

Pu'uhonua o Hōnaunau

Hōnaunau
Many visitors come here because of the national park's cultural and historical significance. But it has good swimming and snorkeling near the boat launch, so bring your beach gear when you visit. Charcoal and picnic tables, restrooms, drinking fountain. Open 8–5. $5 per vehicle—seven days; $3 per individual—seven days.

If you swim at the Punalu'u black sand beach, you may meet sea turtles in the bay.

KAʻU (SOUTH POINT AREA)

Punaluʻu Black Sand Beach
Near Nāʻālehu; off HI 11, follow signs for Sea Mountain Resort
This is the island's most accessible black-sand beach. The sand is truly black, and the contrast with green palms and translucently blue/green water creates a vision you wouldn't accept as real unless you saw it with your own eyes. The area's justly famous for the presence of sea turtles that nest here. If the water's calm, swim in the bay, but leave the turtles alone. Restrooms, showers, camping, some food, drinks available.

PUNA

Ahalanui Park
Off HI 137, near mile marker 10

A spring-fed warm-water pool separated from the ocean by a man-made wall and an all-natural inlet. There are ladders leading into the geothermal pool, which is usually very calm even when the ocean beyond is rough. It's surrounded by palm trees, and you can look out into the ocean while fish swim around you. It's a bit surreal and occasionally smells of sulfur. Like the Waiʻōpae Ponds, be careful if you have cuts or skin conditions. There have been problems with bacterial contamination, so heed posted signs or check with the lifeguard. Restrooms, showers, picnic tables, grills, shade, lifeguard.

Isaac Hale Beach Park
Off HI 137, near mile marker 11

This is a very local park, meaning you may not feel totally welcomed. But if you're exploring the Puna, it is good to know it has restrooms and, on the busy weekends, lunch trucks catering to folks launching their boats or hanging out in the shade. Waves make for better surfing than swimming.

Kapoho Tide Pools
Off III 137 at Kapoho-Kai Rd. near mile markers 9, then right at Hoʻolaiʻi Rd., which leads to the coast via Waiʻōpae Rd.

This area is marked by spring-fed pools. Many are in backyards, but the big Waiʻōpae Ponds are on public property. The waters are calm, the swimming is easy, and the teeming marine life makes for good snorkeling, but these large ponds can get crowded on the weekend. If you have open cuts or a skin condition like psoriasis, don't go in. No facilities.

Kehena Beach
Off HI 137, near mile marker 19

If you've never seen a naked human frolicking in the surf, this is where you might be able to. For those who prefer bathing suits, the vibe is tolerant, and the scene is rather sweet. Expect to encounter drumming circles and what I think was a group of ecstatic dancers. The beach is below the turnout by the roadside. The path is easy to spot at the left end of the stone wall, and it's quite steep, painfully so if muddy. Stay out of the water if the surf is high. No facilities. Lock your car.

HILO

Hilo Bay Beach Park
Fronting downtown Hilo

Hilo Bay is a popular site for the traditional Hawaiian sport of canoe racing. Teams practice early in the morning and in the late afternoons. It's a nice place to sit and absorb some local culture. Weekends can be crowded.

Leleiwi Beach Park, Richardson Ocean Beach Park, Onekahakaha Beach
Kalaniana'ole Ave., about 3 miles east of downtown Hilo

These three beaches mesh together along the irregular lava coastline of Hilo Bay. None are typical picture-postcard beaches, but they're very popular with local people, and kids like them because the waters are calm and the tide pools rich in things to see. At lunchtime, you'll spot people driving in with to-go bags to enjoy a quick meal by the water. All these beaches have restrooms, showers, picnic facilities, lifeguards, and ample weekday parking. The surface water at Leleiwi can be chilly because of freshwater springs, but this doesn't discourage fish and other marine life from making this bay a good snorkeling spot. The beach itself is tiny, but it is all you need for getting in and out of the water. Richardson features a cove protected by a lava rock breakwater that sea turtles frequent, lots of tide pools for children to explore with adults, and good snorkeling. Families with young children head to Onekahakaha, which features a large shallow, sand-bottomed ocean pool protected by a boulder breakwater. It is one of the safest shoreline swimming spots in the area. However, beyond the breakwater, the offshore currents are dangerously, sometimes fatally, strong. High winter surf can flood the park.

Boating & Cruises

Being on an island almost dictates that you should get out on the water. And it is easy enough to do on half-day cruises—one in the morning, one in the afternoon—most of them on the Kona side. The offerings have some similarities: Meals or snacks are provided. Snorkeling and other equipment is provided. If you want to upgrade to scuba diving, you usually can for an additional fee. Afternoon outings are slightly less expensive. Advance online bookings merits a slight discount. Custom itineraries are available, as are private group voyages. Whale-watching excursions are available from December to April when the humpbacks are in local waters. Sunset cruises may sound hokey, but they're fun. Always call ahead for departure times and weather conditions.

KAILUA-KONA

Atlantis Submarine
800-548-6262
www.atlantisadventures.com/kona.cfm

This is very cool, even though you might roll your eyes at the thought of a 35-minute dive that takes you through a 25-acre coral reef teeming with marine life on a high-tech submarine. Once you're in this magical world, the eye-rolling stops. You're too busy taking everything in. Add on another 35 minutes for a to-and-fro shuttle bus ride. There are three dives a day. Children must be at least 3 feet tall for this trip. Prices start at $80 per adult, $40.50 per child.

Body Glove Cruises
808-326-7122, 800-551-8911
www.bodyglovehawaii.com

The *Body Glove*, a 65-foot catamaran certified for 149 passengers, runs half-day cruises to Pawai Bay, a marine sanctuary. They offer round-trip transportation from the Waikoloa resorts for an extra fee. Prices start at $73 per adult, $53 for children 6–17.

Captain Zodiac
808-329-3199
www.captainzodiac.com

Captain Zodiac has a fleet of inflatable 24-foot Zodiacs powered by twin outboard motors. You sit on the side pontoons, a maximum of 16 per trip. The ride from Honokōhau Harbor to Kealekakua Bay can be an adventure in itself. Zodiacs are terrific fun, but if you have history of back trouble, this might not be the cruise for you. Prices start at $90 per adult, $75 for children ages 4–12.

Fair Wind Cruises
808-322-2788, 800-677-9461
www.fair-wind.com

Fair Wind Cruises has added the luxury catamaran *Hula Kai* to its offerings. The five-and-a-half-hour morning and afternoon cruises are upscale, from the smoothness of the ride to the food served. The afternoon cruise includes a sunset barbeque, which means departure is later in the day. These trips are restricted to those 18 and over with the exception of whale-watching season, when the minimum age is 8. Prices start at $109 per adult, $69 for children 4–12. *Hula Kai* trips start at $125.

Kamanu Charters
808-329-2021, 800-348-3091
www.kamanu.com

This cruise is aboard a 36-foot-long catamaran that sails from Honokōhau Harbor to Pawai Bay, which means less intrusive noise so you can hear the water and the wind. It can carry 24 people. Prices start at $80 per adult, $50 for children 12 and under.

Sea Quest
808-329-7238
www.seaquesthawaii.com

Sea Quest offers what they call the "eXpress Adventure" three times a day for those who are short of time. Two leave in the morning. It's a two-and-a-half-hour trip rather than a full half-day, and the last one leaves at 1:30 PM, so you can squeeze it in before a night flight. There's no alcohol on any Sea Quest trip. Prices start at $89 per adult ($64 for the shorter trip).

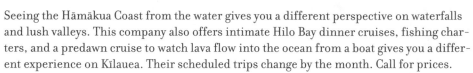

HILO

Lava Ocean Adventures
808-990-0553
www.lavaocean.com
All trips depart from Hilo's Wailoa River boat ramp

Seeing the Hāmākua Coast from the water gives you a different perspective on waterfalls and lush valleys. This company also offers intimate Hilo Bay dinner cruises, fishing charters, and a predawn cruise to watch lava flow into the ocean from a boat gives you a different experience on Kīlauea. Their scheduled trips change by the month. Call for prices.

Waʻakaulua
808-938-5717
www.waakaulua.com

If the wind dies down, expect to paddle this waʻakaulua, or double-hull Hawaiian sailing canoe. The usual trip is three hours, but the starting place varies—Hilo, Kailua-Kona, Puʻakō, or Kawaihae—depending on sea conditions—and you can arrange longer or overnight excursions. The captain, Kiko Johnston-Kitazawa, has a vast knowledge of the local waters and shores. Prices start at $100 per person with a minimum of four per trip.

Kayaking

On the Big Island, it's ocean kayaking or no kayaking at all. And for ocean kayaking, Kealakekua Bay is the place because the water's calm, the spinner dolphins ever-present, and, as an added bonus, the snorkeling never fails to amaze. It's about a mile each way to the Captain Cook Monument from the main launch, but your mileage may vary, depending on how much you want to paddle about. The downside is that it can be a bit of a kayak-jam unless you get there early or late enough for sunset. There are other good places; one favorite is the Keauhou Bay area, going south. Or launch at Kohala beaches such as the Old Kona Airport. Hilo Bay is nice as well. However, the usual warnings apply: Only paddle when it's calm, and if you have doubts, stay out.

Many ocean sport companies rent kayaks as well as other gear for water and beach fun. Rentals usually include paddles, backrests, life vests, gear bags, leash, dry bags, cooler, a car rack, and suggestions on where to go.

Aloha Kayak
808-322-2868, 877-322-1444
www.alohakayak.com
79-7428 Māmalahoa Hwy., Honalo, HI 96750

Single rentals start at $35 for 24 hours to $160 weekly; tandems are $60–210. Guided tours start at $59 per adult, $29.50 per child. They have glass kayak tours that start at $30 per adult for an hour and can provide custom tours. Online reservations accepted.

Hawaiʻi Pack and Paddle
808-328-8911
www.hawaiipackandpaddle.com
87-3187 Honu Moe Rd., Captain Cook, HI 96704

Betsy Morrigan offers day trips and overnights up to a week long that combine camping, B&B stays, hiking, and snorkeling with kayaking. The trips can be fully customized, and prices start at $91.25 per person for one-day outings with a minimum of four. Children 3–12 half price. Custom trips with camping start at $295 per person per day; with B&B stays, $320. Equipment rental is also available at $35 per day for a single, $50 for a tandem, with a three-day minimum.

Kona Boys
808-324-1234
www.konaboys.com
79-7539 Māmalahoa Hwy., Kealakekua, HI 96750

Single kayak rentals start at $47 for 24 hours to $150 for the week; tandems are $67–275. Pricing varies on tours, which include group overnight camping trips and custom tours. No online reservations.

Scuba Diving

If you're a scuba diver, you'll need to show your card to local shops if you want to rent equipment, fill tanks, or go on a charter dive. The Big Island, with its clear water and abundant marine life, is an unparalleled place to earn your PADI scuba or open-water certification, or if you are certified, refresh your skills, learn new ones like night diving, or explore special dive areas. These operators focus on scuba diving and certification, but they also offer introductory dives to those without experience or certification.

One of the best experiences you may ever have after dark is a night dive among manta rays. If you've never made a dive before and don't plan to again, this is the dive to take. Manta rays are graceful sea creatures. Their side or pectoral fins have evolved into triangular wings with spans reaching up to 14 feet across, suggesting the sweep of a dancer's fluid skirts. Most of the time the rays can be found from Keauhou Bay north to the waters off the Kona International Airport at Keāhole. The agreed-upon etiquette is to give the manta rays their space. They'll reward you for it with flips, dips, turns, and wonderful improbable moves. They get disconcertingly up close and personal because nobody told them to give you your space. Relax and flow with the show. Jack's has manta ray dives every night but Tues. and Sat.

Jack's Diving Locker (808-329-7585, 800-345-4807; www.jacksdivinglocker.com) 75-5813 Ali'i Dr., Kailua-Kona, HI 96740

Nautilus Dive Center (808-935-6969; www.nautilusdivehilo.com) 382 Kamehameha Ave., Hilo, HI 96720

Snorkeling

To come to Hawai'i and not snorkel is to miss out on one of the Big Island's great pleasures. If you're not much of a swimmer, this may make you an enthusiast. It's easy, and you don't need to splurge on a boat trip to gain access to special hidden places. If you can swim and all you want to do is look down and see fish, you need to wear sunblock and a T-shirt to protect your back from a vacation-ruining sunburn more than you need formal lessons.

When you rent gear, dive shop attendants can tell you enough to get you started. Or you can watch other snorkelers to see how they do it. The big caution is that because the fins give you much more propulsion than your feet ever could, and you don't move your head or arms much, you can find yourself going farther than you would swimming without getting as tired. Suddenly, you're far from where you started. My safety precaution when starting out is to set a course parallel to the shore. I figure that way I can always get to land rather than heading out and exceeding my limits. And while that's the big argument for going out on a snorkel cruise—you can go into deeper or more varied waters—truly you can have a magical experience just by renting equipment and wading in at the right places. Some are better than others at different times of year. Ask at a dive shop which areas are best for the season and what the conditions are like.

 Kealakekua Bay State Underwater Park in Kailua-Kona is the best place to snorkel, but it can get crowded unless you're there early in the morning.

KOHALA
ʻAnaehoʻomalu Bay, Hāpuna Beach, Ka-paʻa Beach County Park, Mahukona Beach County Park, Mauna Kea Beach, the **Puakō area** (it can be difficult to find the beach access paths, so look for worn-down grass rather than signs), and **Spencer Beach County Park**

KAILUA-KONA
Kahaluʻu Beach Park, Kekaha Kai State Park, Magic Sands Beach, Pāwai Bay, and **Puʻuhonua O Hōnaunau** in Hōnaunau Bay

For renting beach equipment like masks, fins, and snorkels and other beach toys like boogie boards, **Snorkel Bob**'s is a statewide institution. He's easy: Rent on one island, return on another, which can be a real timesaver if your plans include other islands. He's cheap: Weekly scuba gear packages start around $10. Masks with corrective lenses are available. Pony up; they're worth every cent. There are two locations on the Big Island, both in Kailua-Kona: 73-4976 Kamanu St. (808-329-0771) and 75-5831 Kahakai St. (808-329-0770). You can reserve gear online in advance: www.snorkelbob.com.

Hotels and resorts may rent equipment as well, but the prices are higher. Sporting goods stores and retailers like Costco and Wal-Mart sell equipment at a variety of price points if you'd rather own than rent.

PUNA
The Kapoho tide pools

HILO
Leleiwi Beach County Park, Richardon's Beach County Park

Surfing Lessons
From children to people who've harbored a dream of riding waves for decades, learning to surf can be the highlight of a visit to the Big Island.

Hawai'i Lifeguard Surf Instructors (808-324-0442; www.surflessonshawaii.com; Walua Plaza, 75-159 Lunapule Rd., Kailua-Kona, HI 96740) Group, private, and custom packages available. They will also arrange surfing vacations. Prices start at $75.

Kona Boys (808-324-1234; www.konaboys.com; 79-7539 Māmalahoa Hwy., Kealakekua, HI 96750) Group, private, and multiple lessons. Prices start at $75.

Ocean Eco Tours 808-324-7873, www.oceanecotours.com; 74-425 Kealakehe Pkwy., Kailua-Kona, HI 96740) Group, private, and series of lessons available. Prices start at $95.

Surfer Bear Hawai'i (808-936-3654; www.surferbearhawaii.com; Kahalu'u Beach Park, Kailua-Kona, HI 96740) Group, private, or multiple lessons. Prices start at $85.

Surf Board Rentals

Rates to start around $25 a day, with weekly rates in the $100 range.

Pacific Vibrations (808-329-4140; 75-5702 Likana Lane, Kailua-Kona, HI 96740)

Whale-Watching

There are whales in Big Island waters year-round, but if you want to see humpbacks, the season is December through April. No matter what tour operators say, there's no way to guarantee you'll see whales. It's not as if the whales are getting paid to show up on time. However, chances are good you'll see them. These two operators run tours all year.

Capt. Dan McSweeney's Whale Watch (808-322 0028, 888-942-5376; www.ilove whales.com; Holualoa, HI 96725) Captain Dan McSweeney began his love affair with whales in the early 1970s. Tours aboard a custom-designed craft depart from Honokōhau Harbor. Prices start at $79.50.

Living Ocean Adventures (808-325-5556; www.livingoceanadventures.com; 72-1085 Pu'u Kala Rd., Kailua-Kona, HI, 96740) Captain Tom Bottrell's passion is the outgrowth of a 1975 whale and dolphin study trip. From May through November, he also runs lines for sportfishing from his boat, a 31-foot Bertram Sportfisherman. Prices start at $75. No credit cards.

8

Shopping

Island Style

For an island where the natural wonder is the main attraction, it's easy to be distracted by the shops—both everyday and extraordinary—on the Big Island. Kailua-Kona and Hilo, the two population centers, both have rich retail offerings. Hilo has been a trading center since 19th-century whaling crews walked the streets. In Kailua-Kona, growth took off in the 20th century. In between, there are small towns, each with a main street lined with shops that once catered to agricultural or industrial workers. With wooden sidewalks and false-front buildings, many look like something out of a classic Western movie, except for the palm trees and the Pacific vistas. No matter the location, old-time retail offered a mix of useful and more frivolous items, clothes for work and for show.

Retail today now includes boutiques, galleries, old-fashioned family-owned general stores, up-to-date chain-owned department stores, and specialized outlets catering to the special needs of those drawn to the Big Island to cycle, hike, or enjoy a variety of water sports.

Few are discrete in their offerings. A shop may stock delicate ceramics made down the road and a careful selection of sportswear best suited for the rough 'n' tumble action of a resort dining room. Hmmm, a boutique. As you look around, you'll find a few jars of jam made within walking distance. And the furnishings you thought were for display, they're for sale as well, so maybe it's an antiques store. If only there were fishing tackle and snacks, it would be easy to decide it is a general store.

We've tried to categorize stores as best we can. Depending on what you find inside, you may feel a boutique is really a gallery or a gallery is a crafts shop. To each his or her own. What we've done is concentrate on places that reflect a personality or a sensibility. We've sought quality, even in tropical kitsch, and realized that some of our favorite keepsakes have been everyday items like a keychain made special because of a design or materials that remind us constantly of a special place.

Good Hawaiian crafts are expensive. A Hawaiian quilt created locally takes months to design and stitch. Given the amount of work, a price tag in the low five figures is reasonable. A Hawaiian-style quilt fabricated overseas using a pattern and partially machine stitched costs much less but may still seem expensive.

If you like an item, don't assume that it is locally made based on price or the name on the door. Ask. There's been a noticeable increase in the number of souvenir and gift items that would be familiar to anybody who has explored night markets in Phuket or Bali. The tie-dyed sarongs with patterns of smiling, leaping dolphins or a stand of tall palms. The ceramics painted with banana leaves. The clothing made of wild beachin' print fabrics.

The covered sidewalks in Honoka'a shield shoppers from sun and rain but not temptation.

The oh-so-Zen dinnerware. The vintage textiles circa last year. You may have already hauled these home from other destinations.

Most stores keep Monday through Saturday hours. Many are open Sunday as well. But the variations on hours and closing days are many, so if you decide to make a special trip to visit a certain shop, call ahead. Shops in the smaller towns are most likely to have idiosyncratic hours. Stores in Kailua-Kona along Ali'i Drive stay open late every night to accommodate after-dinner strollers. Downtown Hilo shops close earlier. Mall stores are open later. Ask if the store will ship your purchases for you. It will make life much easier flying home. If not, consider the flat-rate boxes available at every U.S. Post Office.

ANTIQUES & VINTAGE

Alan's Art & Collectibles (808-969-1554; 202 Kamehameha Ave., Hilo, HI 96720) An ever-changing, wide-ranging inventory that includes old photographs, Taisho-era Japanese household items, Hawaiian kitsch, and shabby chic island-style items. It's the perfect place to duck into during one of Hilo's daily showers, but you may find yourself staying a while.

Antiques and Orchids (808-323-9851; HI 11, Captain Cook, HI 96704) Collectibles— vintage Hawaiiana, kimono—mixed in with 19th- and early-20th-century antiques all highlighted by fresh orchids. It all hangs together beautifully, and on Saturday, high tea is served in this green building with white trim.

Discovery Antiques (808-323-2239; 81-6593 Māmalahoa Hwy., Kealakekua, HI 96704) You can't miss the red façade of this shop, which focuses on collectible and antique items that mirror the presence of many ethnic groups on the Big Island. There's often a jumble of items outside under the awning.

Honoka'a Trading Company (808-775-0808; Māmane St., Honoka'a, HI) What will you find in this collection of the unusual and the unique? If you visit often enough, probably everything your heart desires, as long as it's inanimate. Vintage ukuleles can be the starting point, and the list goes on. Dedicated hunters can spend hours here poking around for treasure, and, oftentimes, finding it.

ART

The Big Island supports a thriving art scene, and you'll find work in a wide variety of styles and materials. Check listings on gallery Web sites, in local newspapers, and on flyers for special exhibitions and events.

Ackerman Galleries (808-889-5971; www.ackermangalleries.com; Akoni Pule Hwy., Kapa'au, HI) There are two shops to the Ackerman empire. One, across from the Kamehameha statue, features gift and craft items. The jewelry is striking yet affordable. Across the street and a few blocks away, the emphasis is on pieces by local artisans that put the art in craft, as well as Gary Ackerman's paintings and prints.

Art in the Iron Works (808-935-6080; www.artintheironworks.com; 1266 Kamehameha Ave., Hilo, HI 96720) Located in the second floor of the historic Iron Works Building designed by Charles W. Dickey, one of Hawai'i's most notable architects, the gallery space mounts shows of work by artists such as Beverly Jackson, David Hubbard, Ralph Curtis Royer, and Elfie Wilkins-Nacht.

Eternal Wave Gallery (808-322-3203; 79-7407 Mālamahoa Hwy., Kainaliu, HI) An artist-owned space, the constantly changing work includes paintings, prints, ceramics, glass, jewelry, and woodwork by local artists and craftspeople.

Gallery of Great Things (808-885-7706; Parker Square, Waimea, HI) Work by local artists and artisans such as Yvonne Cheng and Kathy Long is displayed amid Hawaiian and Pacific Rim artifacts and treasures including baskets, boxes, glass art, jewelry, and vintage kimonos. You never know what to expect, but it's always worthy of attention.

Harbor Gallery (808-882-1510; www.harborgallery.biz; Kawaihae Shopping Center, CR 270, Kapaʻau, HI) There's a crisp, almost New England feel to the exterior, but inside, the work is all Hawaiian—the graphic prints of Michael Cassidy, the finally turned koa furniture by Frank Chase, Deborah Thompson's acrylic and watercolor paintings, and Joe Neil's Hawaiian playing cards. Baskets, ceramics, and jewelry round out the mix; all the elements are very fine.

Hōlualoa Gallery (808-322-8484; 76-5921 Māmalahoa Hwy., Hōlualoa, HI) A collection of paintings, jewelry, glasswork, and raku ceramics curated by owner-artists Mary and Matthew Lovein. The bright blue gallery has its own Kona coffee grown nearby.

Kim Taylor Reece Gallery (808-331-2433; 79-7412 Māmalahoa Hwy., Kainaliu, HI) Images, posters, and books celebrating *hula kahiko* by Kim Taylor Reece, the fine-arts photographer who has studied the ancient dance for 25 years.

Lavender Moon Gallery (808-324-7708; 79-7404 Māmalahoa Hwy., Kainaliu, HI) Ellen Crocker, who uses Japanese ink brush and batik techniques to create quilts and paintings, is just one of the local artists who show here. Worth a stop.

L. Zeidman Gallery (808-889-1400; www.lzeidman.com; Akoni Pule Hwy., Hāwī, HI) Larry Zeidman works in a variety of Hawaiian woods, not just koa, to create bowls, plates, and sculptures. The vases for ikebana arrangements are particularly striking, as the flat surfaces allow the grains to glow.

Parker Square in Waimea has a nice mix of shops and easy parking.

Silk Road Gallery (808-885-7474; Parker Square, Waimea, HI) It's easy to drop real money here on serious Asian art and antiques, including furniture, netsuke, lacquer ware, tansu, and samurai armor. But there are enough delights for mere mortals that it's worth a stop, even if you walk out with a lovely handmade card rather than a lovely handmade woodblock print.

Studio 7 Gallery (808-324-1335; 76-5920 Māmalahoa Hwy., Hōlualoa , HI) Printmaker Hiroki Morinoue, whose work is in the Contemporary Museum in Honolulu, the Fine Arts Museum of San Francisco, and the Mori Museum in Tokyo, owns this intimate gallery where he shows his own work with that of other local artists.

2400 Fahrenheit (808-985-8667; www.2400f.com; Old Volcano Rd., Volcano, HI) The gallery and glassblowing studio of Michael and Misato Motara is a fascinating introduction to their nationally recognized work and how they make it.

Upcountry Connection (808-885-0623; Mauna Kea Center, CR 190 at the Shell Station, Waimea, HI) An eclectic, sophisticated mix of fine art, antiques, and crafts, along with home accessories and gifts. There are koa items, traditional Hawaiian instruments, silver jewelry, and some clothing.

Volcano Art Center (808-967-7565, 808-967-8222; www.volcanoartcenter.org; next to visitor center, Hawai'i Volcanos National Park, Volcano, HI) Housed in the original Volcano House Hotel, the gallery showcases the work of local artists and offers a rich schedule of classes and cultural events.

Wai-pi'o Valley Artworks (808-775-0958; www.waipiovalleyartworks.com; Kukuihale Rd., Kukuihale, HI) Locally made koa bowls and furniture, ceramics, hand-blown glass, and jewelry, as well as prints and original work by island artists. Lots of information on Waipi'o Valley tours, many of which leave from here.

BOOKS

Most Big Island bookstores have sections devoted to Hawaiian history, culture, and arts. Oftentimes browsing will provide additional insight on what you've seen elsewhere on your visit. There's often a section devoted to local authors, and if you want fiction set in Hawai'i, you'll find that, too.

Basically Books (808-961-0144; www.basicallybooks.com; 160 Kamehameha Ave., Hilo, HI 96720) Carries an extensive selection of books about Hawai'i—everything from children's books to antiquarian scholarly works—and so many maps that some locals refer to the store as "the map shop." Their own imprint, Petroglyph Press, produces books on Hawai'i entirely in Hilo. The staff has an encyclopedic knowledge of the Big Island, and the shop's a good place to find notices of local events.

Kohala Book Shop (808-889-6400; www.kohalabooks.com; 54-3885 Akoni Pule Hwy., Kapa'au, HI) The largest used bookstore in the state has a vast collection of books, prints, maps, and other ephemera on Hawai'i and Oceania. It's easy to spend several hours browsing here, and for every rare volume of missionary writings printed by the American Tract Society, there's a used copy of a mystery by Martha Grimes, Tony Hillerman, or John Burdett.

Kona Stories (808-324-0350; www.konastories.com; Mango Court, 79-7460 Māmalahoa Hwy., Kainaliu, HI 96750) A lovely shop with a quiet, ocean-view lanai in the rear for reading over a cup of Kona coffee and homemade baked goods. The Hawaiiana and

New Age offerings are strong. There are regular events with local authors and story times for children.

CLOTHING

There will come a giddy moment when you decide aloha wear, that symbol of Hawai'i as universal among travelers as the air-writing gesture for "may I have the check now, please," is something you must have. You want to wear a floral shirt all day before the sun sets. You want to wear another even gaudier one as you relax after sunset, umbrella drink in hand.

You are not alone. This urge began hitting the pale and pudgy in the 1930s, after Watamull's East India Store in Honolulu commissioned a local artist, Elsie Das, to create fabric designs that captured Hawai'i's floral and scenic heritage. From that yardage came the aloha shirt as we know it. And, less directly, the matching dress, or muumuu, oftentimes based on a cover-it-up missionary fashion sense.

Today, aloha wear comes in many guises. Prized by collectors, vintage shirts and dresses come in styles specific to the genre. The big name is Hilo Hattie. A lesser-known name is Tori Richard. Some of the most elegant aloha wear comes from Sig Zane, who opened a small Hilo shop in 1978. He's expanded since then—there's a second shop on Maui—but the mother lode remains in Hilo, and aside from a Web site, that's it. No department stores. No mall shops. No resort boutiques.

Western wear is also a style you'll encounter. The Big Island is ranch country, where the cowboys, or *paniolo,* rule. Their horses as well as their Stetsons appear bedecked with lei on special occasions. Look for Western-tailored shirts in tropical prints at the shops in Waimea.

As Hāwī Turns (808-889-5023; Akoni Pule Hwy., Hāwī , HI) There's always something wonderful in this shop, but you never know what it might be. The clothing's a happy island mix of fun and funky, the accessories just a little bit more outrageous than that, but there's nothing so "island" that you won't feel happy to wear it at home.

Crazy Shirts (808-329-2176; 75-5719 Ali'i Dr., Kailua-Kona, HI 96740) T-shirts and more from a statewide business known for their long-lasting cotton clothing emblazoned with designs that change seasonally.

The Cutlery (808-934-7500; 141 Mamo St., Hilo, HI 96720) "Always Hi, Never Lo" is just one of the T-shirt slogans at this tiny shop, shaped like a slice of pizza. It features limited-edition sneakers, T-shirts, hoodies, and other cool clothing that would fit into the hippest clubs of Tokyo, Los Angeles, or New York.

Hilo Hattie (808-875-7200; 75-5597 Palani Rd., Kailua-Kona, HI 96740, and Prince Kuhio Plaza, 808-961-3077; 111 E. Pū'ainakō St., Building G, Hilo, HI 96720) Hilo Hattie is practically synonymous with aloha wear. She was a popular entertainer born Clarissa Haili who took the name Hilo Hattie after a song she popularized, "When Hilo Hattie Does the Hula Hop." That was in the 1950s, and the first store of what was to become Hilo Hattie's opened on Kauai in 1963. But it wasn't until 1979 that Kaluna Hawai'i Sportswear purchased the rights to the name Hilo Hattie. By 1992, Hilo Hattie stores throughout Hawai'i were attracting 1 million people a year. Today, Hilo Hattie has stores in California and Nevada, and the company has expanded beyond aloha wear to make uniforms for businesses and schools. You, however, are after aloha wear. And Hilo Hattie's has it, for men, women, and children. Both Big Island stores are big, with gifts—including lei for dogs— jewelry, and gourmet treats, all made in Hawai'i.

Na Makua (808-969-7985; 107 Waianuenue Ave., Hilo, HI 96720) Casual clothing for men and women by Kainoa and Nelson Makua, a father-and-son design team from the Puna district. Nelson Makua designed the official Merrie Monarch Hula Festival posters for 2003, 2004, 2005, 2006, and 2008. Each depicts a chapter in the story of Pele. They are striking and worth seeing.

Persimmon (808-889-1050; www.persimmon-shop.com; 55-3455 Akoni Pule Hwy., Hāwī, HI 96719) A sweet collection of women's clothing in a cunning shop. The selection captures the North Kohala sensibility—hip, fun, lighthearted—and runs the gamut from yoga wear to cocktail dresses. There's a mix of island and West Coast designers represented.

Sandal Tree (808-886-7884; Hilton Waikoloa Village, 425 Waikoloa Beach Dr., Waikoloa, HI 96738) A truly vast array of sandals for men and women, from sturdy walkers by Clarks to Ramon Tenza fantasies with strawberry-shaped heels.

Sig Zane Designs (808-935-7077; www.sigzane.com; 122 Kamehameha Ave., Hilo, HI 96720) An elegant light-filled space, the shop's usually calm atmosphere explodes during the Merrie Monarch Hula Festival, when sales clerks serve cookies and brownies from nearby Big Island Candies to dancers and hula fans crowding in, many leaving with more than three bags full. They're there, in part, because Zane, whose ancestors came to the Big Island from China, is of their universe. His wife, Nalani Kanaka'ole, is an internationally renowned *kumu hula*, or hula master. His mother-in-law was the late Edith Kanaka'ole, one of the most influential *kumu hula* and Hawaiian cultural preservationist/revivalists of the 20th century. An awareness of the depth of Hawaiian culture infuses Zane's work. He designs the fabrics, often using indigenous plants for inspiration, prints them in very lim-

The shop facades in laid-back Honoka'a give the place a Wild West feel.

ited runs, and creates garments that are as chicly suitable for summer in Kalamazoo as they are year-round in Kailua-Kona. The men's shirts come in several designs, even with long sleeves. As well as shirts for women, there are dresses in a variety of traditional and modern styles flattering to many body types. (For proof, ask to see some wedding photographs.) The shop also stocks Zane-designed kids' wear, small leather accessories, and a limited home selection that includes wool rugs with simple native-plant designs. The rugs, like everything else, can be shipped to your home.

CRAFTS

Spend time looking and training your eye before you buy. These shops, where exquisite workmanship is the norm, are more like galleries, and staffers are often craftspeople themselves, so they can answer questions from deep knowledge. While the larger items can be seriously pricey, most shops have less expensive smaller examples of their work that serve as grace-filled reminders of your visit.

Burgado's Fine Woods (808-969-9663; S. Hata Building, 308 Kamehameha Ave., Hilo, HI 96720) Beautiful koa furniture and home accessories that are more like art pieces than furniture even though they stand up to everyday use (with care).

Dan De Luz Woods (808-935-5587; HI 11, near mile marker 12, Mountain View, HI and 64-1013 Māmalahoa Hwy., Waimea, HI 96743) Dan De Luz has been turning bowls from koa, mango, kamani, kou, hau, Norfolk pine, and other island woods for decades. While he makes trays and other items, the bowls are the star attraction. Some are almost translucent; all take advantage of the wood's natural grain and coloring. The bowls are stunning—so are some of the prices—but they are worth every cent.

Fabric Impressions (808-961-4468, 206 Kamehameha Ave., Hilo, HI 96720) An eye-popping inventory of Hawaiian fabrics, from surfboard prints to florals resembling mid-century bark cloth prints; quilts; and quilt kits. If you live in a cold climate, look for the Hawaiian-print fleece. The handmade quilts on display are often for sale, and the coverlets on the racks in front, notable for their exuberant colors and designs, always are.

Kama'aina Woods (808-775-7722; www.hulihands.com; Lehua St., Honoka'a, HI 96727) Bill and Lois Keb's company makes calabash-style bowls, but what they're known for, indeed, what they trademarked, is the "huli hands" salad and pasta tossers. The shop is adjacent to the workroom, so you can watch craftspeople working. The Kebs stock tables, plant stands, boxes, and trays made by other Big Island woodworkers, but you don't want to leave without your hands.

Kīlauea Kreations (808-967-8090; www.kilaueakreations.com; Old Volcano Rd., Volcano, HI 96785) This co-op sells quilts, baby quilts, quilted pillow covers, and quilted wall hangings all using traditional Hawaiian quilt patterns, often using hand-dyed fabrics that capture the unique colors and textures of a community living near lava flows. Hawaiian quilts have a graphic quality that make the pillows suited to ultramodern interiors as well as more traditional ones.

Kimura Lauhala Shop (808-324-0053; Māmalahoa Hwy. at Hualalai Rd., Hōlualoa, HI 96725) Hats, mats, coasters, tote bags, purses—all are little masterpieces of the craft of weaving with the fragrant leaves of the pandanus tree. The items soften with use. Everything's genuinely local. The Kimura family and the folks they hire have been doing this for decades.

A turned bowl, like this one in Norfolk pine, makes a magnificent souvenir.

Topstitch (808-885-4482; Holomua Center, 64-1067 Māmalahoa Hwy., Waimea, HI 96743) Ellie Erickson oversees a quilt makers' heaven with sterling examples of Hawaiian quilts made by some of the state's most talented craftspeople. If you want to commission a piece, she can help arrange contacts.

Woodshop Gallery and Café (808-963-6363; Old Māmalahoa Hwy., Honomū, HI 96728) This is a not-what-it-seems kind of place that rewards anyone who spends a bit of time looking at what's on offer, such as work by local artists like Carla Crow, glass and ceramic crafts, exquisite koa furniture from McLaren Woodwords, and koa by the board foot for woodworkers.

FLOWERS AND ORCHIDS

Akatsuka Orchid Gardens (808-967-8234; www.atkasuraorchid.com; HI 11, near mile marker 22, Volcano, HI 96785) They'll ship anything you select from the vast nursery, and if you want more, they'll set up a customized orchid-of-the-month program. Yes, tour buses stop here, but so should you.

Fuku-Bonsai (808-982-9880; www.fukubonsai.com; 17-856 Ola'a Rd., Kurtistown, HI 96785) Everything you need and need to know to grow true indoor bonsai.

Orchids of Hawai'i (808-959-3581; 2801 Kīlauea Ave., Hilo, HI 96720) Specialists in tropical flowers, not just orchids, they ship worldwide. The variety is delicious.

General Stores

Throughout the island, family-owned general stores keep rural folks fed and supply their daily needs. Many of them have a gas pump or two out front, and some have hot food inside to go. They're usually a more interesting stop for a snack than a convenience store. Be on the lookout for Lava Tube ice pops and other local or old-fashioned treats when you go in to grab bottled water.

Kimura Store (808-322-3771; 79-7408 Māmalahoa Hwy., Kainaliu, HI 96750) At this old-fashioned general store, you'll find everything you need for a day of fishing, for cooking the catch, setting the table, and dressing up for the party. Cosmetics to cookware, it's all here with some condiments thrown in, just in case. There's an extensive fabric and notions section.

Volcano Store (808-967-7210; Haunani Rd. and Old Volcano Rd., Volcano, HI 96785) Worth a stop for the *poha* jam, *liliko'i* bread, and *liliko'i* butter, which makes a very good gift. It travels well; if the butter separates, stir, then spread on English muffins or pound cake or gingerbread. Of course there's loads more, including orchids and gasoline, because it's a store with a little bit of everything.

Gifts

Bentley's Home & Garden Collection (808-885-5565; Parker Square, Waimea, HI 96743) The elegant tableware collections of glassware, crystal, and linens have expanded to include casual clothing, bath treats, and Western wear in a cohesive, luxurious, and scented whole.

Blue Ginger (808-322-3898; 79-7391 Māmalahoa Hwy., Kainaliu, HI 96750) This shop is an intriguing collection of paintings, ceramics, textiles, jewelry, stained glass, fused glass, and wood by local artists mixed with imported Asian arts and crafts. Look for the happy cat who enjoys napping in the sun atop piles of textiles.

Chawan Shop (808-934-0902; 176 Mamo St., inside the Mamo Mart, Hilo, HI 96720) Gift baskets for birthdays, births, graduations, and such are the main event here, but it's worth stopping by to peruse the elegant Japanese gift items, some made locally, some imported from Japan. The kanji mugs are particularly nice.

For the right person, a bobbing dashboard hula dancer makes the perfect gift.

Dreams of Paradise (808-935-5670; S. Hata Building, 308 Kamehameha Ave., Hilo, HI 96720) Sometimes a shop never fails you. For many shoppers, that's the case here with the art and gifts. With a bit of looking, you'll find things to please people who are notoriously hard to please. One older woman I know delighted in a print of a papaya set on a banana leaf. The composition? The colors? What made her like it so? I know only that I managed to find the perfect gift.

Honoka'a Marketplace (808-775-8255; www.maryguava.com; 45-3586 Māmane St., Honoka'a, HI 96727) A general store of gifts and souvenirs, this very full store stocks kitschy tropical souvenirs and clothing. You can find locally made items and browse as long as you like.

Kathryn's of Kona (808-326-4120; www.kathrynsofkona.com; 75-5660 Kopiko St., Kailua-Kona, HI 96740) Candles, glassware, tableware, stationery, women's clothing, accessories, and shoes, all artfully displayed to inspire thoughts of terrific dinner parties where nothing goes wrong. If you lived on the Big Island, this is one of those places you'd turn to for hostess gifts or help finding just the right accessory to give a blah room a boost. Just because you're visiting doesn't mean you won't find the same thing that will work with your decor at home.

Kohala Winds of Change Health & Tea (808-889-0809; Akoni Pule Hwy., Hāwī, HI 96719) This is one of those blissfully unclassifiable Big Island shops. Marc and Janet Melton created a space with the ambience of a traditional Chinese teahouse—the lacquered doors open onto a high-ceilinged interior that is soothing and cool. They stock organic teas—white, green, oolong, red, black, scented, pu-erhs, herbals, and medicinals—which you can sample. But they also sell such a lovely selection of tea ware—lacquer, porcelain, metal—that it seems like a specialized gift shop.

Most Irresistible Shop (808-935-9644; 256 Kamehameha Ave., Hilo, HI 96720) Gifts, kitsch, treasures, and souvenir items from around the Pacific. A browser's delight.

The Quilted Horse (808-887-0020; High Country Traders Building, HI 19, Waimea, HI 96743) This shop caters to a sophisticated audience with items made of koa wood, locally made gourmet treats, and many Hawaiian-style quilts.

Waimea General Store (808-885-4479; Parker Square, Waimea, HI 96743) Oh my. There are baskets hanging from the ceiling. The big round tables are filled with goodies. The choices are overwhelming. Calm down and find all kinds of things you didn't know you needed. Santas take note: The collection of Hawai'i-themed children's books is well selected.

HAWAIIANA

Alapaki's Hawaiian Gifts (808-322-2007; Keauhou Shopping Center, 78-6831 Ali'i Dr., Kailua-Kona, HI 96740) A wonderful place to find traditional drums, feather work, and other work by Hawaiian artisans.

The Grass Shack (808-323-2877; Māmalahoa Hwy., Kealakekua, HI 96750) If you're expecting something cutesy that goes with the 1933 Johnny Noble hit with the refrain "I want to go back to my little grass shack in Kealakeua, Hawai'i where the humuhumunukunukuapua'a goes swimming by," well, there's some of that, but mostly you'll find here beautiful Hawaiian items like the resonant gourds used in hula and exquisite lei from shells collected on Ni'ihau.

Hana Hou (808-935-4555; 164 Kamehameha Ave., Hilo, HI 96720) Beautiful treasures including lauhala hats and vintage-style clothing are displayed in a jewelbox of a shop owned by Michele Zane-Faridi. She designs much of the clothing and finds the vintage accessories, which may include increasingly collectible pieces from the long-shuttered Ming's, a Honolulu jeweler known for pieces depicting Hawaiian flowers and plants. They're snapped up quickly by the smart set.

Ipu Hale Gallery (808-322-9096; Māmalahoa Hwy., Hōlualoa, HI 96725) Michael Barburg decorates *ipu* (gourds) with geometric, almost modern Polynesian-style motifs. He uses an ancient method unique to the Hawaiian island of Niʻihau that died out at the turn of the 20th century, only to be revived by scholars almost 100 years later.

Hawaiian quilt pillow

Quilters also make pillows in traditional patterns.

HOME DECOR

Dragon Mama (808-934-9081; www.dragonmama.com; 266 Kamehameha Ave., Hilo, HI 96720) "Simple living products from nature" is the shop's motto, and it helps to know that they supply many of the Zen centers and Vipassana groups in Hawaiʻi. A tranquil oasis filled with Japanese, Hawaiian, and Chinese fabric that can be used for decorating or clothing, it's also a workroom for seamstresses making futon and pillow covers. The stacks of new tatami mats scent the space, and it's a wonder people aren't napping on the bedding displays—the shop is that calming.

Dovetail Gallery & Design (808-322-4046; 76-5982 Māmalahoa Hwy., Hōlualoa, HI 96725) Owner Gerald Ben is a ceramicist who is also a woodworker and furniture designer. He does custom work for interior designers, architects, and local collectors. Don't miss this shop.

Kathmandu Trading Company (808-935-4000; 35 Waiānuenue Ave., Hilo, HI 96720) An interesting, must-see collection of furniture, rugs, and religious objects from Tibet and elsewhere in the Himalayas sought out by owner Gregory Lippold.

JEWELRY

Double Joy Designs (808-889-0645; www.doublejoydesigns.com; 889-5555 Akoni Pule Hwy., above Bamboo restaurant, Hāwī, HI 96719) Claire Trester makes jewelry with an Asian flavor, using jade, cinnabar, porcelain, cloisonné, silver, and silk. Many of her pieces incorporate symbols believed to have protective powers, and whether or not you believe that, you can't deny they're very lovely.

Elements (808-889-0760, 800-686-0760; www.kahiko.com; Nanbu Building, 54-3885A Akoni Pule Hwy., Kapa'au, HI 96755) Lovely handmade pieces inspired by Hawai'i's flowers and plants by John Flynn in silver, niobium, and gold. The endless loop gold "Waterfall" earrings are timelessly elegant with or without pearls. The less expensive Kahiko pieces in sterling silver are based on petroglyphs. The shop also carries an interesting idiosyncratic collection of gift items, from stuffed animals to tote bags, as well as works by local artists such as Margaret Ann Hoy.

Kamuela Goldsmiths (808-885-9244; Parker Square, Waimea, HI 96743) A co-op of craftspeople well known in Hawai'i who specialize in elegant custom pieces and some very limited production of popular designs.

Traditional craftspeople weave seeds into elegant necklaces.

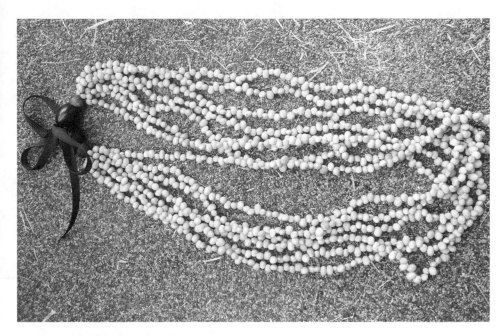

A multi-strand lei is handmade of seeds.

MALLS & SHOPPING CENTERS

Shopping on the Big Island becomes more like that on the mainland every year, which is good for local residents, who can trim the cost of living in paradise by patronizing places like Costco in Kailua-Kona. The malls include all the familiar names—Old Navy, Macy's, Borders, Barnes & Noble, Jamba Juice—with the frequent addition of live entertainment, particularly on Friday, when many people sport aloha wear. The resorts on the Kohala Coast have spawned clusters of high-end shops, again with many familiar names such as Tiffany, Coach, and Louis Vuitton.

Crossroads Shopping Center (808-664-1111; 75-1000 Henry St., in Keauhou area, Kailua-Kona, 96740) Among the tenants is FedEx (808-329-0038).

Coconut Grove Market Place (808-326-2555; 5825 Ali'i Dr., Kailua-Kona 96740) A warren of shops and eateries notable for a sand volleyball court that's well used by local players.

Keauhou Shopping Center (808-322-3000; 78-6831 Ali'i Dr., Kailua-Kona, HI 96740) There's a celebration of aloha each Fri. with Hawaiian music, lei making, and free ukulele lessons. Pineapples Boutique (808-324-1200) carries an island-themed inventory ranging from clothes to home decor.

King's Shops (Waikoloa Beach Resort, Waikoloa Beach Dr., Waikoloa, HI 96738) Stores include: Blue Ginger Resort Apparel (808-886-2020), which has clothing for everyone in the family made from fabrics designed in Hawai'i; Honolua Surf Co. (808-886 6422), for those who surf and wannabes, offering boards, equipment, and clothing; Kubuku (808-886-8581), which sells sarongs, short and long, in silk, cotton, and voile (be sure to check out the tapa clothes from throughout the Pacific region); Making Waves (808-886-1814), with women's swimwear up to size 28 and children's wear; Haimoff & Haimoff, Jewelers (808-886-0088), offering original and custom-designed pieces; Under the Koa Tree (808-886-7444), which features furniture made of koa wood by local artisans and Hawaiian quilts; and Walking in Paradise (808-886-2600), which banishes blisters with comfortable shoes, including Mephistos.

Kona Inn Shopping Village (808-329-6573; 75-5744 Ali'i Dr., Kailua, HI 96740) Built as an upscale hotel in the 1920s, it is now a warren of gift shops, clothing boutiques, and eateries. For those who aren't hunters and gatherers, the lawn by the water is a pleasant place to wait for those who are.

Makalapua Center (808-541-5192; Makalapua Ave., just north of town off HI 19, Kailua-Kona, HI 96740) A large Macy's anchors this mall.

Parker Ranch Shopping Center (808-885-5669; 67-1185 Māmalahoa Hwy., Kamuela, HI 96743) The Parker Ranch Store features Western wear with a *paniolo* flair, gifts, gourmet foodstuffs, clothing, and locally made Ola body spa products made with cane sugar, Hawaiian salt, and volcanic pumice. The ginger scrub followed by the lotion made with Hawaiian kukui, macadamia nut, and virgin coconut oils will cure jet lag coming and going.

Parker Square (HI 19, Kamuela, HI 96743) A restored plantation-style building with many nice shops and a café. Worth exploring.

Prince Kuhio Shopping Plaza (808-959-3555; off HI 11, heading toward the volcanoes, Hilo, HI 96720) Hilo Hattie's, Macy's, and Sears are the anchors at a mall that includes familiar shops such as General Nutrition Center and Radio Shack.

Shops at Mauna Lani (www.shopsatmaunalani.com; 68-1330 Mauna Lani Dr., Kohala Coast, HI 96742) Among the many shopping and dining options here is Tori Richard by Quiet Storm (808-885-4978), a name to know in Hawaiian resort wear for men and women since the 1950s. The company designs the fabrics for their fashions, which elegantly allude to Hawai'i rather than jump up and yell about it.

Waiākea Center (808-792-7200; off HI 11, heading toward the volcanoes, Hilo, HI 96720) Anchor stores include Border's Books, Wal-Mart, Office Max, and Ross.

Waimea Center (65-1158 Māmalahoa Hwy., Kamuela, HI 96743) A low-key, old-fashioned complex with a Radio Shack, a drive-through McDonald's, and FedEx (808-885-8810).

SPORT SHOPS

A'Ama Surf & Sport Shop (808-326-7890; www. aamasurf.com; 75-5741 Kuakini Hwy., Kailua-Kona, HI 96740) The name says it all.

Big Island Surf (808-935-1430; 244 Kamehameha Ave., Hilo, HI 96720) Boards of all kinds, gear, and helpful staff.

Hilo Surplus Store (808-935-6398; 148 Mamo St., Hilo, HI 96720) Camping equipment and supplies suited to local conditions.

Melton International Tackle (808-329-0800; www.meltontackle.com; 74-5035D Queen Ka'ahumanu Hwy., at Kealake'he Pkwy. intersection, Kailua-Kona HI 96740) Equipment and clothing for anglers going after big fish.

Orchidland Surfboards (808-935-1533; 262 Kamehameha Ave., Hilo, HI 96720) Boards, boards, and more boards, plus some cool clothing.

Pacific Rim Fishing Supplies (808-326-1443; www.pacificrimfishing.com; 74-425 Kealakehi Pkwy., Kailua-Kona, HI 96740)

Sports Zone (808-885-7280; 64-1035 Māmalahoa Hwy., Kamuela, HI 96743) Sports shoes, clothing, and equipment.

9

Best Bets

If Time Is Short

Don't Miss

Hawai'i Volcanoes National Park
Mauna Kea stargazing
Pu'uhonua O Hōnaunau National Historical Park

Worth Your Time

Lapakahi State Park—North Kohala
Pacific Tsunami Museum—Hilo
Puakō Petroglyph Area—Kohala Coast

Hawai'i Volcanoes National Park, with its other worldly landscape, is not to be missed.

One of the peacocks at the Wood Valley Temple puts on a display.

St. Benedict's Painted Church—Hōnaunau
Wood Valley Temple—Pāhala

Food with Flair

Aloha Angel Café—Kainaliu
Café 100—Hilo
Café Pesto—Hilo and Kawaihae
The Coffee Shack—Captain Cook
Huli Sue's—Waimea
Ken's House of Pancakes—Hilo
Kiawe Kitchen—Volcano
Kona Brewing Company—Kailua-Kona
Manago Hotel—Captain Cook
Nori's Saimin & Snacks—Hilo
Sushi Rock—Hāwī

Fine Dining (outside a resort)

Fujimamas—Kailua-Kona
Hilo Bay Café—Hilo

Kenichi Pacific—Kailua-Kona
Kīlauea Lodge—Volcano
Merriman's—Waimea

Special Shops

Elements—Kapaʻau (handmade jewelry by local designer John Flynn)
Hano Hou—Hilo (locally designed clothing and vintage jewelry)
Kimura Store—Kainaliu (everything a general store should be)
Kohala Winds of Change—Hāwī (all things tea)
Kona Stories—Kainaliu (a bookstore with reading lanai)
Sig Zane—Hilo (aloha wear to wear anywhere)

Wonderful Views

On an island rich in vistas, some *do* stand out:

Hāmākua Coast, including Onomea Dr. and Old Mamalahoa Hwy.
Ka Lae
Kīlauea Caldera
Kohala Mountain Hwy.

In Ocean View, homes on an old lava flow come in many sizes.

The big sky views on the Kohala Mountain Rd. include dormant volcanoes.

Mauna Kea at dawn seen from Hilo Bay front
Pu'uhonua O Honaunau National Historical Park at sunset

Crafty Options

Dan De Luz Woods—Mountain View and Waimea (the master of turned wood bowls)
Kīlauea Kreations—Volcano (a quilters' co-op)
Kimura Lauhala Shop—Hōlualoa (traditional pandanus weavings)
Topstitch—Waimea (Hawaiian quilts)

Tasty Treats

Atebara taro chips—widely available
Humpback Blue Beer—widely available
Liliko'i butter—Volcano Store or farmers' market
Malasadas—Tex Drive Inn, Honoka'a
Mochi—Two Ladies Kitchen, Hilo
Spam *musubi*—widely available
Sesame almond cookies—Big Island Candies, Hilo
Tropical Dreams—the Big Island's own ice cream, available islandwide

A row of stately palms enhances the landscaping at the Pāhala Plantation House.

The Parker Ranch Center in Waimea blends Hawaiian and Western cowboy cultures.

Childish Fun
To Do and See

Ellison S. Onizuka Center, Mauna Kea (9,300-foot elevation may not be safe for very young children)
Imiloa Astronomy Center, Hilo
Kīlauea Visitor Center, Hawai'i Volcanoes National Park (evening lava walk may not be safe for young children)
Pacific Tsunami Museum and Lili'uokalani Gardens, Hilo
Parker Ranch and Museum, Waimea
Petroglyph walk
Pu'uhonua O Hōnaunau National Historical Park
Snorkling or kayaking in Kealekekua Bay
Waipi'o Valley wagon tour

Kids' Menu
Huli huli chicken
Kālua pork
POG (we're not giving any clues other than it's a juice)
Portuguese sweetbread
Saimin (slurrrrrrrp!)
Shave ice
Spam *musubi*
Strawberry mochi

BEST BEACHES FOR FAMILIES

'Anaeho'omalu Beach
Hāpuna Beach
Kahalu'u Beach
Richardson Beach
Spencer Beach

MOST ROMANTIC LODGING

Kona Village—Kohala Coast
Kīlauea Lodge—Volcano
Palms Cliff House—Honomū
Shipman House—Hilo
Tara Cottage—Kealakekua

BEST LODGING VALUES

Dolphin Bay Hotel—Hilo
Hilo Hawaiian Hotel—Hilo
Kohala Vista Inn—Kawaihae
Kona Village—Kohala Coast
Marriott Waikoloa Resort—Kohala Coast
Outrigger Keauhou Beach Resort—Kailua-Kona

Steep hilly pastures frame a classic Waimea residence.

Best Day Trips

For wandering, stopping, and seeing the sights. For details, see chapter 5, Sacred Sites, Ancient Ruins, and Natural Wonders.

Head north from the Kohala Coast resorts to explore the rich Hawaiian heritage of North Kohala along CR 270, stopping in Kapaʻau and Hāwī for shopping and a meal before heading back before sunset via CR 250, the Kohala Mountain Rd.

From either Hilo or Kailua-Kona, drive to Waimea for lunch in one of the ranching town's sophisticated restaurants. If you're based in Kailua-Kona, be sure to take CR 190 through coffee farms and up-country enclaves in one direction. If you're based in Hilo, sneak off HI 19 for some wandering on the old highway

From the Kohala Coast or Kailua-Kona, combine education with recreation by heading up-country along CR 190 for some Kona coffee tasting and gallery hopping, then dropping down to sea level for time at Kealakekua Bay and sunset at Puʻuhonua O Hōnaunau National Historical Park.

Get lost in the Puna. Turn off HI 11 to CR 130 at Keaʻau to explore Pāhoa, then carry on until you meet the sea. There's some backtracking involved to reach CR 136, the "Red Road," but there's also verdant jungle and awesome views.

If Time Is Short

These itineraries are based on the earliest possible arrival flight and the last flight out. Note: These are unsuitable for families with young children or those who want to stop and smell the plumeria.

There are many scenic pull-outs along the Kohala Mountain Rd.

One-Day Wonder

Fly into Hilo as early as possible.

Rent a car.

Stop at a grocery store for picnic fixings.

Stop at the Hilo Coffee Mill off HI 11 for coffee tasting.

Go to Hawai'i Volcanoes National Park. Spend the day.

Fly out.

Dining options: Ken's House of Pancakes for a big breakfast, Hilo Bay Café for an early dinner.

Two-Day Flying Leap

Day 1

Fly into Kona International Airport.

Rent a four-wheel drive from Harper's.

Early check-in at the Outrigger Keauhou Beach Resort for an ocean-view, high-floor room.

Breakfast at Aloha Angel Café.

Head south on III 11, stopping for a coffee tour at Greenwell Farms.

Continue to Kealakekua Bay; frolic in the waves.

Continue to Pu'uhonua O Hōnaunau National Historical Park for exploring and sunset.

Dinner at Fujimamas or Kenichi Pacific.

Sleep with the windows open to hear the surf below.

Day 2

Wake up. Quick swim.

Check out.

Java on the Rocks for Kona coffee and breakfast.

Drive to the Waikoloa Heliport.

Take the two-hour Big Island Spectacular helicopter tour offered by Blue Hawaiian.

Drive to Waimea via HI 19 for lunch at Merriman's or Huli Sue's.

Take the Kohala Mountain Road to Hāwī to explore.

Take CR 270 heading south.

Beach time at 'Anaeho'omalu.

Fly out.

OR

After lunch, take CR 190, stopping for coffee tasting and galleries in up-country enclaves.

Continue down toward the ocean, turn right onto HI 11, and take a swim at Old Airport Beach Park.

Fly out.

Three-Day Have It All

Day 1

Fly into Hilo.

Rent a car.

The Art Deco Nāʻalehu Theatre had the southernmost movie screens in the United States.

Breakfast at Ken's House of Pancakes.

Go to Hawai'i Volcanoes National Park. Spend the day.

Check into Hilo Hawaiian hotel.

Dinner in Hilo: Café Pesto or Nori's Saimin & Snacks to suss out the local scene.

Day 2

A pleasant morning Hāmākua Coast drive to Waipi'o Valley lookout. Be sure to stop at What's Shakin'.

You'll be spending the night in Waimea, but you must check in early enough to meet a Mauna Kea stargazing tour at the Saddle Road junction. The timing suggests a late lunch at Huli Sue's.

Day 3

Late-start morning through up-country coffee farms along CR 190.

Continue to Pu'uhonua O Hōnaunau National Historical Park for exploring.

Fly out from the Kona International Airport.

Palms reach for the sun above the roadside jungles on the Hāmākua Coast.

10

Information

Practical Matters

Ambulance, Fire, and Police

The general emergency number (fire, police, ambulance) for Hilo, Kailua Kona, and Waimea is 911. The combined nonemergency number is 808-935-3311.

  Other emergency numbers are as follows:

Kailua-Kona police: 808-326-4646
Hilo police: 808-961-2213
Domestic Violence Crisis Intervention: 808-322-7233
Poison Control: 800-222-1222
Rape Crisis Center: 808-935-0677
Suicide Prevention: 800-784-2433
Civil Defense: 808-935-0031 for tsunami or earthquake information

Banks

Bank of Hawai'i

Hilo: 808-935-9701, 120 Pauahi St., 808-959-8447, 50 E. Puainako St.; 808-961-0681, 417 E. Kawili
Honoka'a: 808-775-7218; 45-3568 Māmane St.
Kapa'au: 808-889-6217; 54-3888 Akoni Pule Hwy.
Kailua-Kona: 808-326-3900, 75-5595 Palani Rd.; 808-322-3380, 78-6831 Ali'i Dr.
Pāhala: 808-928-8356; 96-3163 Pikake St.
Waimea: 808-885-7995; 67-1191 Māmalahoa Hwy.

First Hawaiian Bank

Honoka'a: 808-775-7276; 45-3538 Māmane St.
Hilo: 808-969-2211; 345 Kekuanoa St.
Kailua-Kona: 808-329-2461; 74-5593 Palani Rd.
Pāhoa, 808-965-8621; Government Main Rd.
Waikoloa: 808-883-8555; Waikoloa Highlands Center, 68-1845 Waikoloa Rd.
Waimea: 808-885-7991; 67-1189 Māmalahoa Hwy.

  ATMs from these banks and others, as well as private operators, are found at convenience stores, gas stations, grocery stores, shopping malls, and elsewhere. Every major network is serviced.

BIBLIOGRAPHY

Many travelers enjoy reading about a destination as well as exploring it. Here's a list of some books about the Big Island and Hawai'i that will be useful before, during, or after your trip. (For information on booksellers on the Big Island, see chapter 8, Shopping.)

Art and Design

Brown, Desoto. *The Art of the Aloha Shirt*. Honolulu: Island Heritage Publishing, 2005.

Fujii, Jocelyn. *Tori Richard: The First Fifty Years*. Honolulu: TR Press, 2006.

———. *Under a Hula Moon*. New York: Crown, 1992.

Hibbard, Don. *Designing Paradise: The Allure of the Hawaiian Resort*. Princeton, NJ: Princeton Architectural Press, 2006.

Horikawa, M., J. Saville, and D. Severson. *Finding Paradise: Island Art in Private Collections*. Honolulu: University of Hawai'i Press, 2002.

Jay, Robert. *The Architecture of Charles W. Dickey: Hawai'i and California*. Honolulu: University of Hawai'i Press, 1992.

McGrath, Mary Philpotts. *Hawai'i, A Sense of Place: Island Interior Design*. Honolulu: Mutual Pub, 2005.

Miles, Richard. *A Printmaker in Paradise: The Art and Life of Charles W. Bartlett*. Arts Media Resources, 2003.

Nakayama, Nobu. *Hawaiian Light: The Tao of the Islands*. VIZ Media, 1997.

Treib, Marc. *Hawaiian Modern: The Architecture of Vladimir Ossipoff*. New Haven, CT: Yale University Press, 2007.

Astronomy

Bryan, E. H. *Stars over Hawai'i*. Hilo, HI: Petroglyph Press, 1977. An introduction to astronomy, featuring the stars filling the night sky in Hawai'i, by month.

Cooking

Beeman, Judy, and Martin Beeman. *Joys of Hawaiian Cooking*. Hilo, HI: Petroglyph Press, 1977.

Choy, Sam. *Cooking from the Heart with Sam Choy*. Honolulu: Mutual Publishing, 1995.

Corum, Ann Kondo. *Hawai'i's Spam Cookbook*. Honolulu: Bess Press, 1987.

———. *Hawai'i's 2nd Spam Cookbook*. Honolulu: Bess Press, 2001.

Fukuda, Sachi. *Pupus, An Island Tradition*. Honolulu: Bess Press, 1995.

Hawai'i Farm Bureau. *Hawai'i Farmers Market Cookbook: Fresh Island Products from A to Z*. Honolulu: Watermark Publishing, 2006.

Junior League of Honolulu. *Aloha Days Hula Nights*. Junior League of Honolulu, 2006.

———. *A Taste of Aloha: A Collection of Recipes from the Junior League of Honolulu*. Junior League of Honolulu, 1983.

———. *Another Taste of Aloha*. Junior League of Honolulu, 1994.

Keys, Jean. *We the Women of Hawai'i Cookbook*. Press Pacifica, 1987.

Kinro, Gerald. *Cup of Aloha: The Kona Coffee Epic*. Honolulu: University of Hawai'i Press, 2003.

Philpotts, Kaui. *Great Chefs of Hawai'i*. Honolulu: Mutual Publishing, 2003.

Shimabukuro, Betty. *By Request: The Search for Hawai'i's Greatest Recipes*. Honolulu: Mutual Publishing, 2006.

Wong, Alan. *Alan Wong's New Wave Luau*. Berkeley: Ten Speed Press, 2003.

Yamaguchi, Roy. *Roy's Fish & Seafood: Recipes from the Pacific Rim*. Berkeley: Ten Speed Press, 2005.

Crafts

Arbeit, Wendy. *What Are Fronds For?* Honolulu: University of Hawai'i Press, 1985.

Brandon, Reiko. *The Hawaiian Quilt*. Honolulu: Honolulu Academy of Arts, 1993.

Brandon, R., and L. Woodard. *Hawaiian Quilts: Tradition and Transition*. Honolulu: Honolulu Academy of Arts, 2004.

Buck, Peter. *Arts and Crafts of Hawai'i: Plaiting*. Honolulu: Bishop Museum Press, 1957.

Heckman, Marsha. *Lei Aloha*. Honolulu: Island Heritage, 2001.

Holt, John. *The Art of Featherwork in Old Hawai'i*. Honolulu: Bishop Museum Press, 1985.

Kekuewa, Mary Louise, and Paulette Kahalepuna. *Feather Lei as an Art*. Honolulu: Mutual Publishing, 2005.

McDonald, Marie. *Ka Lei: The Leis of Hawai'i*. Honolulu: Ku Pa'a Publishing, 1995.

Pay attention when you see signs like this one near Laupāhoehoe.

Cultural Studies

Barrere, Dorothy, Marion, Kelly, and Mary Pukui. *Hula: Historical Perspectives*. Honolulu: Bishop Museum Press, 1980.

Blackburn, Mark. *Tattoos from Paradise: Traditional Patterns*. Atglen, PA: Schiffer Publishing, 2000.

Craighill Handy, E. *The Polynesian Family System of Kau'u, Hawai'i*. Polynesian Society, 1950.

Dudley, Michael Kioni. *Man, Gods, and Nature*. Honolulu: No Kane O Ka Malo Press, 1990.

Emerson, Nathaniel. *Unwritten Literature of Hawai'i: The Sacred Songs of Hula*. Honolulu: Mutual Publishing Co., 2007.

Finney, Ben, and James D. Houstin. *Surfing: A History of the Ancient Hawaiian Sport*. Los Angeles: Pomegranate Communications, 1996. Features many early etchings and old photos.

Gutmanis, June. *Kahuna La'au Lapa'au: A guide to the use of Hawaiian herbal medicines*. Honolulu: Island Heritage, rev. ed. 2001.

———. *Na Pule Kahiko: Ancient Hawaiian Prayers*. Editions Ltd., 1983.

Hartwell, Jay. *Na Mamo: Hawaiian People Today*. Honolulu: Ai Pohaku Press, 1996. Profiles 12 people practicing Hawaiian traditions in the modern world.

Hawaiian Studies Institute. *Life in Early Hawai'i: The Ahupua'a*. 3rd ed. Honolulu: Kamehameha Schools Press, 1994. An explanation of traditional land allocation.

Kahalewai, Nancy. *Hawaiian Lomilomi: Big Island Massage*. Island Massage Publishing, 2005.

Kwiatkowski, P. *The Hawaiian Tattoo*. Halona, Incorporated, 1996.

Lebra, Joyce Chapman. *Women's Voices in Hawai'i*. Boulder: University Press of Colorado, 1991.

McBride, L. R. *The Kahuna: Versatile Masters of Old Hawai'i*. Hilo, HI: Petroglyph Press, 2000.

Phillips, Kathy. *This is a Picture I'm Holding: Kuan Yin*. Honolulu: University of Hawai'i Press, 2004.

Stillman, Amy. *Sacred Hula: The Historical Hula Ala'Apapa*. Honolulu: Bishop Museum, 1998.

History

Baily, B., and D. Farber. *The First Strange Place: Race and Sex in World War II Hawai'i*. Baltimore: The Johns Hopkins University Press, 1994.

Barnes, Phil. *A Concise History of the Hawaiian Islands*. Hilo, HI: Petroglyph Press, 1999.

Bergin, Billy. *Loyal to the Land: The Legendary Parker Ranch*. Honolulu: University of Hawai'i Press, 2003.

Budnick, Rick. *Stolen Kingdom: An American Conspiracy*. Honolulu: Aloha Press, 1992.

Daws, Gavan. *Shoal of Time, A History of the Hawaiian Islands*. Honolulu: University of Hawai'i Press, 1974.

Dorrance, William H., and Francis S. Morgan. *Sugar Islands: The 165-Year Story of Sugar in Hawai'i*. Honolulu: Mutual Publishing, 2000.

Fornander, Abraham. *An Account of the Polynesian Race: Its Origins and Migrations, and the Ancient History of the Hawaiian People to the Times of Kamehameha I*. Rutland, VT: C. E. Tuttle Co., 1969.

I'i, John Papa. *Fragments of Hawaiian History*. Honolulu: Bishop Museum, 1959.

Kimberley, Sandy. *Duke: A Great Hawaiian*. Honolulu: Bess Press, 2004.

Kirch, Patrick. *Feathered Gods and Fishhooks: An Introduction to Hawaiian Archaeology and Prehistory*. Honolulu: University of Hawai'i Press, 2000.

Kurisu, Yasushi. *Sugar Town, Hawaiian Plantation Days Remembered*. Honolulu: Watermark Publishing, 1995.

Lili'uokalani. *Hawai'i's Story by Hawai'i's Queen*. Reprint. Honolulu: Mutual Publishing, 1990.

McBride, Likeke. *Petroglyphs of Hawai'i*. Hilo, HI: Petroglyph Press, 1997. A revised and updated guide to petroglyphs found in the Hawaiian Islands. A basic introduction to these old Hawaiian picture stories.

Oaks, Robert. *Hawai'i: A History of the Big Island*. Charleston, SC: Arcadia Publishing, 2003.

Stauffer, Robert. *Kahana: How the Land Was Lost*. Honolulu: University of Hawai'i Press, 2003.

Takaki, Ronald. *Pau Hana: Plantation Life and Labor in Hawai'i*. Honolulu: University of Hawai'i Press, 1983. The story of immigrant labor and the sugar industry in Hawai'i until the 1920s from the worker's perspective.

Language

Pukui, Mary, Samuel Elbert, and Esther T. Mookini. *Place Names of Hawai'i*. Honolulu: University of Hawai'i Press, 1974. Gives the pronunciation, spelling, meaning, and location.

———. *'Olelo No'eau: Hawaiian Proverbs & Poetical Sayings*. Honolulu: Bishop Press Museum, 1997.

Mythology and Legends

Beckwith, Martha. *Hawaiian Mythology*. Reprint. Honolulu: University of Hawai'i Press, 1976. First printed in 1940, this is the definitive text on Hawaiian mythology.

———. *The Kumulipo*. Reprint. Honolulu: University of Hawai'i Press, 1972.

Carol, Rick. *Madame Pele: True Encounters with Hawaii's Fire Goddess*. Honolulu: Bess Press, 2003.

Kalakaua, His Hawaiian Majesty, King David. *The Legends and Myths of Hawai'i*. Edited by R. M. Daggett, with a foreword by Glen Grant. Honolulu: Mutual Publishing, 1990.

Maguire, Eliza. *Kona Legends*. Whitefish, MT: Kessinger Publishing, 2007.

Westervelt, W. D. *Hawaiian Legends of Volcanoes*. 1916. Reprint. Boston: Ellis Press, 1991.

Natural Science and Geography

Beckwith, Meredith. *Kepelino's Traditions of Hawai'i*. Honolulu: Bishop Museum Press, 2007.

Ching, Patrick. *Sea Turtles of Hawai'i*. Honolulu: University of Hawai'i Press, 2002.

Cox, J., and E. Stasack. *Hawaiian Petroglyphs*. Honolulu: Bishop Museum Press, 1970.

Crowe, Ellie. *Exploring Lost Hawai'i: Places of Power, History, Magic & Mystery*. Honolulu: Island Heritage, 2001.

Evenhuis, Neal. *Barefoot on Lava: The Journals and Correspondence of Naturalist R. C. L. Perkins in Hawai'i, 1892–1901*. Honolulu: Bishop Press Museum, 2007.

Fredericks, Anthony. *Tsunami Man: Learning about Killer Waves with Walter Dudley*. Honolulu: University of Hawai'i Press, 2001.

On the Big Island's back roads, sometimes the local sights stare right back at you.

Guthrie, Loye, and John Mertus. *Images of Hawaii's Flowers*. Honolulu: Hawaiian Service, 1996.

Hazlett, Richard, and Donald Hyndman. *Roadside Geology of Hawai'i*. Missoula, MT: Mountain Press Publishing, 1996.

Howe, K. R. *Vaka Moana, Voyages of the Ancestors: The Discovery and Settlement of the Pacific*. Honolulu: University of Hawai'i Press, 2007.

Joesting, Edward. *Hawai'i: An Uncommon History*. New York: W. W. Norton, 1978.

Juvik, Sonia. *Atlas of Hawai'i*. Honolulu: University of Hawai'i Press, 1998.

Littschwager, D., and S. Middleton. *Archipelago: Portraits of Life in the World's Most Remote Island Sanctuary*. Washington, DC: National Geographic, 2005.

———. *Remains of a Rainbow: Rare Plants and Animals of Hawai'i*. Washington, DC: National Geographic, 2003.

Miyano, Leland. *A Pocket Guide to Hawai'i's Flowers*. Honolulu: Mutual Publishing, 2001.

Pratt, Douglas. *A Pocket Guide to Hawai'i's Birds*. Honolulu: Mutual Publishing, 1996.

Valier, Kathy. *Ferns of Hawai'i*. Honolulu: University of Hawai'i Press, 1995.

Literature

Bird, Isabella. *Six Months in the Sandwich Islands*. Honolulu: Mutual Publishing, 1998.

Blandings, Don. *Leaves from Grass House*. 2nd Anniversary Edition. Hilo, HI: Petroglyph Press, 2007.

Davenport, Kiana. *House of Many Gods: A Novel*. New York: Ballantine Books, 2007.

———. *Songs of Exiles*. New York: Ballantine Books, 2000.

Michner, James. *Hawai'i*. New York: Random House, 1959.

Murayama, Milton. *All I Asking for is My Body*. Honolulu: University of Hawai'i Press, 1988.

Stevenson, Robert. *Travels in Hawai'i.* Honolulu: University of Hawai'i Press, 1991.

Twain, Mark. *Mark Twain in Hawai'i: Roughing It in the Sandwich Islands.* New Edition. Honolulu: Mutual Publishing, 1990.

Yamanaka, Lois-Ann. *Behold the Many: A Novel.* New York: Picador, 2007.

———. *Saturday Night at the Pahala Theatre.* Honolulu: Bamboo Ridge Press, 1993.

CHILDREN

Kids are welcome almost everywhere on the Big Island. Most restaurants have children's menus and high chairs available, but calling ahead to ask is always wise. Children often stay free in their parents' hotel or resort rooms, but this isn't a given. Ask if there's an extra charge for a cot.

Do, however, use common sense about bringing young children to the most formal, expensive restaurants. Would you want a cranky child at the table next to you as you celebrate a special anniversary? Many resorts have special seatings for families, and almost all have babysitting or children's programs available for guests.

Attractions and activities usually charge less for children, but, again, this varies, often by age. Some activities have age and height requirements, so be sure to ask. There are a number of B&B and rental properties with age restrictions due to safety concerns about steep cliffs, deep gulches, or other natural features that can't be childproofed.

If you're traveling with an infant or toddler, be sure to book a child-safety seat when you book your rental vehicle. If you prefer not to travel with all the other equipment or forget something, **Baby's Away** (808-987-9237, 800-996-9030; www.babysaway.com) offers rental cribs, strollers, high chairs, beach equipment, and more. They deliver. Sitters **Unlimited of Hawai'i** can provide CPR and First Aid–certified babysitters who have undergone background checks. Advance bookings suggested (808-674-8440; www.sitters hawaii.com). **People Attentive to Children** (808-325-3864 in Kona, 808-961-3169 in Hilo; www.patchhawaii.org) can refer you to babysitters who have taken a training course on child care. The concierge at your hotel may also have a roster of screened and certified babysitters.

CLIMATE AND WEATHER REPORTS

Your location on the Big Island will determine the climate. On the Kailua-Kona side, it's hot and dry, while the Hilo side gets lots of showers—which means lots of rainbows—but it is rare for it to rain all day. Climate also varies by elevation, and the higher you go, the cooler it gets. In Waimea and Volcano, it can be foggy, chilly, and drippy. November through March are the rainy months, and storms can be wild. But the temperature will vary only by about 10 degrees from the summer months, so with the exception of Mauna Kea, where it can be freezing or close to it year-round, the range of temperatures is from about 65 degrees Fahrenheit in winter in Volcano to above 90 degrees Fahrenheit on the Kohala Coast.

Weather updates: 808-935-6268

ELECTRICITY

The same electrical current is in use in Hawai'i as on the U.S. mainland and is uniform throughout the islands. The system functions on 110 volts, 60 cycles of alternating current (AC).

HOLIDAYS

Federal, state, and county government offices and banks are closed on all federal holidays: January 1 (New Year's Day), the third Monday in January (Martin Luther King Jr., Day), the third Monday in February (President's Day, Washington's Birthday), the last Monday in May (Memorial Day), July 4 (Independence Day), the first Monday in September (Labor Day), the second Monday in October (Columbus Day), November 11 (Veterans Day), the fourth Thursday in November (Thanksgiving Day), and December 25 (Christmas).

State and county offices are closed on local holidays, including Prince Kuhio Day (March 26), honoring the birthday of Hawai'i's first delegate to the U.S. Congress; King Kamehameha Day (June 11), a statewide holiday commemorating Kamehameha the Great, who united the islands and ruled from 1795 to 1819; and Admissions Day (third Friday in August), which honors the admittance of Hawai'i as the 50th state on August 21, 1959.

Other special days celebrated in Hawai'i that do not involve official closings of federal, state, and county offices and banks but can mean businesses and restaurants close altogether or early are the Chinese New Year (which can fall in January or February), Girls' Day (March 3), Buddha's Birthday (April 8), Father Damien's Day (April 15), Boys' Day (May 5), Samoan Flag Day (in August), Aloha Festivals (in September and October), and Pearl Harbor Day (December 7).

There are ancient fishponds and tidepools to explore in Keauhou.

Hospitals and Pharmacies

Hospitals
Hale Hoʻola Hāmākua: 808-775-7211; 45-547 Plumeria St., Honokaʻa, HI
Hilo Medical Center: 808-974-4700; 1190 Waiānuenue Ave., Hilo, HI
Kaʻu Hospital: 808-928-2027; 1 Kamani St., Pāhala, HI
Kohala Hospital: 808-889-6211; 54-383 Hospital Rd., Kapaʻau, HI
Kona Community Hospital: 808-322-9311; 79-1019 Haukapila St., Kealakekua, HI
North Hawaiʻi Community Hospital: 808-885-4444; 67-1125 Māmalahoa Hwy., Waimea, HI
Straub Clinic & Hospital: 808-329-9744; 75-170 Hualālai Rd., Kailua-Kona, HI

Pharmacies
Long's Drugs, in many shopping centers, and KTA Super Stores throughout the island have pharmacies.

Costco: 808-331-4833; 73-5600 Maiau St., Kailua-Kona, HI 96740
Foodland: 808-885-2022; Parker Ranch Center, Kamuela, HI 96743
Hilo Pharmacy: 808-961-9267; 82 Puʻuhonu Pl., Hilo, HI 96720
Kamehameha Pharmacy: 808-889-6161; 54-3877 Akoni Pule Hwy., Kapaʻau, HI 96755
Kaʻu Community Pharmacy: 808-928-6252
Waikoloa Pharmacy: 808-883-8484; Highlands Shopping Ctr., Ste. 113, Waikoloa Village, Kohala Coast, HI 96738
Wal-Mart: 808-334-0466; 2321 75-1015 Henry St., Kailua-Kona, HI 96740
Wal-Mart Pharmacy: 808-961-9115; 2473 325 Makaʻala St., Hilo, HI 96720

Media

Magazines and Newspapers
Hawaiʻi Tribune-Herald (808-935-6621; www.hawaiitribune-herald.com; P.O. Box 767, Hilo, HI 96721).
West Hawaiʻi Today (808-329-9311; www.westhawaiitoday.com; P.O. Box 789, Kailua-Kona HI 96745)

Music
Hawaiian music is varied. To get a taste of what you like, listen to an online radio station like www.alohajoe.com, www.pipeline2paradise.com, or www.hawaiianrainbow.com. For a survey of Hawaiian music, a good starting place is at honolulumagazine.com: *Honolulu Magazine* June 2007 "The 50 Greatest Hawaiʻi Songs of All Time" June 2007, and "The 50 Greatest Hawaiʻi Albums of All Time" June 2004.

Here some CD suggestions to get you started. All are available at www.mele.com:

The 50 Greatest Hawaiʻi Music Albums Ever, Vol. I & II
Best of the Cazimero Brothers, Vol. I, II, III
Best of Sun. Manoa, Vol. I, II
Keola & Kapono Beamer: *Honolulu City Lights*
Sonny Ching: *Hoʻoulu I Ka Naʻauao*
Amy Hanalaliʻi: *Gilliom*

Israel "IZ" Kamakawiwo'olo: *Facing Future*
Hokule'a: *The Legacy*
Ho'okena: *Thirst Quencher*
Mark Keali'i Ho'omalu: *Call It What You Like and Po'okela Chants*
Ledward Kaapana: *Black Sand*
Eddie Kamae & the Sons of Hawai'i: *Folk Music of Hawai'i*
Genoa Keawe: *By Request*
Makaha Sons of Ni'ihau: *Ho'oluana*
Peter Moon Band: *Cane Fire*
Cyril Pahinui: *He'eia, 6 & 12 String Slack Key, Cyril Pahinui*
Gabby Pahinui: *Rabbit Island Festival*
Keali'i Reichel: *Kawaipunahele, Kamahiwa*

For listening to Hawaiian music as you travel, find KIPA–620 or HHBC–1060 on the AM dial or KHWI–92.7 and KAPA–100.3 on FM.

Road Services

Here is a listing of some road services:

AAA: 800-736-2886 (24-hour statewide dispatch)

Hilo
Don's Big Island Towing: 808-967-7688
Ken's Towing: 808-959-3361, 808-969-3000
Trouble Call: 808-329-1800

Kailua-Kona and Around
Don's Big Island Towing: 808-967-7688
Joe's Towing Service: 808-324-4869
Roberts Repair & Service: 808-328-8578

Waimea
Tow Guys: 808-885-8697, 808-885-4133
Waimea Auto Center: 808-885-1245

Staying Safe

At the Beach
If in doubt, stay out.

If you're at a beach with lifeguards or beach attendants, ask them about conditions and follow their advice. If you're at a beach without lifeguards or attendants, and local people aren't going in the water, follow their lead and stay ashore.

Obey warning signs. If they say don't go in the water, don't.

Study the water before you enter. Swim where others are swimming or snorkeling. Don't swim alone. Come in before you get tired. If the wind picks up, get out. If the surf is high, don't go in.

Stay off coral. It damages easily, so don't stand on it. If you don't respect coral, coral can

At Mahukona Beach Park, a ladder provides access for snorkelers and swimmers.

give you a nasty infection so look, don't touch.

Let fish, turtles, seals, and other creatures of the deep do what they do without you. Leave them alone. If you knowingly disturb green sea turtles and seals, you face a stiff fine because they are endangered species.

If you're exploring tide pools, wear reef shoes or sneakers, because if you step on a sea urchin with a bare foot, you'll be in pain. Pour vinegar or wine on the wound to stop the burn. The traditional Hawaiian antidote is urine.

If you're exploring reefs, watch out for moray eels. They'll use their razor-sharp teeth on you if disturbed.

If you're around fresh water, take precautions to avoid leptospirosis, a bacteria. Stay out of streams and ponds where cattle and other animals wade and drink, particularly if you have an open cut. Do not drink stream water.

In the Sun

Use sunblock. Nothing can ruin a holiday in Hawai'i faster than a bad burn. Any Long's Drugs is a good source of sunblock with a higher SPF than you may have brought from home. Don't limit use to broiling on the beach. If you're out in the sun during the day— hiking, in and out of shops along a cloudy street, in a convertible with the top down—be sure to reapply SPF 25 or higher every few hours. The sun is most intense either side of high noon, 11–3, so be extra careful then. Use waterproof sunblock while swimming or wear a T-shirt to protect your back. Yes, you can get a sunburn watching the sunset.

Drink plenty of liquids. Dehydration can be a big problem after a long flight, and being in hot weather exacerbates it.

Wear your sunglasses and a brimmed hat. If the brim doesn't cover the back of your neck and you're outdoors without sunblock, drape a towel or a T-shirt over the exposed area between your shirt and hairline.

Securing Property

Be as security conscious as you are at home.

Do not leave anything of value unattended or in plain sight in your car, or anywhere—on the beach, in restaurants, or in lobbies. Lock valuables or temptations in your trunk before arriving at the destination if you must leave them behind.

Leave valuable or important items at your hotel's safe, or in your room safe. Use ATMs for daily withdrawals rather than carry cash.

Tsunami

Be prepared for tsunami waves. Tsunami have killed more Hawaiians than all other natural disasters combined.

Check the telephone book in your room for a map of low-lying areas that can be threatened by tsunami waves. Follow the instructions. In brief, a warning will be sounded at least three hours before the waves are expected to reach the shore if the triggering event is out of state.

When you stay in coastal areas, be aware of signs pointing out the evacuation route.

If you hear the Civil Defense sirens (a steady siren tone for three minutes, repeated as necessary), listen to your radio for emergency information and instructions broadcast by Civil Defense. Note: Civil Defense sirens are tested at 11:45 AM on the first working day of each month.

Weather
Be aware of the weather. The hurricane season runs from June 1 to November 30, and winter storms through March can be unpredictable. They're rare, but when storm watches and warnings are issued, monitor the radio or TV for official bulletins.

TELEPHONES
The 808 area code includes all the Hawaiian islands, but to call from one island to another, you must dial 808. You don't need to dial the area code when making a call on the same island. There are pay phones at beaches, parks, and most shopping centers, although there seem to be fewer every year as cell phone coverage improves. It does not yet cover the entire island. Expect to lose coverage if you go off the main roads outside population centers. If you're dialing a number from a cell phone and get a recording saying the number is out of service, call again from a different location. You may find you get through.

TIME
There is no daylight saving time in Hawai'i. When daylight saving time is not observed on the mainland, Hawai'i is two hours behind the West Coast, four hours behind the Midwest, and five hours behind the East Coast.

TOURIST INFORMATION
The Big Island Visitor's Bureau (800 648 2441; www.bigisland.org) has a wealth of information online. There are two local offices:

Hilo: 808-961-5797; 250 Keawe St.
Waikoloa: 808-886-1655; 69-250 Waikoloa Beach Dr.

The tourist-directed publications *This Week*, the *Beach and Activity Guide*, and *101 Things to Do on Hawai'i the Big Island* are loaded with information as well as discount coupons for activities. Copies are easy to find.

TOURS
There are circle-the-island tours that speed you past the highlights in one very full day, and the same operators offer daylong tours of Hawai'i Volcanoes National Park. Prices vary according to pickup point, and these include the Kohala Coast, Kailua-Kona, and Hilo.
  Jack's Hawai'i (808-969-9507, 800-442-5557; www.jackstours.com) Reservations are required. Customized limousine tours are available, as are tours of historic Kona and nighttime Mauna Kea and Hawai'i Volcanoes National Park outings. Prices start at $60, and online discounts are available.
  Polynesian Adventure Tours (808-833-3000, 800-622-3011; www.polyad.com) Reservations are required. Prices start at $65, and there are discounts for booking online.
  Roberts Hawai'i (808-329-1688, 866-898-2519; www.robertshawaii.com) Reservations are required. Prices start at $65, and there are discounts for booking online.

Sun breaks through the clouds on the slopes of Mauna Kea behind Hilo Bay.

Your hotel concierge or B&B host may know of private tour guides as well. Specialized tour operators providing hiking or other kinds of specific activities are listed in chapter 7, Recreation. Unless you are determined to see everything in one 250-mile day, I suggest that you do one tour in depth, such as visit the volcanoes, enjoy Waipiʻo Valley, or ascend Mauna Kea to stargaze. Even a slow drive along the Hāmākua Coast or over the Kohala Mountain Road beats rushing around in a circle.

WEDDINGS

No waiting period, no residency requirement, and no blood tests—what a cinch to get married in Hawaiʻi. If you jump through a few legal hoops and have an intended, that is. First, after deciding you're truly, madly, absolutely in love, you must obtain a license from an authorized agent, who can be found through the Big Island office of the state Department of Health: 808-974-6008. The bride and groom are required to appear together in person before a marriage license agent to apply for a marriage license. There is no requirement that you hold hands. Both of you must have proof that you're over 18—a driver's license is fine—and the state imposes various conditions for those who are younger. (Parents or their stand-ins are involved. You've been warned.)

The prospective bride and groom must prepare an official application and file it in person with the marriage license agent. The agent may have the application, or it can be downloaded from www.hawaii.gov/health/vital-records/marriage/index.html#eligible. A completed application will not be accepted if it is submitted by mail or by e-mail.

The $60 marriage license fee is payable in cash at the time the application is made, and the license is issued immediately. Valid throughout the state of Hawaiʻi, it expires 30 days from, and includes, the date it was issued.

It's important to remember that the person performing your wedding must be licensed by the Hawaiʻi Department of Health even if they are an ordained minister or other spiritual leader. A marriage certificate will be mailed to you after the wedding.

Resorts, hotels, and other accommodations have experience planning a Big Island wedding for visitors. If they don't have somebody on staff who can help, they will have local contacts for helpers, from planners to florists. Subscriptions to *Hawaiʻi Bride & Groom* (808-428-1596; www.hawaiibride.com) and *Pacific Rim Weddings* (808-233-3310; www.pacificweddings.com) are also useful for getting a sense of what's available on the Big Island before you arrive.

General Index

A

A-1 Taxi, 42
AAA (American Automobile Association), 264
A'Ama Surf & Sport Shop, 240
AARP, senior discounts, 201
Abundant Life Natural Foods and Café, 174, 194
accommodations. *See* bed-and-breakfasts; condo rentals; lodging; rental properties; *and* Lodging by Price Index
Ackerman Galleries, 228
activities. *See* recreational activities; *and specific activities*
Admissions Day, 126
agricultural inspection, 37
Ahalanui Park, 219
Ahhh, the Views, 91
Ahualoa: coffee farms, 188; lodging, 90–91
Ahu'ena Heiau, 137–38
air (helicopter) tours, 209
air travel, 37, 39–41
airlines, 40–41
airport shuttles, 42
Akaka Falls, 153
Akatsuka Orchid Gardens, 234
Akebono Farmers' Market, 192
Aki's Café, 164
Akoni Pule Highway, 130–31
Alan's Art & Collectibles, 228
Alapaki's Hawaiian Gifts, 236
Ali'i Garden Market Place, 192
Aloha Angel Café, 168
Aloha Cottage (Volcano), 78
Aloha Festival, 126
Aloha Guest House (Captain Cook), 70
Aloha Kayak, 222
Aloha Outpost, 183
Aloha Performing Arts Company, 115
Aloha Sundays, 115
Aloha Theatre and Performing Arts Center, 115
aloha wear, 231–33
ambulances, 255
American Express Travel, 40
Amy B. H. Greenwell Ethnobotanical Garden, 201–2
'Anaeho'omalu Beach, 214

ancient sites. *See* sacred sites
animal quarantine, 37
antiques, 228
Antiques and Orchids, 228
aquaculture, 122, 134, 167, 177–78
aquarium, 121
archeological sites. *See* sacred sites
art books, 256
art galleries, 109, 228–30
Art in the Iron Works, 228
art museums, 112–15
As Hāwī Turns, 231
astronomy, 118–21; books about, 256
Atebara Chips, 189
Atlantis Submarine, 220
ATM machines, 255
Audubon Society, 199, 210

B

Baby's Away, 261
babysitters, 261
Backroads, 198
bakeries, 182–83
Ba-Le, 164–65
Bamboo, 179
Bank of Hawai'i, 255
banks, 255
Banyan Massage Hale, 213
Basically Books, 210, 230
Batik, 164
Bay House Bed and Breakfast (Hilo), 86
Beach Tree Bar and Grill (Kailua-Kona), 158
beaches, 214–20; safety tip, 214, 264, 266; best for families, 249; Hilo, 220; Honolulu, 47; Kailua-Kona, 217–18; Kailua-Kona south, 218; Ka'u, 219; Kohala Coast, 214–17; Puna, 219; Pu'uhonua o Honaunau, 218. *See also specific beaches*
Bears' Café, 183
bed-and-breakfasts (B&Bs), 54; Captain Cook, 70–71; Hilo, 88; Kailua-Kona, 70; Ocean View, 75
Bentley's Home & Garden Collection, 235
best bets, 243–53
Bicycle Adventures, 198

bicycling, 45, 197–98
Big Island Candies, 194
Big Island Film Festival, 97
Big Island Grill, 165
Big Island Motorcycle Rentals, 43, 45
Big Island Mountain Bike Association, 198
Big Island Music Festival, 124
Big Island Surf, 240
Big Island Visitor's Bureau, 267
Billfish Tournament, 126, 201
birds (birding), 23, 199; books about, 260;
   Hakalau Forest National Wildlife Refuge, 23,
   153, 199; tours, 199, 210
Bishop Museum (Oahu), 47, 49
Black Bamboo Hawaii, 54
Black Rock Café, 173
Blockbuster, 97
Blue Ginger, 235
Blue Hawaiian, 209
boating and cruises, 220–22. *See also* whale-
   watching
Body Glove Cruises, 221
Boiling Pots, 152
Bong Brothers and Sistah, 183, 185
books, recommended, 256–61
bookstores, 230–31
Born of Fire, Born of the Sea (film), 147
botanical gardens, 201–4
Bougainvillea B&B, 75
breweries, 183
Broke the Mouth, 190
Brown's Beach House, 161; hula, 107
Burgado's Fine Woods, 233
buses, 41
business hours, 228

C

cabs, 41–42
Café 100, 174
Café Il Mondo, 178, 185
Café Pesto (Hilo), 174; (Kawaihae), 179
cafés, 183–87
camping, 200
candy, 194–95
Canoe House, 161
Cape Kumukahi, 22
Capt. Dan McSweeney's Whale Watch, 225
Captain Cook: antiques, 228; coffee, 185; eat-
   ing, 168–69; farmers' markets, 192; gardens,

201–2; historic sites, 101–2; kayaking,
   222–23; lodging, 70–74; sacred sites, 138
Captain Cook Monument, 100
Captain Zodiac, 221
car rentals, 39, 42–43; Honolulu, 47, 49
car travel, 39; best maps, 42, 152; driving
   times, 45; driving tips, 43; road services, 264
Caretakers of Our Land Farmers' Market, 192
Casa de Emdeko, 68–69
caverns, 150–51
Cedar House Coffee Farm B&B, 70–71
centers, shopping, 239–40
Chain of Craters Road, 145, 149
Charter Services Hawaii, 201
Chawan Shop, 235
Cheap Tickets, 40
children: best bets with, 248–49; travel tips,
   261
chips, 189
churches, 99–102, 104, 105–6
cinemas, 97
Civil Defense, 255, 266
Cliff House (Kukuihaele), 89
climate, 261
clothing stores, 231–33
Coast Grille & Oyster Bar (Kohala Coast), 164
Coconut Cottage, 82
Coconut Grove Marketplace, 239; nightlife,
   117–18
Coconut Island, 201
coffee: about, 184; cafés and roasters, 183,
   185–87; farms, 188; Kona Coffee Cultural
   Festival, 127; Kona Coffee Living History
   Farm, 112, 114
The Coffee Shack (Captain Cook), 168
Coffees 'n' Epicurea, 185
Colony One at Sea Mountain, 75
condo rentals, 54–56; Kailua-Kona, 55–56,
   68–69; Kohala Coast, 62–63; owners, agents,
   and agencies, 54–56
Cook, James, 26–27, 29, 31, 138; Monument,
   100
cookbooks, 256–57
Costco, 68, 263
Costco Travel, 40
Cowboys of Hawai'i, 211
craft galleries, 233–34, 246
crafts, books about, 257
Crater Rim Trail, 209

Crazy Shirts, 231
Creation Chant, 130
Cronies, 174–75
cross-country skiing, 212
Crossroads Shopping Center, 239; eating, 167; groceries, 68, 167
Crosswinds Shopping Center: groceries, 194
cruises, 220–22. *See also* whale-watching
cuisine, 155–57; cookbooks, 256–57; glossary of terms, 162–63. *See also* dining; food purveyors
culture, 95–127; books about, 258; cinema, 97–98; galleries, 109; historic buildings and sites, 98–106; hula, 106–9; libraries, 110; lū'aus, 110–12; museums, 112–15; nightlife, 117–18; performing arts, 115–17; science and technology, 118–22; seasonal events, 122–27
The Cutlery, 231

D

Da Kine Bike Shop, 198
Dahana Ranch, 211
Daifukuji Soto Zen Mission, 101
Dan De Luz Woods, 233
dance, 115–17
Daniel Thiebaut, 179–80
Dave's Bike & Triathlon Shop, 198
Daylight Donuts, 195
Devastation Trail, 147
Diamond Head Beach Hotel (Oahu), 48
dining, 155–82; best bets, 244–45; by cuisine, 274–76; by price, 271–74; glossary of terms, 162–63; hours, 155; price codes, 157; with children, 248; Hawai'i Volcanoes National Park, 171–73; Hilo, 174–78; Honolulu, 48–49; Kailua-Kona, 164–68; Kailua-Kona south, 168–70; Kohala Coast, 158–61, 164; North Kohala, 179–82; Puna area, 173–74; Waimea, 179–82
Disappearing Sands Beach, 218
Discount Hawaii Car Rental, 43
Discovery Antiques, 228
diving, 223
Dolphin Bay Hotel, 86
Dolphin Days, 124
Dolphin Quest, 200
dolphins, 200
Donatoni's, 159
Donkey Hike, 209–10

Donkey Mill Art Center, 109
Double Joy Designs, 238
Dovetail Gallery & Design, 238
Dragon Mama, 237
Dreams of Paradise, 236
driving. *See* car travel
drugstores, 263
Durty Jake's, 117

E

Earthquake Trail, 209
East Hawai'i Cultural Center, 109, 115
eating, 155–82; best bets, 244–45; best tasty treats, 246; by cuisine, 274–76; by price, 271–74; glossary of terms, 162–63; hours, 155; price codes, 157; with children, 248; Hawai'i Volcanoes National Park, 171–73; Hilo, 174–78; Honolulu, 48–49; Kailua-Kona, 164–68; Kailua-Kona south, 168–70; Kohala Coast, 158–61, 164; North Kohala, 179–82; Puna area, 173–74; Waimea, 179–82. *See also* farmers' markets; food purveyors
electricity, 262
Elements, 238
Emerald Orchid, 118
Emerald View Bed and Breakfast, 86–87
emergencies, 255
Eternal Wave Gallery, 229

F

Fabric Impressions, 233
Fair Wind Cruises, 221
Fairmont Orchid, 61; eating, 161; hula, 107; lū'aus, 111; spa, 212; tennis, 214
farmers' markets, 189–93
FedEx, 239, 240
Ferguson-Ota, Amy, 167
festivals, 122–27
film festivals, 97–98
fire, 255
First Hawaiian Bank, 255
First Hawaiian Bank Building (Hilo), 102, 114–15
fishing, 201; International Billfish Tournament, 126, 201
fishponds, 134–36
flower shops, 234
food purveyors, 182–95; bakeries, 182–83; breweries, 183; cafés and coffee roasters,

183–87; chips, 189; coffee farms, 188; glossary of terms, 162–63; groceries, 193–94; sweets, 194–95; wine and liquor, 195. *See also* farmers' markets
Foodland, 193, 194, 263
Ford Ironman World Championship, 127, 197
Four Seasons Resort Hualālai, 57–58; eating, 158–59; golf, 205; spa, 212
Francis H. I'i Brown North Course, 204
Francis H. I'i Brown South Course, 204–5
Fujimamas, 165
Fuku-Bonsai, 234

G

galleries. *See* art galleries; craft galleries
Gallery of Great Things, 229
gardens, 201–4
Gathering of the Kings, 111
gay and lesbian travelers: lodging, 54
general stores, 235
geography, 23; books about, 259–60
George Na'ope Kane Hula Festival, 109
gift shops, 235–36
Gold Coast. *See* Kohala Coast
golf, 204–7
The Grass Shack, 236
Green Sand Beach (Papakolea Beach), 218
Greenwell Ethnobotanical Garden, 201–2
Greenwell Farms, 188
Greenwell Store, 112
The Grill (Kohala Coast), 161
grocery stores, 193–94
guided tours. *See* tours

H

H. N. Greenwell Store, 112
Haili Congregational Church, 104
Hakalau Forest National Wildlife Refuge, 23, 153, 199
Hakone Steakhouse Sushi Bar, 164
Hale Hualālai, 71
Hale 'Ōhi'a Cottages, 78–79
Hale Samoa, 159
Halema'uma'u Overlook, 147
Hāmākua Artisans Guild, 109
Hāmākua Coast, 149–50; camping, 200; eating, 178–79; farmers' markets, 190; golf, 207; helicopter tours, 209; historic sites, 105; lodging, 89–91; natural wonders, 152–53

Hāmākua Coast Drive, 152–53
Hāmākua Country Club, 207
Hana Hou (Hilo), 237
Hana Hou Restaurant (Na'alehu), 170
Hāpuna Beach, 216
Hāpuna Beach Prince Hotel, 62; eating, 164
Hāpuna Golf Course, 205
Harbor Gallery, 229
Hard Rock Café, 117–18
Harper's Car and Truck Rental, 42
Harrington's, 175
Hata Building, 105; eating, 174
Hau Tree Lanai (Oahu), 49
Hawai'i Audubon Society, 199, 210
Hawai'i Belt Road, 39
Hawai'i Calls (radio program), 35
Hawai'i Calls (restaurant), 160
Hawai'i Concert Society, 116
Hawai'i Forest and Trail, 121, 199, 210
Hawai'i Gateway Energy Center, 122
Hawaii Healing Ohana, 213
Hawaii Island B&B Association, 54
Hawai'i Island Chinese Film Festival, 97
Hawai'i Lifeguard Surf Instructors, 225
Hawai'i Pack and Paddle, 222–23
Hawai'i Preparatory Academy, 109
Hawai'i Tribune-Herald, 263
Hawai'i Tropical Botanical Gardens, 202
Hawai'i Volcanoes National Park, 142–49; art galleries, 230; attractions, 145–49; birding, 199; campgrounds, 200; eating near, 171–73; hiking, 147, 209; hula festival, 108–9; lodging, 79, 81; map, 16; natural history, 21; planning tips, 144–45; safety tips, 142, 144
Hawai'i Wood Guild Show, 122
Hawaiian Airlines, 40–41
Hawaiian Homestead Farmers Market, 190
Hawaiian International Billfish Tournament, 126, 201
Hawaiian music, 115–17, 263–64
Hawaiian Pedals, 198
Hawaiian Telephone Building, 104
Hawaiian Trail and Mountain Club, 210
Hawaiian Walkways, 210
Hawaiiana, 236–37
Hawai'iana Live, 115–16
Hāwī: art galleries, 229; clothing stores, 231, 232; coffee, 186; eating, 179, 181, 182; farmers' markets, 192; gift shops, 236; groceries,

194; ice cream, 195; jewelry stores, 238; lodging, 94; natural wonders, 150
Hele-On (bus), 41
helicopter tours, 209
Hikiau Heiau, 138
hiking, 209–10; Hawai'i Volcanoes National Park, 147, 209; safety tips, 207
Hilo: antiques, 228; art galleries, 109, 228; bakeries, 182–83; banks, 255; beaches, 220; bicycling, 198; bookstores, 230; breweries, 183; chips, 189; clothing stores, 231–33; coffee, 183–88; craft galleries, 233; cruises, 222; eating, 174–78; emergencies, 255; farmers' markets, 190; flower shop, 234; gardens, 202, 204; gift shops, 235–36; golf, 206–7; groceries, 193; Hawaiiana, 237; historic sites, 102–5; home decor, 237–38; hospitals, 263; hula, 107–9, 123; ice cream, 195; libraries, 110; liquor stores, 195; lodging, 86–89; map, 15; motorcycle rentals, 43; movie rentals, 97; movie theaters, 97; museums, 112, 114–15, 121; natural foods, 194; natural wonders, 152; nightlife, 118; performing arts, 115–17; pharmacies, 263; planetarium, 118; road services, 264; scuba diving, 223; shopping center, 240; shopping plaza, 240; snorkeling, 224; spas, 213; special events, 123, 124; sport shops, 240; sweets, 194; taxis, 41–42; tourist information, 267; waterfalls, 152
Hilo Art Museum, 112
Hilo Bay: kayaking, 222
Hilo Bay Beach Park, 220
Hilo Bay Café, 175
Hilo Bike Hub, 198
Hilo Chamber Music Festival, 123
Hilo Coffee Mill, 185
Hilo Farmers' Market, 189–90
Hilo Federal Building, 104
Hilo Harry's, 42
Hilo Hattie, 231–32
Hilo Hawaiian Hotel, 87, 213
Hilo Homemade, 195
Hilo International Airport, 37, 40; car rentals, 43
Hilo Medical Center, 263
Hilo Municipal Golf Course, 206–7
Hilo Pharmacy, 263
Hilo Post Office, 104
Hilo Public Library, 110

Hilo Seaside Hotel, 87
Hilo Surplus Store, 240
Hilton Waikoloa Village, 58–59; Dolphin Days, 124; Dolphin Quest, 200; eating, 159–60; golf, 206; lū'aus, 112; shopping, 232
historic buildings and sites, 98–106. *See also* sacred sites
history, 21–35; books about, 258–59
Hobbit House, 75–76
Holei Pali Lookout, 149
holidays, 262
Holuakoa Café, 168, 186
Hōlualoa: café, 186; coffee farms, 188; eating, 168; galleries, 109, 229–30, 233, 237; home decor, 238; lodging, 65, 71; whale-watching, 225
Hōlualoa Gallery, 229
Hōlualoa Inn, 65
Hōlualoa Kona Coffee Company, 188
home decor, 237–38
Honalo: kayaking, 222
Honauau: lodging, 74–75
Honaunau: coffee, 183, 185; lodging, 71–72
Hōnaunau Beach, 218
Honoka'a: antiques, 228; banks, 255; coffee, 185, 188; craft galleries, 233; eating, 178–79; farmers' markets, 190; gift shops, 236; golf, 207; horseback riding, 211; hospitals, 263; lodging, 89–91
Honoka'a Farmers' Market, 190
Honoka'a Marketplace, 236
Honoka'a People's Theater, 97
Honoka'a Trading Company, 228
Honokohau Marine Charters, 201
Honolulu, 47–49
Honolulu International Airport, 39
Honomu: craft galleries, 234; gardens, 204; lodging, 90
Honpa Hongwanji Hilo Betsuin, 104
Horizon Guest House, 71–72
horseback riding, 211
hospitals, 263
hotels. *See* lodging; *and specific hotels*
HP Bikeworks, 198
Hualālai Golf Course, 205
Hualālai Grille by Alan Wong, 158
Huggo's, 118, 165
hula, 106–9; books about, 258; Merrie Monarch Hula Festival, 108, 123

Hula Mana and Savai'i, Origins of Polynesia, 112

Huli Sue's BBQ and Grill, 180–81

Hulihe'e Palace, 98–99, 107

hunting, 211

I

I Ka Pono Farmers' Market, 192

ice cream, 195

Imari, 159

'Imiloa Astronomy Center, 118

'Imiola Congregational Church, 105

information, 255–69

International Billfish Tournament, 126, 201

Ipu Hale Gallery, 237

Ironman Triathlon, 127, 197

Isaac Hale Beach Park, 200, 219

Isaacs Art Center, 109

Island Breeze Lū'au, 111

Island Fruits (Mountain View), 193

Island Lava Java (Kailua-Kona), 186

Island Naturals (Hilo), 194

itineraries, best, 250–53

Itsu's Fishing Supplies, 194

J

Jacaranda Inn, 92

Jackie Ray's Ohana Grill, 166

Jack's Diving Locker, 223

Jack's Hawai'i, 267

Jaggar (Thomas) Museum, 142, 147

Jameson's by the Sea, 166

Java on the Rocks, 186

jewelry stores, 238

K

K. Takata Store, 194

Ka Lae, 22, 142

Ka'awa Loa Plantation, 72

Kadota's Liquor, 195

Kahalu'u Beach Park, 217

Kahapapa Fishpond, 135

Kahilu Theatre, 116

Kahilu Theatre Gallery, 109

Kailua Candy Company, 194–95

Kailua Pier, 67, 217

Kailua Village Farmer's Market, 192

Kailua Village Walking Tour, 112, 114

Kailua-Kona: banks, 255; beaches, 217–18;
bicycling, 198; breweries, 183; clothing
stores, 231–32; coffee, 127, 183–88; cruises,
220–21; eating, 158–59, 164–68; emergencies, 255; farmers' markets, 192; fishing, 201;
gift shops, 236; golf, 206; groceries, 194;
Hawaiiana, 236; historic sites, 98–100; hospitals, 263; hula, 107; ice cream, 195; liquor
stores, 195; lodging, 65–70; vacation rentals,
55–56, 68–69; lū'aus, 111; map, 17; motorcycle rentals, 43; movie rentals, 97; movie theaters, 97; museums, 112, 114; natural foods,
194; nightlife, 117; pharmacies, 263; road
services, 264; sacred sites, 135–38; science
and technology, 122; scuba diving, 223, 224;
shopping malls, 239–40; spas, 213; special
events, 122, 126, 127, 201; sport shops,
240–41; submarine tours, 220; surfing, 225;
sweets, 194–95; taxis, 41–42; tennis, 214;
whale-watching, 225

Kainaliu: art galleries, 229; bookstores,
230–31; eating, 168, 170; general store, 235;
gift shops, 235; performing arts, 115

Kakua Ranch, 211

Kalaekilohana, 76

Kalahikiola Congregational Church, 105–6

Kalahuipua'a Fishponds and Historical Trail,
135

Kalakaua, King, 33–34, 99, 107

Kalakekua: eating, 169

Kalani Oceanside Retreat, 82, 84

Kaloko Fishpond, 135–36

Kaloko-Honokohau National Historic Park,
135–36

Kālōpa Cabins, 89

Kālōpa State Recreation Area, 200; cabin
rentals, 89

Kama'aina Woods, 233

Kamaha'o "The Wondrous Myths of Hawai'i,"
111

Kamakahonu Beach, 217

Kamanu Charters, 221

Kamehameha I, 29, 31, 66, 105, 129, 134–35,
137; birthplace, 132; Day, 123–24, 262

Kamehameha III, 33

Kamehameha Pharmacy, 263

Kamuela. *See* Waimea

Kamuela Airport, 40; car rentals, 43

Kamuela Goldsmiths, 238

Kamuela Inn, 92

Kamuela Liquor, 195
Kamuela Philharmonic, 116
Kamuela Provision Company, 159–60
Kanaloa at Kona, 69
Kapa'au: art galleries, 228, 229; banks, 255;
  bookstores, 230; eating, 181–82; historic
  sites, 105–6; hospitals, 263; jewelry stores,
  238; lodging, 94; pharmacies, 263
Kapoho Tide Pools, 219
Kathmandu Trading Company, 238
Kathryn's of Kona, 236
Ka'u coffee, 184, 185, 187
Ka'u Community Pharmacy, 263
Ka'u District, 22; beaches, 219; camping, 200;
  eating, 170–71; farmers' markets, 192; fish-
  ing, 201; gardens, 202; golf, 206; lodging,
  75–78; natural wonders, 150–51; sacred sites,
  142
Ka'u Hospital, 263
Kauna'oa Beach, 217
Ka'upulehu Petroglyphs, 136
Kawaihae: eating, 179; gardens, 202, 204; lodg-
  ing, 63, 65; special events, 126
Kawaihae Coast: sacred sites, 130–32
kayaking, 222–23
Kea'au: farmers' market, 193; groceries, 194
Kea'au Shopping Center: groceries, 194
Kea'au Village Farmers' Market, 193
Keahole-Kona International Airport, 37,
  39–40; car rentals, 43
Kealakekua: antiques, 228; coffee farms, 188;
  eating, 169–70; flea market, 192; Hawaiiana,
  236; historic sites, 101; horseback riding, 211;
  hospitals, 263; kayaking, 223; lodging, 72;
  museums, 112; surfing, 225
Kealakekua Bay: lodging, 73
Kealakekua Bay State Historical Park, 138, 224
Kealakekua Flea Market, 192
Keanakoko'i Overlook, 147
Keauhou: beaches, 217–18; church, 100; eating,
  166; groceries, 194; lodging, 67–68; lū'aus,
  111; movie theater, 97; shopping centers, 239;
  tennis, 214
Keauhou 7 Cinemas, 97
Keauhou Bay: kayaking, 222; scuba diving, 223
Keauhou Bay Resort & Spa. See Sheraton
  Keauhou Bay Resort & Spa
Keauhou Beach Resort. See Outrigger Keauhou
  Beach Resort

Keauhou Shopping Center, 239; eating, 166;
  groceries, 194; Hawaiiana, 236; movies, 97
Keei Café, 169
Kehena Beach, 219; lodging, 82, 84
Kekaha Kai State Park, 216
Kenichi Pacific, 166
Ken's House of Pancakes, 175
Kiawe Kitchen, 171
kids: best bets with, 248–49; travel tips, 261
Kīlauea Drama and Entertainment Network,
  116
Kīlauea Iki Overlook, 145
Kīlauea Iki Trail, 209
Kīlauea Kreations, 233
Kīlauea Lodge, 79; eating, 171–72
Kīlauea Visitor Center, 142, 145
Killer Tacos, 166
Kim Taylor Reece Gallery, 229
Kimura Lauhala Shop, 233
Kimura Store, 235
King Kamehameha. See Kamehameha I
King Kamehameha Day, 123–24, 262
King Kamehameha Kona Beach Hotel, 66;
  lū'aus, 111
King Kamehameha Statue, 123–24
King's Shops, 239–40; eating, 160–61; hula,
  107
King's Trail Rides, 211
Kipuka Puaulu Bird Preserve, 199
Koehnen's Interiors, 104
Kohala: farmers' markets, 190; lodging, 63, 65
Kohala Book Shop, 230
Kohala Club Hotel, 94
Kohala Coast: banks, 255; beaches, 214–17; eat-
  ing, 158–61, 164; emergencies, 255; golf,
  204–6; hospitals, 263; hula, 107; lodging,
  56–65; lū'aus, 111–12; pharmacies, 263;
  sacred sites, 134–37; scuba diving, 224; spas,
  212–13; special events, 124; tennis, 214
Kohala Coffee Mill, 181, 186, 195
Kohala Historical Sites States Monument, 132
Kohala Hospital, 263
Kohala Mountain Lookout, 150
Kohala Pacific Realty, 55
Kohala Rainbow Café, 181
Kohala Village Inn, 94
Kohala Vista Inn, 63, 65
Kohala Winds of Change Health & Tea, 236
Kona: lodging, 70–75. See also Kailua-Kona

Kona Beach Hotel. *See* King Kamehameha Kona Beach Hotel
Kona Boys, 223, 225
Kona Brewing Co., 183
Kona Chocolate Festival, 122
Kona Coast Shopping Center: eating, 164–65; groceries, 194; movie rentals, 97
Kona coffee: about, 184; cafés and roasters, 183, 185–87; farms, 188
Kona Coffee Cultural Festival, 127
Kona Coffee Living History Farm, 112, 114
Kona Community Hospital, 263
Kona Country Club, 206
Kona Farmers' Market, 192
Kona Forest National Wildlife Reserve, 199, 202
Kona Historical Society & Museum, 112, 114
Kona Inn Restaurant, 166–67
Kona Inn Shopping Village, 240; bike rentals, 198; eating, 166–67; hula, 107
Kona International Airport, 37, 39–40; car rentals, 43
Kona Joe, 188
Kona Marketplace: nightlife, 117–18
Kona Music Society, 117
Kona Natural Foods, 167, 194
Kona Pacific Farmers' Co-op, 192
Kona Seaside Hotel, 66
Kona Stories, 230–31
Kona Tiki Hotel, 66
Kona Village Resort, 58; eating, 159; lū'aus, 112; petroglyphs, 136
Kona Wine Market, 195
Kope Kope, 187
Kress Building, 104
Kress Cinemas, 97
Kuamo'o Battlefield, 138
Ku'emanu Heiau, 138
Kukuihaele: lodging, 89
Kula Kai Caverns, 150–51
Kulanaokuaiki Campground, 200
Kumulipo, 130
Ku'uali'i Fishpond, 135
Kyoto House, 70

L

L. Zeidman Gallery, 229
language: books about, 259; food terms, 162–63; sacred site terms, 134

Lapakahi State Historical Park, 131–32
Laupāhoehoe, 129; camping, 200; farmers' market, 190; historic site, 105; museum, 114
Laupāhoehoe Market, 190
Laupāhoehoe Train Museum, 114
lava, 144–45, 147, 149; map of hazard zones, 19; types of, 142
Lava Ocean Adventures, 222
Lava Rock Café, 172
Lava Tree State Monument, 151
Lavender Moon Gallery, 229
"Legends of the Pacific," 112
Lei Day, 123
leis, 124–25
Lekeleke Burial Grounds, 138
Leleiwi Beach Park, 220
Liberty Travel, 40
libraries, 110
Liholiho, King, 31, 32, 99
Lili'uokalani, Queen, 34, 107
Lili'uokalani Gardens, 202
liquor stores, 195
literature, 260–61
Living Ocean Adventures, 225
loco moco: about, 156
lodging, 51–94; best bets, 249; by price, 269–71; deposits and cancellations, 53; handicapped access, 54; minimum stay, 53; price codes, 53; Hamakua Coast, 89–91; Hilo, 86–89; Honolulu, 47, 48; Kailua-Kona, 65–70; Ka'u, 75–78; Kohala Coast, 56–65; North Kohala, 94; North Kona, 70–75; Puna area, 82–84; South Kona, 70–75; Volcano, 78–82; Waimea, 91–94
Long Ears Coffee, 188
Lono, 27, 137–38
Louis Vuitton Hawai'i International Film Festival, 98
Luana Ola Cottages, 89–90
lū'aus, 110–12
Lulu's, 118
Luquin's Restauant, 173
Lyman House Museum, 114

M

MacArthur & Company, 55
McCandless Ranch, 71
McKenzie State Recreation Area, 200
McSweeney's (Capt. Dan) Whale Watch, 225

magazines, 263
Magic Sands Beach, 218; eating, 166
Mahukona Beach Park, 216–17
Makalapua Center, 240
Makalapua Stadium Cinema, 97
Makalei Hawaii Country Club, 206
Maku'u Farmers' Market, 192
malasadas, 162, 170–71, 179
malls, shopping, 239–40
Māmane Street Bakery, 178
Manago Hotel, 72; eating, 169
Manukā State Wayside Park, 200, 202
maps: best to buy, 42, 152; Big Island, 6;
   Hawai'i Volcanoes National Park, 16; Hilo, 15;
   Kailua-Kona, 17; lava hazard zone, 19; Puna
   District, 18
marriage licenses, 269
Mauna Kea, 119–21, 153; skiing, 212
Mauna Kea Beach, 217
Mauna Kea Beach Hotel, 61–62; eating, 164;
   golf, 205
Mauna Kea Golf Course, 205
Mauna Kea Mountain Bikes, 198
Mauna Kea SRA, 200
Mauna Kea State Park, 153
Mauna Kea Summit Adventures, 121
Mauna Kea Telescopes, 119–21
Mauna Lani Point, 62–63
Mauna Lani Resort, 59, 61, 240; attractions,
   135, 136–37; eating, 161; golf, 204–5; gro-
   ceries, 193; hiking, 210; shopping, 240; spa,
   212
Mauna Loa, 22, 153, 199
Mauna Loa Strip Road, 209
Mehana Brewing Company, 183
Melton International Tackle, 240
menehune, 132, 135–36
Merrie Monarch Hula Festival, 108, 123
Merriman, Peter, 160–61, 181
Merriman's, 181
Merriman's Market Café, 160–61
Mid-Pacific Wheels, 198
Miloli'i, 200, 202
missionaries, history on the Big Island, 32–33
Miyo's, 176
Moku Loa Group, 210
Moku o Keawe International Festival, 109
Moku'aikaua Church, 99
Moku'aweoweo Cabin, 200

Mokupapapa Discovery Center, 121
Monkeypod Tree, 150
Mo'okini Heiau, 132
Most Irresistible Shop, 236
motorcycle rentals, 43, 45
mountain biking, 197–98
Mountain View: bakeries, 183; cafés, 185; craft
   galleries, 233; farmers' markets, 193
Mountain View Bakery, 183
movie rentals, 97
movie theaters, 97
museums, 112–15
music, 115–17, 263–64
mythology: books about, 259

N
Na Makua, 232
Na Mea Hawai'i Hula Kahiko, 108–9
Na'alapa Stables, 211
Na'alehu: beaches, 219; eating, 170–71; farmers'
   market, 192; lodging, 76
Na'alehu Farmers Market, 192
Namakani Paio Cabins, 81
Namakani Paio Campground, 200
Nanbu Courtyard, 181–82
Nancy's Hideaway, 72–73
Naniloa Country Club Golf Course, 207
Naniloa Volcanoes Resort, 88
Nasturtium Café, 169
Natural Energy Laboratory of Hawai'i Authority
   (NELHA), 122, 167
natural food stores, 194
natural history, 22–23; books about, 259–60
Naung Mai, 176
Nautilus Dive Center, 223
nene, 199
New Otani Kaimana Beach Hotel (Oahu), 48
newspapers, 263
nightlife, 117–18
Nihon Restaurant & Cultural Center, 176
Ni'ihau leis, 236
Ning's Thai Cuisine, 173–74
Nori's Saimin and Snacks, 176–77
North Hawai'i Community Hospital, 263
North Kohala: camping, 200; eating, 179–82;
   historic sites, 105–6; horseback riding, 211;
   lodging, 94; natural wonders, 150; sacred
   sites, 130–32
North Kona: lodging, 57–58

nudist beach, 219

O

Oahu: Honolulu, 47–49
Ocean Eco Tours, 225
ocean kayaking, 222–23
Ocean Song, 73
Ocean Sushi Deli (Hilo), 177
Ocean View Inn (Kailua-Kona), 167–68
O'Keefe and Sons Bakery and Garden Café, 182
Old Jodo Mission, 105
Old Kona Airport Beach, 217
Old Mamalahoa Highway, 152–53
Onekahakaha Beach, 220
Onizuka International Astronomy Visitor
   Center, 118–21
Ono Kona Coffee, 187
Onomea Bay Scenic Drive, 153
Opelo Plaza: eating, 181
Orchid Isle Bicycling, 198
Orchidland Surfboards, 240
orchids, 234
Orchids of Hawai'i, 234
organized tours. See tours
O's Bistro, 167
Ossipoff, Vladimir, 109, 256
Outrigger Keauhou Beach Resort, 67–68; ten-
   nis, 214

P

Pacific Rim Fishing Supplies, 241
Pacific Tsunami Museum, 114–15
Pacific Vibrations, 225
package tours, 40
Pāhala: banks, 255; eating, 170–71; golf, 206;
   hospitals, 263; lodging, 76–77, 78
Pāhala Plantation Cottages, 76–77
Pāhala Town Café, 170–71
Pāhoa: banks, 255; eating, 173–74; farmers'
   markets, 192; groceries, 174, 194; lodging, 82,
   84
Pāhoa Marketplace: coffee, 183
Pāhoa Natural Foods, 174
Pahu i'a, 158–59
Palace Theatre, 97, 115
Palms Cliff House Inn, 90
Paniolo Adventures, 211
Paniolo Cottage, 92–93
Papakōlea Beach, 218

Parker Ranch, 105; books about, 258; horseback riding, 211; hunting, 211; Visitors Center
   and Museum, 115
Parker Ranch Independence Day Rodeo,
   125–26
Parker Ranch Rodeo, 126
Parker Ranch Shopping Center, 240
Parker Square, 240; coffee, 187; galleries,
   229–30; general store, 236; gift shops, 235;
   jewelry store, 238
pa'u riders, 125
Pe'epe'e Falls, 152
People Attentive to Children, 261
Peoples Advocacy for Trails Hawai'i, 198
Pepe'ekeo: eating, 178
performing arts, 115–17
Persimmon, 232
pet quarantine, 37
petroglyphs, 135, 136–37
pharmacies, 263
planetarium, 118
plate lunches: about, 156
Pleasant Hawaiian Holidays, 40
Pohakuloa Military Training Area, 153
Pohakunani, 84
poi, 25, 111
Poison Control, 255
police, 255
Pololū Valley Lookout, 150
Polynesian Adventure Tours, 267
potato chips, 189
Prince Kūhiō Day, 123
Prince Kūhiō Shopping Plaza, 240; clothing,
   231–32; natural foods, 194
Prince Kūhiō Stadium Cinema, 97
Property Network, 55
Pua Mau Botanical Gardens, 202, 204
Puakō Bed and Breakfast, 65
Pu'akō Petroglyph Archeological District,
   136–37
Puka Puka Kitchen, 177
Pukui, Mary Kawena, 107, 258, 259
Puna coffee, 183, 184, 185, 187
Puna District: beaches, 219; camping, 200;
   eating, 173–74; farmers' markets, 192; lodg-
   ing, 82–84; map, 18; natural wonders,
   151–52; snorkeling, 224
Puna Fresh Foods, 194
Punalu'u: lodging, 75

Punaluʻu Bake Shop, 171
Punaluʻu Black Sand Beach, 219
Puʻu Uʻlaʻula Cabin, 200
Puʻuhonua O Honaunau National Historical
    Park, 138, 140, 142; beach, 218
Puʻukoholā Heiau National Historic Site, 137;
    Cultural Festival, 126

Q

The Quilted Horse, 236
quilts, 229, 233–34, 236, 257

R

Rainbow Falls, 152
Rainbow Falls Connection, 190
Ramashala, 84
Rape Crisis Center, 255
reading, recommended, 256–61
recreational activities, 197–225; beaches,
    214–20; bicycling, 197–99; birding, 199;
    boating and cruises, 220–22; camping, 200;
    dolphin watching, 200–201; fishing, 201;
    gardens, 201–4; golf, 204–7; hiking, 209–10;
    horseback riding, 211; hunting, 211; kayaking,
    222–23; scuba diving, 223; skiing, 212; snor-
    keling, 223–24; spas, 212–13; surfing,
    224–25; tennis, 214; whale watching, 225
Red Hill, 209
Red Road, 151–52
rental properties: Kailua-Kona, 55–56, 68–69;
    Kohala Coast, 62–63; owners, agents, and
    agencies, 54–56
resorts. See lodging; and specific resorts
restaurants. See dining; and specific restaurants
Richard, Tori, 231, 240
Richardson Ocean Beach Park, 220
road services, 264
Roberts Hawaiʻi, 267
Royal Sea Cliff Resort, 69
Royal Siam Thai Restaurant, 177
Roy's Waikoloa Bar and Grill, 160

S

S. Hata Building, 105; eating, 174
Sack 'n' Save, 193
sacred sites, 129–42; books about, 258–59;
    glossary of terms, 134; Kaʻu, 142; Kohala
    Coast, 134–37; Kona Coast, 137–38; North
    Kohala, 130–32; South Kona, 138–42

Saddle Road, 153
safety tips, 264, 266–67
Safeway (Hilo), 193; (Kailua-Kona), 68, 194
St. Benedict's Painted Church, 101–2
St. Michael's Church, 99–100
St. Peter's Church, 100
Sam's Hideaway, 118
Sandal Tree, 232
Scandinavian Shave Ice, 195
science and technology, 118–22
scuba diving, 223
sea kayaking, 222–23
Sea Mountain Golf Course (Pāhala), 206
Sea Quest, 221
sea turtles, 217, 219, 220, 259
Seaside Restaurant and Aquafarm (Hilo),
    177–78
seasonal events, 122–27
seasons, 52–53
senior discounts, 201
Shaka Restaurant, 171
shave ice, 163, 194–95
Sheraton Keauhou Bay Resort & Spa, 68; lūʻaus,
    111; trolley, 67
Shipman House Bed and Breakfast, 88
shopping, 226–41; antiques and vintage, 228;
    art galleries, 228–30; best bets, 245; book-
    stores, 230–31; clothing, 231–33; crafts,
    233–34; flowers and orchids, 234; general
    stores, 235; gift shops, 235–36; Hawaiiana,
    236–37; home decor, 237–38; hours, 228;
    jewelry stores, 238; malls and shopping cen-
    ters, 239–40; sport shops, 240–41
Shops at Mauna Lani, 240; groceries, 193
Shores at Waikoloa, 63
Sierra Club, 210
Sig Zane Designs, 232–33
Silk Road Gallery, 230
Simply Natural, 178
Ski Guides Hawaii, 212
skiing, 212
Snorkel Bob's, 224
snorkeling, 223–24
snowboarding, 212
South Kohala Management, 55
South Kona: camping, 200; farmers' markets,
    192; lodging, 70–75; sacred sites, 138–42
South Kona Forest Reserve, 199, 202
South Kona Fruit Stand, 192

South Kona Hideaway, 73–74

South Point (Ka'u), 22; beaches, 219; camping, 200; eating, 170–71; farmers' markets, 192; fishing, 201; gardens, 202; golf, 206; lodging, 75–78; natural wonders, 150–51; sacred sites, 142

South Point Banyan Tree House, 77–78

Spam, 157, 256

spas, 212–13

special events, 122–27

Speedishuttle, 42

Spencer Beach Park, 217

sport shops, 240–41

sports. See recreational activities; water sports

Sports Zone, 241

Standard Bakery, 170

Starbucks, 187

stargazing, 119–21; books about, 256

steam vents, in Hawai'i Volcanoes National Park, 146

Straub Clinic & Hospital, 263

Studio 7 Gallery, 230

Sulphur Banks, 146

sun precautions, 266

SunQuest Vacations, 55

Sure Save Supermarket, 194

surf shops, 240

Surfer Bear Hawai'i, 225

surfing, 224–25

Sushi Rocks, 182

sweets, 194–95

T

Tako Taco Taqueria, 182

Tara Cottage, 74–75

taro chips, 189

taxis, 41–42

telephones, 267

tennis, 214

Teshima's, 170

Tex Drive-In, 179

Thai Thai Restaurant, 172

theater, 115–17

Thomas Jaggar Museum, 142, 147

Thurston Lava Tube, 147, 149

tide pools, 219, 220, 266

time zone, 267

Tong Wo Society, 106

Topstitch, 234

tourist information, 267

tours, 267, 269; bicycling, 198; birding, 199; helicopter, 209; hiking, 210; kayaking, 222–23; Mauna Kea, 120–21; package, 40; skiing, 212; whale-watching, 225

transportation, 37–45; to Big Island, 39–41; within Big Island, 41–45

trolley, 67

Tropical Dreamin', 195

tsunami: safety tips, 266

Tsunami Museum, 114–15

Twain, Mark, 51, 261; Monkeypod Tree, 150

2400 Fahrenheit, 230

Two Ladies Kitchen, 182–83

2Papayas, 55

U

Ukulele & Slack Key Guitar Festival, 127

Uncle Billy's Hilo Bay Hotel, 88–89; hula, 107; nightlife, 118

Uncle Billy's Kona Bay Hotel, 67

Under the Banyans Farmers' Market, 192

University of Hawai'i at Hilo Botanical Gardens, 204

University of Hawai'i-Hilo Performing Arts Center, 117

Upcountry Connection, 230

Upolu Point Airport, 132

V

vacation home rentals. See rental properties

Vacation Rental By Owner (VRBO), 56

Victor Emanuel Nature Tours, 199

views, best, 245–46

vintage clothing, 228

visitor information, 267

vog, 199

Volcano: art galleries, 230; craft galleries, 233; eating, 171–73; farmers' markets, 193; general store, 235; golf, 206; lodging, 78–82; performing arts, 116; wineries, 195. See also Hawai'i Volcanoes National Park

Volcano Art Center, 142, 145, 230

Volcano Festival Chorus, 116

Volcano Golf and Country Club, 206; eating, 172–73

Volcano House, 51, 146; eating, 173; lodging, 81

Volcano Places, 81

Volcano Store, 235

Volcano Teapot, 81–82
Volcano True Value Hardware, 173
Volcano Village Farmers Market, 193
Volcano Winery, 195
Volcanoes National Park. *See* Hawai'i Volcanoes
National Park

W

Wa'akaulua, 222
Waiakea Center, 240
Waianuhea, 90–91
Waikiki (Oahu), 47–49
Waikoloa: banks, 255; clothing stores, 232; eat-
ing, 159–61; golf, 205–6; groceries, 193; hula,
107, 109; lodging, 58–59, 63; lū'aus, 112;
pharmacies, 263; sacred sites, 135; shopping
malls, 239–40; spas, 212–13; tourist informa-
tion, 267
Waikoloa Beach Marriott Resort, 59; beach,
214; eating, 160; fishponds, 135; hula, 107,
109; shopping, 239; spa, 212
Waikoloa Highlands Center: groceries, 193
Waikoloa Pharmacy, 263
Waikoloa Resort Golf-Beach Course, 205
Waikoloa Resort Golf-King's Course, 205
Waikoloa Village Golf Club, 206
Wailoa Center, 109
Wailuku River, 152; fishing, 201
Waimea (Kamuela): art galleries, 109, 229, 230;
banks, 255; bicycling, 198; coffee, 187; craft
galleries, 233, 234; eating, 164, 179–82;
emergencies, 255; farmers' markets, 190,
192; gift shops, 235–36; golf, 205, 207; groceries, 194; historic sites, 105; horseback
riding, 211; hospitals, 263; jewelry stores,
238; liquor stores, 195; lodging, 61–62, 65,
91–94; movie theaters, 97; museums, 115;
performing arts, 116–17; pharmacies, 263;
road services, 264; shopping malls, 240; special events, 125–26, 127; sport shops, 241
Waimea Center, 240

Waimea Coffee Co., 187
Waimea Community Theatre, 117
Waimea Country Club, 207
Waimea Gardens Cottage, 93–94
Waimea General Store, 236
Waimea-Kohala Airport, 40; car rentals, 43
Wai'ohinu, 150; lodging, 75–78
Waipi'o on Horseback, 211
Waipi'o Ridge Stables, 211
Waipi'o Valley, 149–50; horseback riding, 211
Waipi'o Valley Artworks, 149, 230
Waipi'o Valley Shuttle, 149
Waipi'o Wayside Bed and Breakfast, 91
Waldron Ledge, 209
Wal-Mart, 263
water sports, 214–25; beaches, 214–20; boating
and cruises, 220–22; kayaking, 222–23; scuba
diving, 223; snorkeling, 223–24; surfing,
224–25; whale watching, 225
waterfalls, 152, 153
weather, 261, 267
weddings, 269
West Hawaii Property Services Inc., 56
West Hawai'i Today, 263
whale-watching, 132, 225
What's Shakin', 178
White Sands Beach, 218
W Honolulu-Diamond Head (Oahu), 48
wine (liquor) stores, 195
wineries, 195
Womantours, 198
Wong, Alan, 156, 158, 256
Wood Guild Show, 122
Wood Valley Temple Retreat and Guest House,
78
Woodshop Gallery and Café, 234
World Botanical Garden, 204
World War II, 35

Y

Yamaguchi, Roy, 160, 257

LODGING BY PRICE

INEXPENSIVE	Up to $100
MODERATE	$100–225
EXPENSIVE	$225–350
VERY EXPENSIVE	Over $350

Kohala Coast

MODERATE
Kohala Vista Inn
Puakō Bed and Breakfast

MODERATE–EXPENSIVE
The Shore at Waikoloa
Waikoloa Beach Marriott Resort

EXPENSIVE
Mauna Lani Point

EXPENSIVE–VERY EXPENSIVE
The Fairmont Orchid
Hilton Waikoloa Village

VERY EXPENSIVE
Four Seasons Resort Hualālai
Hāpuna Beach Prince Hotel
Kona Village Resort
Mauna Kea Beach Hotel
The Mauna Lani Resort

North & South Kona

INEXPENSIVE
Kona Seaside Hotel
Kona Tiki Hotel
Manago Hotel
Uncle Billy's Kona Bay Hotel

MODERATE
Aloha Guest House
Casa de Emdeko
Cedar House Coffee Farm B&B
Nancy's Hideaway
South Kona Hideaway

MODERATE–EXPENSIVE
Hale Hualālai
King Kamehameha Kona Beach Hotel

Outrigger Keauhou Beach Resort
Royal Sea Cliff Resort
Tara Cottage

EXPENSIVE
Hōlualoa Inn
Horizon Guest House
Kyoto House
Ocean Song
Sheraton Keauhou Bay Resort and Spa

VERY EXPENSIVE
Kanaloa at Kona

Ka'u (South Point Area)

INEXPENSIVE
Bougainvillea B&B
Colony One at Sea Mountain
Wood Valley Temple Retreat

MODERATE
The Hobbit House
Kalaekilohana
Pāhala Plantation Cottages
South Point Banyan Tree House

Volcano

MODERATE
Aloha Cottage
Volcano Teapot

MODERATE–EXPENSIVE
Hale 'Ōhi'a Cottages
Kilauea Lodge
Volcano House Hotel
Volcano Places

In and around Puna

INEXPENSIVE
Hale Kukui Ola
Pohakunai

MODERATE
Coconut Cottage
Ramashala

Hilo

INEXPENSIVE
Hilo Seaside Hotel
Uncle Billy's Hilo Bay Hotel

MODERATE
Bay House Bed and Breakfast
Dolphin Bay Hotel
Emerald View Bed and Breakfast
Hilo Hawaiian Hotel

EXPENSIVE
Shipman House Bed and Breakfast

Hāmākua Coast

INEXPENSIVE
Kālōpa Cabins

MODERATE
Luana Ola Cottages

MODERATE–EXPENSIVE
Waipi'o Wayside Bed and Breakfast

VERY EXPENSIVE
The Palms Cliff House Inn
Waianuhea

Waimea

INEXPENSIVE
Kamuela Inn

MODERATE
Ahhh, the Views
Jacaranda Inn
Paniolo Cottage
Waimea Gardens Cottage

North Kohala

INEXPENSIVE
Kohala Club Hotel
Kohala Village Inn

DINING BY PRICE

INEXPENSIVE	Up to $20
MODERATE	$20–40
EXPENSIVE	$40–85
VERY EXPENSIVE	$85 or more

Kohala Coast

MODERATE–EXPENSIVE
Beach Tree Bar and Grill
Hawai'i Calls
The Hualālai Grille by Alan Wong
Manua Lani Resort
Merriman's Market Café

EXPENSIVE
Coast Grille & Oyster Bar
Hakone Steakhouse Sushi Bar
Imari
Kamuela Provision Company

EXPENSIVE–VERY EXPENSIVE
Batik
Canoe House
Donatoni's
The Grill
Hale Samoa
Pahu i'a
Roy's Waikoloa Bar and Grill

Kailua-Kona

INEXPENSIVE
Aki's Café
Ba-Le
Killer Tacos
Kona Natural Foods

INEXPENSIVE–MODERATE
Kona Inn Restaurant
Ocean View Inn

MODERATE–EXPENSIVE
Big Island Grill
Fujimamas
Huggo's
Jackie Ray's Ohana Grill

Jameson's by the Sea
Kenichi Pacific
O's Bistro

South Kona

INEXPENSIVE
The Coffee Shack
Standard Bakery
Teshima's

INEXPENSIVE–MODERATE
Holuakoa Café
Manago Hotel
Nasturtium Café

MODERATE
Keei Café

INEXPENSIVE–EXPENSIVE
Aloha Angel Café

Ka'u (South Point)

INEXPENSIVE
Pahala Town Café
Punalu'u Bake Shop

INEXPENSIVE–MODERATE
Hana Hou Restaurant
Shaka Restaurant

Volcano

INEXPENSIVE
Volcano True Value Hardware

INEXPENSIVE–MODERATE
Lava Rock Café
Thai Thai Restaurant
Volcano Golf and Country Club
Volcano House

MODERATE
Kiawe Kitchen

EXPENSIVE
Kīlauea Lodge

Puna

INEXPENSIVE
Ning's Thai Cuisine

INEXPENSIVE–MODERATE
Black Rock Café
Pāhoa Natural Foods

Greater Hilo

INEXPENSIVE
Abundant Life Natural Foods and Café
Café 100
Naung Mai
Nori's Saimin and Snacks
Puka Puka Kitchen
What's Shakin'

INEXPENSIVE–MODERATE
Cronies
Ken's House of Pancakes
Miyo's
Royal Siam Thai Restaurant

INEXPENSIVE–EXPENSIVE
Café Pesto

MODERATE
Harrington's
Ocean Sushi Deli

MODERATE–EXPENSIVE
Hilo Bay Café
Nihon Restaurant & Cultural Center
Seaside Restaurant and Aquafarm

Hāmākua Coast

INEXPENSIVE
Māmane Street Bakery
Simply Natural
Tex Drive-In

INEXPENSIVE–MODERATE
Café II Mondo

North Kohala & Waimea

INEXPENSIVE
Kohala Rainbow Café
Nanbu Courtyard
Tako Taco Taqueria

INEXPENSIVE–MODERATE
Huli Sue's BBQ and Grill
Kohala Coffee Mill

INEXPENSIVE–EXPENSIVE
Café Pesto

MODERATE
Sushi Rocks

MODERATE–EXPENSIVE
Bamboo

EXPENSIVE
Daniel Thiebaut
Merriman's

DINING BY CUISINE

Kohala Coast

AMERICAN
Beach Tree Bar and Grill
The Grill
Hawai'i Calls
Kamuela Provision Company

HAWAIIAN REGIONAL
Batik
Brown Beach Houses
Canoe House
The Grill
Hale Samoa
The Hualālai Grille by Alan Wong
Pahu i'a

ITALIAN
Donatoni's

JAPANESE
Imari

MEDITERRANEAN
Merriman's Market Café

PACIFIC RIM
Roy's Waikoloa Bar and Grill

SEAFOOD
Coast Grille & Oyster Bar
Hakone Steakhouse Sushi Bar

Kailua-Kona

AMERICAN-HAWAIIAN
Big Island Grill
Kona Inn Restaurant
Ocean View Inn

AMERICAN-JAPANESE
Aki's Café
Asian Fusion
Kenichi Pacific

CONTINENTAL
Jameson's by the Sea

EAST-WEST FUSION
Fujimamas

ECLECTIC
Jackie Ray's Ohana Grill

HAWAIIAN REGIONAL
O's Bistro

PACIFIC RIM
Huggo's
Surfer Mex
Killer Tacos

VIETNAMESE
Ba-Le

South Kona

AMERICAN
The Coffee Shack

AMERICAN ECLECTIC
Aloha Angel Café

ECLECTIC HAWAIIAN
Holuakoa Café
Keei Café
Nasturtium Café

JAPANESE
Manago Hotel
Teshima's
Bento
Standard Bakery

Ka'u (South Point)

AMERICAN
Hana Hou Restaurant
Pāhala Town Café
Shaka Restaurant

BAKERY/LIGHT MEALS
Punalu'u Bake Shop

Volcano

AMERICAN
Volcano Golf and Country Club
Volcano House
Volcano True Value Hardware

AMERICAN ECLECTIC
Lava Rock Café

EUROPEAN
Kīlauea Lodge

ITALIAN
Kiawe Kitchen

THAI
Thai Thai Restaurant

Puna

AMERICAN
Black Rock Café

CHINESE
Pāhoa Chop Suey House

THAI
Ning's Thai Cuisine

Greater Hilo

AMERICAN
Cronies
Ken's House of Pancakes

HAWAIIAN REGIONAL
Hilo Bay Café

HEALTHY
Abundant Life Natural Foods and Café
What's Shakin'

ITALIAN
Café Pesto

JAPANESE
Miyo's
Nihon Restaurant and Cultural Center
Nori's Saimin and Snacks
Ocean Sushi Deli
Puka Puka Kitchen

LOCAL
Café 100

SEAFOOD
Harrington's
Seaside Restaurant and Aquafarm

THAI
Naung Mai
Royal Siam Thai Restaurant

Hāmākua Coast

AMERICAN
Café II Mondo

BAKERY
Māmane Street Bakery

HEALTHY
Simply Natural

LOCAL
Tex Drive-In

North Kohala & Waimea

ASIAN FUSION
Bamboo

BBQ
Huli Sue's BBQ and Grill

ECLECTIC
Café Pesto

FRENCH ASIAN
Daniel Thiebaut

HAWAIIAN REGIONAL
Merriman's

LIGHT FARE & COFFEE
Kohala Coffee Mill
Kohala Rainbow Café
Nanbu Courtyard

MEXICAN
Tako Taco Taqueria

SUSHI
Sushi Rocks